S0-BEZ-666

REPUBLICANISM, RELIGION, AND THE SOUL OF AMERICA

ERIC VOEGELIN INSTITUTE SERIES IN POLITICAL PHILOSOPHY:
STUDIES IN RELIGION AND POLITICS

Michael Oakeshott on Religion, Aesthetics, and Politics, by Elizabeth Campbell
    Corey
Jesus and the Gospel Movement: Not Afraid to Be Partners, by William Thompson-
    Uberuaga
The Religious Foundations of Francis Bacon's Thought, by Stephen A. McKnight

OTHER BOOKS IN THE ERIC VOEGELIN INSTITUTE
SERIES IN POLITICAL PHILOSOPHY

The American Way of Peace: An Interpretation, by Jan Prybyla
*Faith and Political Philosophy: The Correspondence between Leo Strauss and Eric
    Voegelin, 1934–1964,* edited by Peter Emberley and Barry Cooper
New Political Religions, or an Analysis of Modern Terrorism, by Barry Cooper
Art and Intellect in the Philosophy of Étienne Gilson, by Francesca Aran Murphy
Robert B. Heilman and Eric Voegelin: A Friendship in Letters, 1944–1984, edited
    by Charles R. Embry
Voegelin, Schelling, and the Philosophy of Historical Existence, by Jerry Day
*Transcendence and History: The Search for Ultimacy from Ancient Societies to
    Postmodernity,* by Glenn Hughes
Eros, Wisdom, and Silence: Plato's Erotic Dialogues, by James M. Rhodes
The Narrow Path of Freedom and Other Essays, by Eugene Davidson
Hans Jonas: The Integrity of Thinking, by David J. Levy
A Government of Laws: Political Theory, Religion, and the American Founding,
    by Ellis Sandoz
Augustine and Politics as Longing in the World, by John von Heyking
Lonergan and the Philosophy of Historical Existence, by Thomas J. McPartland

REPUBLICANISM, RELIGION, AND THE SOUL OF AMERICA

Ellis Sandoz

UNIVERSITY OF MISSOURI
COLUMBIA AND LONDON

Copyright © 2006 by
The Curators of the University of Missouri
University of Missouri Press, Columbia, Missouri 65201
Printed and bound in the United States of America
All rights reserved
5   4   3   2   1   10   09   08   07   06

Library of Congress Cataloging-in-Publication Data

Sandoz, Ellis, 1931–
    Republicanism, religion, and the soul of America / Ellis Sandoz.
        p.   cm. — (Eric Voegelin Institute series in political philosophy)
    Summary: "Explores the role of Christianity, including John Wesley and the
Great Awakening revival, in the formation of the American Republic; also considers
Eric Voegelin's contributions to the philosophy of religious experience. Argues that
modern republicanism grounds human dignity in spiritual individualism, thereby
generating democratic agency for self-government under divine Providence" —
Provided by publisher.
    Includes bibliographical references and index.
    ISBN-13: 978-0-8262-1726-4 (pbk. : alk. paper)
    ISBN-10: 0-8262-1726-5 (pbk. : alk. paper)
    1. United States—Church history—18th century.   2. Christianity and
politics—United States.   3. Republicanism—United States.   I. Title.
II. Series.
    BR520.S26   2006
    261.70973'09033—dc22   2006013487

∞™ This paper meets the requirements of the
American National Standard for Permanence of Paper
for Printed Library Materials, Z39.48, 1984.

Designer: foleydesign
Typesetter: Phoenix Type, Inc.
Printer and binder: The Maple-Vail Book Manufacturing Group
Typeface: Adobe Garamond

Excerpts from "Choruses from 'The Rock'" in Collected Poems 1909–1962 by
T. S. Eliot copyright 1936 and renewed 1964 by T. S. Eliot, and from "The Dry
Salvages" in Four Quartets, copyright 1941 by T. S. Eliot and renewed 1969 by
Esme Valerie Eliot, reprinted by permission of Harcourt, Inc., and by Faber and
Faber Ltd.

Publication of this book has been assisted by a generous contribution from the
Eric Voegelin Institute and the Pierre F. and Enid Goodrich Foundation.

FOR JONATHAN, ERICA, LISA, ELLIS III—AND ALVERNE

Things do not happen in the astrophysical universe; the universe, together with all things founded in it, happens in God.

—ERIC VOEGELIN

Contents

Preface

This book traces the rise of republican government, and the republican spirit of consent and individual dignity, from key sources in Western Christian Protestant civilization—with particular attention to the Bible and to the emergence of the American mind in the eighteenth century culminating in 1776 and the constitutional founding of free government. "There has never been anything like America!" it has been well said by one of our staunchest friends, former British prime minister Lady Margaret Thatcher. Just why and how that may be true is a theme of the present study.

Central to my account is the analysis of the religious debt of the emergent eighteenth-century American community and its elevation of the individual person and citizen as unique in the eyes of his Creator. This grounding of the notion of human dignity, and of the citizen's vocation in spiritual individualism, I have argued, along with the understanding of human capacity for self-government under Providential guidance, emerges as the core distinction of American republicanism. It is to be considered as the seminal matrix of the more familiar so-called "Enlightenment" features, and as integral to the founding and to the heart of *Americanism* itself to this day.

While it is a collection of studies in political philosophy, the thematic unity of the volume arises from the non-reductionist philosophical framework within which the questions I address are examined. A theoretical perspective unifies the book, one for which I am indebted to Eric Voegelin, who figures prominently in the pages that follow. Among other things, this specifically means that the spiritual and noetic dimensions of experience as historically ascertained are seriously attended to and given their deserved empirical weight in the analysis. My purpose is not polemical but diagnostic and therapeutic. This persuasive purpose goes to the heart of the deformations exhibited in a contemporary climate of opinion whose relentlessly reductionist orthodoxy, oppressively bordering on fanaticism, prohibits the asking of philosophical questions and ruthlessly enforces a nihilistic occlusion against the Ground of being as threshold restrictions upon scholarly discourse. In these as in other related matters I politely decline to play the boundary game and so refuse to join the alienated in the sour misery of their own self-imposed prison of closed existence. In the present exercise of window-opening, I have followed the evidence of the sources to the best of my ability so as to make its meaning luminously explicit and true to the various contexts under consideration. Silently underlying the argument at every stage, in effect, is the Socratic invitation to look and see if this is not the case—then and still now the way to truth through the exercise of critical reason in a dispassionate assessment of pertinent experience. In Aristotle's formulation of the decisive epistemological principle of prudential science: "We must examine the conclusions we have reached . . . by applying them to the actual facts of life: if they are in harmony with the facts we must accept them, and if they clash we must assume that they are mere words" (*Nicomachean Ethics* 1179a20–22).

Divided into nine chapters, the first half of the book addresses aspects of American thought influential in the Founding, including the neglected question of the education of the Founders for their unique endeavor, common law constitutionalism, the place of the Greek and Latin classics. The first chapter attempts a searching account of the texture of religious experience from the Great Awakening to the Declaration of Independence, paying detailed attention to the prevalent understanding of human nature (anthropology) and its political implications as powerfully theorized notably by John Wesley and Jonathan Edwards.

The latter half of the book continues with studies of Eric Voegelin's philosophy, itself conditioned by his own early American experience, its relationship to Christianity, the watershed debate with Leo Strauss over the true meaning of *philosophy*, the theory of Gnosticism as basic to radical modernity, and an exploration of the spirit of Voegelin's remarkable late writings. The book concludes with some preliminary reflections on the current epoch in history now unfolding before our eyes and its possible meanings for America and for humankind in an evidently post-ideological global age lived, at present, under the shadow of lethal conflict with Islamist jihadism.

Acknowledgments

Several of the chapters appeared previously in published form and are found here revised and enlarged. Chapter one began as the "John Witherspoon Lecture" (Washington, DC, April 2004) and was published in Italian translation in *Culture costituzionali a confronto. Europa e Stati Uniti dall'età delle rivoluzioni all'età contem Cuporanea,* ed. Fernanda Mazzanti Pepe (NAME Edizioni, 2005). Chapter two began as the Distinguished Research Master Lecture at Louisiana State University and first appeared in *Presidential Studies Quarterly* (Summer 1994). Chapter six was published in *Faith and Political Philosophy: The Correspondence between Leo Strauss and Eric Voegelin, 1934–1964,* trans. and ed. Peter Emberley and Barry Cooper (Pennsylvania State University Press, 1991). Chapter 7 was published as the introduction to Eric Voegelin, *Science, Politics, and Gnosticism* (ISI Books, 2004). Chapter 8 was published as the epilogue to my *The Voegelinian Revolution,* 2nd edition (Transaction Publishers, 2000). I am glad to thank copyright holders for kind permission to reprint here. Last, thanks goes to the able editors and staff of the University of Missouri Press for their hard work and wonderful assistance in bringing the book to publication. A special word of gratitude, of course, goes to my longtime editor Beverly Jarrett, stalwart director and editor-in-chief, as well as to Jane Lago, managing editor (who keeps all the wheels turning); also to the expert freelance help of Julie Schorfheide, the copyeditor, and to Linda Webster, the indexer.

Abbreviations

AR
Eric Voegelin, *Autobiographical Reflections,* ed. Ellis Sandoz. Baton Rouge: Louisiana State University Press, 1989. Revised edition included in *CW* 34.

CW
The Collected Works of Eric Voegelin, in 34 vols. Abbreviated as *CW* 1, etc. (See comprehensive listing in the Bibliographical Appendix.)

GOL
Ellis Sandoz, *A Government of Laws.* 1990. Revised edition, Columbia: University of Missouri Press, 2001.

NSP
Eric Voegelin, *The New Science of Politics: An Introduction.* Chicago: University of Chicago Press, 1952. Included in *CW* 5.

OH
Eric Voegelin, *Order and History,* 5 vols. Baton Rouge: Louisiana State University Press, 1956–87. Reprinted as *CW* 14–18.

VR
Ellis Sandoz, *The Voegelinian Revolution: A Biographical Introduction.* 1981. 2nd edition, New Brunswick: Transaction Publishers, 2000.

WPG/SPG
Eric Voegelin, *Wissenschaft, Politik, und Gnosis* [Inaugural Lecture at the University of Munich]. Munich: Kösel Verlag, 1959. English translation by William J. Fitzpatrick: Eric Voegelin, *Science, Politics, and Gnosticism: Two Essays.* 1968; repr., 1990, and 2004, ed. with and intro. by Ellis Sandoz; Wilmington, DE: ISI Books. Included in *CW* 5.

REPUBLICANISM, RELIGION, AND THE SOUL OF AMERICA

1

Republicanism and Religion
SOME CONTEXTUAL CONSIDERATIONS

§1. Introduction and Contemporary Setting

Despite the Enlightenment's concerted project of doing away with the Bible as the basis of political and social order in favor of "Reason,"[1] religion today continues to condition politics as an undergirding belief foundation: Men always have God or idols, as Luther long ago said. The present war against terrorism with its religious dimensions evident to even the most blinkered secularist underlines the point. Perhaps less evidently, this phenomenon can be seen in the context of a global revival of traditional religiosity, including Christianity, as a major event of the present—following the era of the death and murder of God proclaimed by Hegel and Nietzsche—now called "the revenge of God" by such scholars as Gilles Kepel, Philip Jenkins, and Samuel Huntington.[2]

---

1. Robert C. Bartlett, "On the Politics of Faith and Reason: The Project of Enlightenment in Pierre Bayle and Montesquieu," *Journal of Politics* 63 (Feb. 2001): 1–28. Cf. Robert C. Bartlett, *The Idea of Enlightenment: A Post-Mortem Study* (Toronto: University of Toronto Press, 2001).

2. Cf. Gilles Kepel, *The Revenge of God: The Resurgence of Islam, Christianity, and Judaism in the Modern World,* trans. Alan Braley (University Park: Pennsylvania State University Press, 1994); Philip Jenkins, *The Next Christendom: The Coming of Global Christianity* (New York: Oxford University Press, 2002); Samuel P. Huntington, *The Clash of Civilizations and the Remaking of World Order* (New York: Simon & Schuster, 1996), and Samuel P. Huntington, *Who Are We? The Challenges to America's National Identity* (New York: Simon & Schuster, 2004), esp. chap. 3; also Kenneth D. Wald, *Religion and Politics in the United States,* 4th ed. (Lanham, MD: Rowman & Littlefield, 2003).

Leaving aside the radical Islamists and the contemporary revivals of Christianity and Hinduism for present considerations, the principal intellectual fruit of Enlightenment rationalism's systematic deformation of reality—through occlusion against transcendent divine Being and consequent catastrophic ontological result—has proved to be the ascendancy of various competing political "idealisms" in the form of reductionist ideologies. These are largely comprehensible as forms of intramundane religion and magical operations decked out as "science" that immanentize aspects of the Christian faith. They then generate such familiar belief systems as progressivism, utopianism, positivism, nihilism, and Marxist-Leninist revolutionary activism. Such artifacts of modern and post-modern "egophanic revolt" culminate, for instance, in the radical humanism that proclaims Autonomous Man as the god-men of this or that description and politically in the totalitarian killers of recent memory.[3] Properly they can be understood as manifestations of the recrudescence of superstition, of resurgent apocalypticism, and of the ancient religiosity called Gnosticism that replaces faith with fanatical certitude beyond experience and reason. Eric Voegelin's more intricate analysis[4] of these phenomena was long preceded by that of acute

---

3. For "egophanic revolt" see Eric Voegelin, *OH*, vol. IV, *The Ecumenic Age* (Baton Rouge: Louisiana State University Press, 1974), chap. 5, §2, pp. 260–71; available from University of Missouri Press in *CW* 17). The *ersatz* religions have been studied in a vast literature since Eric Voegelin first published his *Political Religions* in 1938; see the recent edition titled *Modernity without Restraint: The Political Religions; The New Science of Politics; and Science, Politics, and Gnosticism, CW* 5. The horrific consequences of such "Utopian politics" in terms of lives taken ("democide") is authoritatively studied in books by R. J. Rummel, who tabulates that since 1900 "independent of war and other kinds of conflict—governments probably have murdered 119,400,000 people—Marxist governments about 95,200,000 of them. By comparison, the battle-killed in all foreign and domestic wars in this [i.e., the twentieth] century total 35,700,000" (Rummel, *Lethal Politics: Soviet Genocide and Mass Murder since 1917* [New Brunswick, NJ: Transaction Publishers, 1990], ix). See also R. J. Rummel, *Death by Government*, intro. by Irving Louis Horowitz (New Brunswick, NJ: Transaction Publishers, 1994). A more philosophical recent work that continues the study of "revolutionary gnosticism" (p. ix) in the spirit of Voegelin's work is Luciano Pellicani, *Revolutionary Apocalypse: Ideological Roots of Terrorism* (Westport, CT: Praeger, 2003); see esp. chap. 9, "Utopia in Power," and chap. 13, "The Annihilators of the World."

4. Eric Voegelin, *NSP*, esp. chap. 4, pp. 107–31; also Voegelin, "The People of God," in *History of Political Ideas*, vol. IV, *Renaissance and Reformation, CW* 22, chap. 3, pp. 131–214. From a large literature see also Stefan Rossbach, *The Gnostic Wars: The Cold War in the Context of a History of Western Spirituality* (Edinburgh: University

observers of the French Revolution and its bloodlust disguised as the Religion of Reason, such as Edmund Burke[5] and Alexis de Tocqueville— who is especially clear on the point: That civilizational upheaval, he found, was a religious movement clothing murderous zealotry and enthusiasm in the ingratiating mantle of instrumental reason and republicanism. Tocqueville wrote that its ideal "was not merely a change in the French social system but nothing short of a regeneration of the whole human race. It created an atmosphere of missionary fervor and... assumed all the aspects of a religious revival.... It would perhaps be truer to say that it developed into a species of religion, if a singularly imperfect one, since it was without God, without a ritual or promise of a future life. Nevertheless, this strange religion has, like Islam, overrun the whole world with its apostles, militants, and martyrs."[6]

§2. Religious Roots of Whig Republicanism

Since my primary interest here is in the American experience and its unique experiential contexts, I must also leave aside the totalitarian ideologies, even though they loom large in the immediate background. In turning to that subject, then, let us remember Tocqueville's further observation that the men and women who colonized America "brought... a Christianity which I can only describe as democratic and republican.... There is not a single religious doctrine hostile to democratic and republican institutions.... It was religion that gave birth to... America. One must never forget that."[7]

The question to be addressed is this: How can the religious dimension of Anglo-American republicanism best be understood when viewed

---

of Edinburgh Press, 2000); also Barry Cooper, *The New Political Religions, or an Analysis of Modern Terrorism,* Eric Voegelin Institute Series in Political Philosophy (Columbia: University of Missouri Press, 2004).

5. Edmund Burke, *Letters on a Regicide Peace,* 1796, in *The Writings and Speeches of Edmund Burke,* 12 vols. (Boston: Little Brown, 1901), vol. 5; also *Select Works of Edmund Burke,* a new imprint of the Payne edition, ed. Francis Canavan, 4 vols. (Indianapolis: Liberty Fund, 1999), vol. 3.

6. Alexis de Tocqueville, *The Old Regime and the French Revolution* [4th ed., 1858], trans. Stuart Gilbert (Garden City, NY: Anchor Books, 1955), 13–14.

7. Alexis de Tocqueville, *Democracy in America,* ed. J. P. Mayer, trans. George Lawrence, 2 vols. in 1 (Garden City, NY: Doubleday Anchor Books, 1969), 1:46f., 288ff., 2:432.

against the backdrop of radical political movements and doctrines just mentioned? The answer is not simple, and I can attempt only a synoptic sketch. In giving it I am reminded that, if war is too important to be left to the generals, then history is surely too important to be left to the historians—not to mention political scientists, many of whom blithely write as though the Enlightenment dogma of their own complacent persuasion has rightly ruled for the past three hundred years and seldom mention, except disparagingly, religion as having much to do with the rise of modern democratic republicanism. As Perry Miller remarked a generation ago when confronting an attitude he labeled "obtuse secularism" in accounts of American experience, "A cool rationalism such as Jefferson's might have declared the independence of [Americans in 1776], but it could never have persuaded them to fight for it."[8] There is more to reality and politics, dear Horatio, than your philosophy has dreamt of.

What then? The tangle is dense and the terminology ambiguous at best. Advocates of republicanism in the Anglo-American Whig tradition (to be distinguished firmly from French Jacobinism, which was both atheistic and anti-property) assert liberty and justice in resistance against tyranny and arbitrary government and do so in the name of highest truth. To summarize: In varying degrees they attempt, within limits, to apply Gospel principles to politics: The state was made for man, not men for the state (cf. Mark 2:27). The imperfect, flawed, sinful being *Man,* for all his inability, paradoxically yet remains capable with the aid of divine grace of self-government—i.e., of living decent lives as individuals; through understanding and free will able to respond to grace and to accept the terms of eternal salvation; and capable, with providential guidance, of self-government in both temporal and spiritual affairs, in regimes based on consent and churches organized congregationally.

This characteristic attitude has a religious and specifically Protestant Christian root in the conviction that evil in the world must be combated by free men out of the resources of pure conscience, true religion, and reformed institutions of power and authority. The fundamental virtue basic to all others is godliness; and the fundamental source of revealed truth is the Bible—to remember John Milton and the seventeenth-

8. Perry Miller, "From Covenant to Revival," quoted from Sandoz, *GOL,* 111.

century English experience widely revived in eighteenth-century America during the struggle leading up to independence.[9]

Favored institutional arrangements drew from classical sources, to be sure—from Aristotle's description of the mixed regime in *Politics* even more than from Polybius—but they drew also from the republic of the Israelites and the rule of seventy Elders (or Sanhedrin or senate) recounted in the Old Testament (Num. 11:17, Deut. 16:18).[10] The mixed constitution delineated by Aristotle is extolled by Thomas Aquinas, in whom Lord Acton finds "the earliest exposition of Whig theory"; and finding it like the ancient "Gothick polity," it also was favored by Algernon Sidney.[11] English republicanism's brief career followed the Puritan Revolution, civil war, and deposition and execution of Charles I for tyranny when England was declared to be "a Commonwealth or Free-State." Oliver Cromwell sought to fill the void left by the regicide with new governing institutions. He saw the situation under Charles I as analogous to the Israelites' bondage in Egypt and himself as a latter-day Moses leading a confused and recalcitrant people through the Red Sea into a promised liberty Christ would show them. The failed experiment ended after little more than a decade with the Stuart Restoration; and English republicanism itself is said to have died on the scaffold with Algernon Sidney and been "buried in an unmarked grave" by the Settlement of 1689[12]—only to be resurrected and transformed in America a century afterward. All the old arguments and imagery then were reasserted, and fervid sentiments echoed John Milton's convictions that the "whole freedom of man consists in spiritual or civil libertie." "Who can be at rest, who can enjoy any thing in this world with contentment, who hath not libertie to serve God and to save his own soul, according to the best light which God hath planted in him to that purpose, by

9. Cf. Martin Dzelzainis, "Milton's Classical Republicanism," in *Milton and Republicanism*, ed. David Armitage et al. (Cambridge: Cambridge University Press, 1995), 21.

10. See Michael Harrington, *The Commonwealth of Oceana* [1656], in *The Political Works of James Harrington*, ed. with an intro. by J. G. A. Pocock (Cambridge: Cambridge University Press, 1977), 174–77 and *passim*.

11. Acton, *History of Liberty*, ed. Rufus Fears, 2 vols. (Indianapolis: Liberty Fund, n.d.), 1:34; Algernon Sidney, *Discourses concerning Government*, ed. Thomas G. West (Indianapolis: Liberty Fund, 1996), 166–70.

12. Cf. Tony Davies, "Borrowed Language: Milton, Jefferson, Mirabeau," in *Milton and Republicanism*, ed. Armitage et al., 254.

the reading of his revealed will [in scripture] and the guidance of his holy spirit?"[13]

Tyranny and superstition alike were enemies of the "*the Good Old Cause*" of liberty, rule of law, *salus populi*, government based on consent of the people, freedom of speech, press, and conscience. The political theory of republicanism was explicitly identified with Aristotle's mixed regime as the "free commonwealth" he ultimately preferred as the best practicable form of government, because monarchy was too vulnerable to derailment and perversion into tyranny. Along with the New Testament teachings, the whole classical theory of politics especially as given in Aristotle and Cicero was absorbed into Old Whig discourse. This was no merely *Sectarian* affair, Milton stressed, but eagerly drew from all reliable authorities. In abandoning the Commonwealth and allowing restoration of Charles II, Milton thought the English were like apostate Israelites returning to idolatry in Egypt, reversing the Exodus and again installing Nimrod.[14] Thought and speech were "soaked in the Bible," with Magna Carta and Bible quoted side by side and together with the classics. Thus, it was urged in a fast sermon: "You are a free Parliament, preserve your freedom, our laws, and liberties"; "let not England become a house of bondage, a second Egypt."[15] Political and religious liberty were seen to be all of a piece, Edmund Burke and John Witherspoon insisted a century later, still invoking the Good Old Cause. The latter went on to say that "there is not a single instance in history in which civil liberty was lost, and religious liberty preserved entire. If therefore we yield up our temporal property, we at the same time deliver the conscience into bondage."[16] No impiety prompted

13. J. M. [John Milton, 1608–1674], *The Readie & Easie Way to Establish a free Commonwealth, and the Excellence thereof compar'd with the inconveniences and dangers of readmitting kingship in this nation* [London: Livewell Chapman, 1660], in *The Struggle for Sovereignty: Seventeenth-Century English Political Tracts*, ed. Joyce Lee Malcolm, 2 vols. (Indianapolis: Liberty Fund, 1999), 1:503–25, at 520.

14. *Areopagitica and Other Political Writings of John Milton*, ed. John Alvis (Indianapolis: Liberty Fund, 1999), 435, 439, 444, and *passim*.

15. William Greenhill as quoted from his 1643 fast sermon, in Christopher Hill, *The English Bible and the Seventeenth-Century Revolution* (Harmondsworth: Penguin Books, 1993), 92, 371.

16. John Witherspoon, *The Dominion of Providence over the Passions of Men* [1776], in *Political Sermons of the American Founding Era, 1730–1805*, ed. Ellis Sandoz (Indianapolis: Liberty Fund, 1991), 529–58, at 549.

Bishop James Madison occasionally to pray the Lord's Prayer using the words "Thy republic come." Nor did he or the other American patriots ignore the prayer's next clause, lying as it did at the heart of their republicanism: "Thy will be done, on earth as it is in heaven." "Patriotism without piety is mere grimace," one American preacher quaintly asserted.[17]

§3. The Bible, Politics, and Philosophical Anthropology

That multiple pre-modern sources of political culture were complexly woven into foundation of the American representative republics as the most eligible form of government (even if we routinely call it *democracy* today) is, of course, beyond dispute—most especially common law constitutionalism and the Greek and Latin classics, among other neglected sources.[18] But the importance of Bible reading and the spiritual grounding nurtured by it can hardly be overrated. From this perspective it is not the institutional *forms* that were decisive (if they ever are), and like many before him James Madison regarded them as "auxiliary precautions" of consequence. Decisive from antiquity onward is dedication to *salus populi* as supreme law (or *bonum publicum*, the universal or common good) and as the end of government and requisite animating spirit of the political community and of any persons vested with authority. These fundamental matters of community and *homonoia* can be glimpsed in *Federalist No. 2* where Publius (John Jay) remarks that "Providence has been pleased to give this one connected country to one united people—a people descended from the same ancestors, speaking the same language, professing the same religion, attached to the same principles of government, very similar in their manners and customs, and who, by their joint counsels, arms, and efforts, fighting side by side throughout a long and bloody war, have nobly established their general liberty and independence."[19] The supposed hostility between

17. Rev. Thomas Coombe in 1775, quoted in Perry Miller, "From Covenant to Revival," in *Religion in American Life*, ed. J. W. Smith and A. L. Jamison, 4 vols. (Princeton: Princeton University Press, 1961), 1:329.

18. See James R. Stoner Jr., *Common-Law Liberty: Rethinking American Constitutionalism* (Lawrence: University Press of Kansas, 2003).

19. *The Federalist Papers*, ed. Clinton Rossiter (New York: Mentor Books, 1961), 38.

liberal *individualism* and republican communitarianism can be over-drawn and distorted.

At the bottom of republicanism lies a *philosophical anthropology* of the kind I have limned and which must steadily be held in view, one that concretely exists solely in the hearts and minds of individual human beings, the only concrete reality of political existence. That anthropology is basic to the claim of human dignity. To amplify briefly, it is decisively grounded in biblical faith philosophically elaborated as disclosing hegemonic reality, with its appeal to transcendent truth and to eternal Beatitude (blessedness and felicity, happiness) as humankind's *summum bonum* and ultimate destiny. "And God said, Let us make man in our image, after our likeness: and let them have *dominion* ... over all the earth, and over every creeping thing that creepeth upon the earth. So God created man in his *own* image, in the image of God created he him; male and female created he them" (Gen. 1:26–27). The Trinitarian structure of the image reflects that of the godhead of Father, Son, and Holy Spirit theorized by Augustine[20] as the *esse, nosse, velle infinitum* of God mirrored in the image's being, wisdom or knowledge, and will or love *finitum* of the creature. The human being is, therefore, the same through *participation*—a likeness reflecting divine Being. But since the creature is divided into mind and body, will and knowledge tend to be in a conflict which—through the mutilation of the Fall—manifests itself in cupidity, lust, avarice, greed, and other sin. Thus, the creature as *imago dei* is a trinity: *it is, it sees, it loves:* God created it (being); it sees, since God illumined it (knowledge); and it chooses or inclines always to love the Good at least in appearance, if (because of human imperfection) not always in reality. We are drawn to seek and to find true Good because "God first loved us" (1 Jn. 4:19). In Bonaventure (following Augustine) the Trinitarian structure is analyzed in terms of the faculties of memory, intelligence, will and love (the capacity to

---

20. Augustine, *Confessions* 13.11.12; *City of God* 11.26–28; *On the Trinity* bks. 10 and 14. Cf. discussion in John von Heyking, *Augustine and Politics as Longing in the World*, Eric Voegelin Institute Series in Political Philosophy (Columbia: University of Missouri Press, 2001), 187–992. Mediation of this anthropology into English political thought is from many sources, but Fortescue may especially be mentioned; cf. the discussion and literature cited in "Sir John Fortescue as Political Philosopher," in *The Politics of Truth and Other Untimely Essays: The Crisis of Civic Consciousness*, by Ellis Sandoz (Columbia: University of Missouri Press, 1999), 95–103.

choose), which ontologically correlate with eternity, truth, and goodness.[21] The sinful perversions in the creature are identified as the lust of the flesh, lust of the eyes, and the pride of life (1 Jn. 2:16).

Philosophical anthropology in its several versions supplies the core of political theory, and it opens into the heart of the republican argument as that builds on natural law and consent of the people as foundations of any just regime. This is not merely ancient and medieval lore long since forgotten by moderns. Rather, natural law as theorized by Aquinas was mediated lock, stock, and barrel into English Protestant theory by Richard Hooker's great work entitled *Of the Laws of Ecclesiastical Polity* (1593). In Hooker's formulation:

> God alone excepted, who actually and everlastingly is whatsoever he may be, and which cannot hereafter be that which now he is not; all other things besides are somewhat in possibility, which as yet they are not in act. And for this cause there is in all things an appetite or desire, whereby they incline to something which they may be.... All which perfections are contained under the general name of *Goodness*. And because there is not in the world anything whereby another may not some way be made the perfecter, therefore all things that are, are good. Again since there can be no goodness desired which proceedeth not from God himself, as from the supreme cause of all things; ... all things in the world are said in some sort to seek the highest, and to covet more or less the participation of God himself. Yet this doth nowhere so much appear as it doth in man: because there are so many kinds of perfections which man seeketh. The first degree of goodness is that general perfection which all things do seek, in desiring the continuance of their being. All things therefore coveting as much

21. *Itinerarium* of Bonaventure; in English, *The Journey of the Mind to God*, trans. Philotheus Boehner, ed. with an intro. and notes by Stephen F. Brown (Indianapolis: Hackett, 1993), chap. 3, pp. 18–22 and notes. For the anthropology of the Reformers consider John Calvin, *Calvin: Institutes of the Christian Religion*, 2 vols., ed. John T. McNeill, trans. Fred Battles, Library of Christian Classics vol. 20 (Philadelphia: Westminister Press, 1960), bk. 1, chaps. 15–18, and bk 2, chaps. 1–4, 1:183–316. While affirming that even in his deformed nature man's *"soul yet bears, though almost obliterated, the image of God,"* Calvin vaguely distances himself from "that speculation of Augustine, that the soul is the reflection of the Trinity because in it reside the understanding, will, and memory, [as] by no means sound." Instead he settles on the view "that the human soul consists of two faculties, understanding and will" (*Calvin*, 1:183, 190, 194).

as may be to be like unto God in being ever, that which cannot hereunto attain personally, doth seek to continue itself in another way, that is by offspring and propagation. The next degree of goodness is that which each thing coveteth by affecting resemblance with God, in the constancy and excellency of those operations which belong unto their kind. The immutability of God they strive unto, ... by tending unto that which is most exquisite in every particular. Hence have risen a number of axioms in Philosophy showing how *The works of nature do always aim at that which cannot be bettered.* These two kinds of goodness rehearsed are so nearly united to the things themselves which desire them, that we scarcely perceive the appetite to stir in reaching forth her hand towards them. ... Concerning perfections in this kind, that by proceeding in the knowledge of truth and growing in the exercise of virtue, man amongst the creatures of this inferior world, aspireth to the greatest conformity with God, this is not only known unto us, whom he himself hath so instructed, but even they acknowledge, who amongst men are not judged the nearest unto him. With *Plato* what one thing more usual, than to excite men unto the love of wisdom, by showing how much wise men are thereby exalted above [other] men; how knowledge doth raise them up into heaven; how it maketh them, though not Gods, yet as gods, high, admirable and divine?[22]

The key to this theory is its root in the manifestly "self-evident" search for the Good beyond all finite goods as that is exhibited in human *inclinations,* as Hooker and before him Thomas Aquinas observed. These are ranked hierarchically toward *summum bonum* or the transcendent Good itself: rising from the creature's persistent desire for self-preservation of one's very being (subsistence itself); next to the desire to procreate and propagate in continuation of one's being and to educate one's children and protect one's family (which is common to all animals); and ultimately including the desire to know the meaning of existence and the truth about the ground of being (God), and to live in political society. The culmination of this meditative and experiential ascent

22. Richard Hooker, *Of the Laws of Ecclesiastical Polity [1593],* 1.5.1–3, in Cambridge Texts in the History of Political Thought, ed. Arthur S. McGrade (Cambridge: Cambridge University Press, 1989), 66–67.

thereby manifests the *differentia specifica* of human Noetic rationality, conscience, synderesis, desire for communion of the creature with the Creator whose image he bears, and the political essence of man showing him to be more than merely gregarious.[23] To greater or lesser degree, this generalized synthesis of biblical revelation and Aristotelian and Scholastic philosophy passes through Hooker to Jonathan Edwards in eighteenth-century America, and along the way to such astute English republican writers as John Milton and Algernon Sidney, to form the spiritual and intellectual matrix of their theoretical argumentation and conviction. It is a broadly grounded birthright to be remembered and nurtured.

Finally, in the vocabulary and rhetorical idiom of *natural rights* this same constellation of theoretical understanding is exhibited in the thinking of the American Founders themselves. This is achieved by turning the analysis of natural law *inclinations* into a reading of *duties* grounding correlative and reciprocal *rights*. For example, if you have a *duty* to preserve your life (the first law of nature in Locke no less than in Aquinas), liberty, and property, you manifestly also have a *right* to do so.[24] For the purposes of the present illustrative analysis, John Milton's robust prose may again be quoted to emphasize some of the decisive points:

> No man who knows ought, can be so stupid as to deny that all men naturally were borne free, being the image and resemblance of God himself, and were by privilege above all the creatures born to command and not to obey: and that they lived so.... [The] authority and power of self-defence and preservation being originally and naturally in every one of them, and unitedly in them

23. Summarizing Thomas Aquinas, *Summa theologiae* 1–2 Q. 94. See *The Political Ideas of St. Thomas Aquinas*, ed. Dino Bigongiari (New York: Hafner Press, 1953), 44–46. Cf. Thomas Aquinas, *The Disputed Questions on Truth*, trans. James V. McGlynn, 2 vols. (Chicago: Henry Regnery, n.d.), Qq. 16 and 17, 2:300–37; Aristotle *Politics* 1.2.1253a1–17.

24. Sidney, *Discourses*, 406, is explicit on the point: "If all princes are obliged by the law of nature to preserve the lands, goods, lives and liberties of their subjects, those subjects have by the *law of nature a right* to their liberties." See the development of this argument in "American Religion and Higher Law" in *Politics of Truth*, by Sandoz, 104–20.

all. . . . While the Magistrate was set above the people, so the Law was set above the magistrate. . . . A Tyrant whether by wrong or right comming to the Crown, is he who regarding neither Law nor the common good, reigns onely for himself and his faction.[25]

"The law of God does exactly agree with the law of nature" and ordains rule for the common good, i.e., the "preservation of all men's liberty, peace, and safety"; "if any law or custom be contrary to the law of God or of nature, or, in fine, to reason, it shall not be held a valid law"; "nothing that is contrary to the laws of God and to reason can be accounted law, any more than a tyrant can be said to be a king, or the servant of the Devil a servant of God. Since therefore the law is right reason [*recta ratio*] above all else, then if we are bound to obey a king and a servant of God, by the very same reason and the very same law we ought to resist a tyrant and a servant of the Devil."[26]

In sum, therefore, the principal *religious* springs of republican politics are: a paradoxical sense of the dignity yet frailty of every human being as potentially *imago dei;* individual and political liberty fostered through a rule of law grounded in "the nature and being of man" as "the gift of God and nature";[27] government and laws based on consent of the people; and above all resistance to tyranny, whether ecclesiastical or political, in the name of truth, justice, and righteousness. These key elements were directly and essentially fostered by the prevalent ("dissenting," Edmund Burke called it) Christianity of the late eighteenth century and by a citizenry well-schooled in them by devoted Bible reading, from the pulpit, and through an enormous controversial literature made widely accessible by the printing press.

It is worth lingering a moment over the last point as George Trevelyan memorably makes it:

> The effect of the continual domestic study of the book [i.e., Bible] upon the national character, imagination and intelligence for nearly three centuries to come [after William Tyndale's translation in 1526–1534] was greater than that of any literary movement in

25. Milton, *The Tenure of Kings and Magistrates,* in *Areopagitica and Other Political Writings,* ed. Alvis, 58–59, 66.
26. Milton, *Defence of the People of England,* in ibid., 201–3, 263, 270.
27. Sidney, *Discourses,* 510.

our annals, or any religious movement since the coming of St. Augustine.... The Bible in English history may be regarded as a "Renaissance" of Hebrew literature far more widespread and more potent than even the Classical Renaissance which ... provided the mental background of the better educated.[28]

The path to that stage of liberty was less than smooth. Indeed, the rise of Whig liberty, the freedom we cherish, was in no small degree bound up with the efforts of early religious reformers, notably John Wyclif and William Tyndale, to make the text of the Bible available in English — an eminently if inadvertently democratizing effort that expanded the much earlier revolutionary principle already proclaimed in the remarkable *York Tractates,* authored by the person identified as the "Anglo-Norman Anonymous" (ca. 1100), as "the priesthood of all [baptized] believers," with the individual person standing in immediacy to God (1 Pet. 2:9). "Our author is intent upon eliminating the idea of laity which he relates to *publicani,* from the Church, clearly espousing the doctrine of the priesthood of all believers.... He who puts on Christ in baptism, assumes His royal sacerdotal nature.... The Anonymous suggests indeed both the royalty and the priesthood of all believers, reborn in baptism as sons of the heavenly *Rex et Sacerdos.*"[29]

Translation of scripture into English was denounced by the authorities as the work of heretics spreading pearls before swine (Matt. 7:6). Possession of such a Bible was a capital crime in Britain after 1401, one punished (as were the translators themselves) by condemnation, excommunication, burning at the stake, and the scattering of their bones.[30]

---

28. George M. Trevelyan, *History of England* (New York: Longmans, Green, 1928), 367. For a detailed account, see Hill, *The English Bible.* Cf. Northrop Frye, *The Great Code: The Bible and Literature* (San Diego: Harcourt Brace Jovanovich, 1982); Brian Moynahan, *God's Bestseller: William Tyndale, Thomas More, and the Writing of the English Bible—A Story of Martyrdom and Betrayal* (New York: St. Martin's Press, 2003); Adam Nicolson, *God's Secretaries: The Making of the King James Bible* (New York: HarperCollins, 2003), published in the United Kingdom under the title *Power and Glory.*

29. George Huntston Williams, *The Norman Anonymous of 1100 A.D.,* Harvard Theological Studies 18 (Cambridge, MA: Harvard University Press, 1951), 143–44, incorporating n476, and *passim.*

30. "The first execution of a Wycliffite [came under King Henry IV] in 1401, shortly after the passing of *De haeretico comburendo.* The English Bible attributed to Wyclif was prohibited in 1407, and the universal condemnation of Wycliffite doctrine

The reason in an authoritarian age is not far to seek. As Wyclif wrote in the prologue to his and John Purvey's translation of the Bible (as it appears in the edition of ca. 1395):

> All the books of the New Testament . . . be fully of authority of belief; therefore Christian men and women, old and young, should study fast in the New Testament, for it is of full authority, and open to understanding of simple men, as to points that be most needful to salvation; . . . and each place of holy writ . . . teacheth meekness and charity; and therefore he that keepeth meekness and charity hath the true understanding and perfection of all holy writ, as Augustine proveth in his sermon on the praising of charity. There-fore no simpel man of wit be feared unmeasurably to study in the text of holy writ, for why those be words of everlasting life, as Peter said to Christ in the 6th chapter of John; and the Holy Ghost stirred holy men to speak and write the words of holy writ for the comfort and salvation of meek Christian men, as Peter in the 2nd epistle in the end, and Paul in the 15th chapter of Romans witness. And no clerk [clergy/cleric] be proud of the very understanding of holy writ, for why very understanding of holy writ without char-ity, and keeping of God's behests, maketh a man deeper damned/ condemned, and James and Jesus Christ witness; and [the] pride and covetousness of clerks is [the] cause of their blindness and heresy, and depriveth them from [the] very understanding of holy writ, and make them go quick into hell, as Augustine saith on the Psalter, on that word, *Descendant in infernum viventes*.[31]

To be emphasized, and evident in the passage just quoted, is the inordinate importance of the conviction of Christian *egalitarianism* in

---

was secured at the Councils of Pisa and Constance" (*Wyclif: Political Ideas and Prac-tice; Papers by Michael Wilks*, ed. and intro. by Anne Hudson [Oxford: Oxbow Books, 2000], 252). Wyclif's remains were exhumed and burned.

31. Prologue, Wyclif Bible, ca. 1395 edition, modern-spelling edition of the Middle English translation by John Wyclif and John Purvey, done by Terence P. Noble. Sup-plied to the author by a personal communication, since the project is in preparation. Cf. *Wycliffe's New Testament, translated by John Wycliffe and John Purvey: A Modern-Spelling Edition of Their 14th Century Middle English Translation [of the Latin Vul-gate], the First Complete English Vernacular Version, with an Introduction by Terence P. Noble, editor and publisher* (Vancouver, BC: T. P. Noble, 2001). Wyclif's direct role (if any) in the production of the Wyclif Bible itself is explored by Michael Wilks in "Wyclif and the Non-Wycliffite Bible," chap. 5 of *Wyclif: Political Ideas and Practice*, ed. Hudson, 85–99.

the church society, a verity here daringly uttered in the very teeth of a strongly hierarchical society, church, and monarchy. It is nobly emblemized as *every* member's equal and God-given charismatically indelible participation in the one Body of Christ, whatever their gifts or station, as that is nobly stated in Paul's First Letter to the Corinthians (12:12). The symbolism had been variously deployed in theorizing civil liberty and political order by such major figures as John of Salisbury (d. 1180) and later on by Sir John Fortescue (d. ca. 1479) in their respective accounts. It found renewed *political* importance in later centuries as devotion to hierarchy waned and egalitarian sentiments flourished. Thus, Moses was a foundling, David a shepherd boy, the Savior incarnate as a simple carpenter, His apostles fishermen, Saint Paul a tent-maker, the meek, poor in spirit, heavy-laden, and peacemakers were blessed of God, and Christ proclaimed Himself present in "the least of these" (Matt. 25:40, 45). In Virginia, Madison's and Jefferson's fiery Baptist constituent the Elder John Leland ridiculed as arrogant conceit the notion that the ordinary man of common sense is incapable of judging for himself, and he asked: "Did many of the rulers believe in Christ when he was upon the earth? Were not the learned clergy (the scribes) his most inveterate enemies? Do not great men differ as much as little men in judgment? ... Is the Bible written (like Caligula's laws) so intricate and high, that none but the ... learned ... can read it? Is not the vision written so plain that he that runs may read it?"[32] The riddle of spiritual equality's uneasy relationship to politics thereby ultimately tended to dissolve into political populism—for better or worse, and as always feared it would—and powerfully fueled the subsequent rise of democracy in America.

§4. Faith and Civil Theology in Eighteenth-Century America: Great Awakening and Aftermath

Did the alliance of pulpit and republican politics persist throughout the Revolutionary and early national periods in the United States or

---

32. John Leland, *Rights of Conscience Inalienable* [1791], in *Political Sermons*, ed. Sandoz, 1079–99, at 1090. Cf. 1 Cor. 1:18–31: "God hath chosen the foolish things of the world to confound the wise; and God hath chosen the weak things of the world to confound the things which are mighty" (v. 27 [KJV]).

did devotion wane? This is a factual question debated among students of these periods.[33] While the matter cannot be settled here, I think a diversified and robust religiousness remained a cardinal experiential force, one undiminished throughout the historical periods mentioned. The momentum of revival and spiritual vitality that reshaped America itself beginning with the Great Awakening from the 1730s onward, identified especially with Jonathan Edwards, John and Charles Wesley, George Whitefield, Gilbert Tennent, Joseph Bellamy, Isaac and Ezra Stiles (among others), continued in a dynamic of ebb and flow into the later period of the founding, to be renewed shortly thereafter in the Second Great Awakening, which carried well into the nineteenth century.[34] As Mark Noll explains:

> [O]ne of the reasons the War for Independence succeeded was that Protestants sacralized its aims as from God. . . . [T]he patriots' message was embraced by a religious community whose own religious history prepared it for receiving [republicanism]. . . . The Christianity that thrived best in the new democratic America had not dropped from the sky but bore the imprint of its own colonial history. . . . [A]n evangelicalism inspired by face-to-face itinerant preaching, that stressed the all-powerful but also egalitarian grace of God as the source of salvation, that taught converts to connect virtue to the exertions of their hearts instead of to mere social conformity—this was a religion already closer to democracy than

33. Cf. J. H. Hutson, ed., *Religion and the New Republic: Faith in the Founding of America* (Lanham, MD: Rowman & Littlefield, 2000).

34. Pertinent source material is collected in *Political Sermons of the American Founding Era, 1730–1805,* ed. with intro. and notes by Ellis Sandoz, 2 vols., 2nd ed. (1991; repr., Indianapolis: Liberty Fund, 1998), *passim.* On the significance of the Great Awakening as marking an "epoch" in history, see Herbert L. Osgood, *American Colonies in the Eighteenth Century,* 4 vols. (1924; repr., Gloucester, MA: Peter Smith, 1958), 3:409. More fully: Alan Heimert and Perry Miller, eds., *The Great Awakening: Documents Illustrating the Crisis and Its Consequences* (Indianapolis: Bobbs-Merrill, 1967), introduction, xiv–xv: "The Awakening clearly began a new era, not merely of American Protestantism, but in the evolution of the American mind. . . . [It was] a turning point . . . in the history of American civilization." On the Second Great Awakening, see Nathan O. Hatch, *The Democratization of American Christianity* (New Haven: Yale University Press, 1989); also, Jon Butler, *Awash in a Sea of Faith: Christianizing the American People* (Cambridge, MA: Harvard University Press, 1990), and Mark A. Noll, *America's God: From Jonathan Edwards to Abraham Lincoln* (New York: Oxford University Press, 2002), chap. 9, "The Evangelical Surge."

the hierarchical establishmentarian communalism of either clerically ordered Congregationalism or inherited Anglicanism.[35]

§5. Experiential Religion and Human Agency: John Wesley and Jonathan Edwards

The epochal effects of the revival and the evangelism that carried it were politically consequential in many ways but especially in two that are of fundamental importance here: (1) experiential formation of the rudiments of an *American* community of shared convictions rooted in faith rising above and beyond colonial and merely British identities; and (2) by what has been termed a *Second Reformation* that conceptually drove home in unique ways the political implications of Christianity as a core element of man's imitation of God as part of his vocation to perfect through faith-grace his life as *imago dei,* the heart of the redemptive process as pursued in the In-Between of historical existence. By these two factors spiritual rebirth came to be gingerly associated with political as well as spiritual and intellectual like-mindedness *(homonoia)*.[36] The eschatology of salvation was thereby broadened, quite aside from millenarian expectations, to include civic duty along with stewardship in the creature's emulation of, and participation in, God's loving governance of his Creation, as that is reflected and modestly extended through

35. Noll, *America's God,* 192. For details on the revival from the 1760s onward, see Anne Taves, *Fits, Trances, and Visions: Experiencing Religion and Explaining Experience from Wesley to James* (Princeton: Princeton University Press, 1999), chap. 3, "Shouting Methodists," and the sources cited therein.

36. *Homonoia* is found in Plato *(Republic* 545c–d; *Statesman* 311b–c) and in Aristotle *(Nicomachean Ethics* 1167a23, 1167b5; cf. *Politics* 1306a10), where it is translated as *concord,* meaning being of the same mind, thinking in harmony, or likeminded; it is "primarily a political concept" (Martin Ostwald, "Glossary" in his translation of *Aristotle's Nicomachean Ethics* [Indianapolis: Library of Liberal Arts, 1962], 309). "When men live in harmonious existence, in agreement with their true self, and when agreement between them is based on such agreement with themselves, then the relation prevails between them which Aristotle calls *homonoia*—which may be translated as a friendship [*philia*] based on likeness in actualization of the *nous*" (Eric Voegelin, *OH* III, *Plato and Aristotle* [Baton Rouge: Louisiana State University Press, 1957], 321, see 357, 364). However, *contra* Voegelin (ibid., 321n2 and elsewhere), the word *homonoia* seems not to occur in the New Testament, where *likeminded* in the King James Version (Rom. 15:5, Phil. 2:2, 20) translates *isopsuchos,* and *concord* (2 Cor. 6:15) translates *sumphonesis.* See James Strong, ed., *The New Strong's Exhaustive Concordance of the Bible* (Nashville: Thomas Nelson, 1984).

human agency in time and history. "And God said, Let us make man in our image, after our likeness: and let them have *dominion* [râdâh] over... all the earth" (Gen. 1:26). "What is man, that thou art mindful of him?... Thou madest him to have *dominion* [mâshal] over the works of thy hands; thou has put all *things* under his feet" (Ps. 8:4, 6).[37] Yet all that is done serves not man primarily but God: "God's glory is the ultimate end of the creation of the world." It is theophany not egophany that is celebrated, God who is glorified, not man, despite his celebrated high nobility among the creatures of the moral world.[38] This applies especially to the Elect, anciently to Israel and then to the Christians who now are newly chosen to glorify God under the New Covenant of Love, implying progressive revelation of the living God as manifested in the providential unfolding of history.

> This [glorification of God] is spoken of as the end of the good [i.e., blessed, not reprobate] part of the moral world, or as the end of God's people in the same manner as the glory of God. Is. 43:21, "This people have I formed for myself, they shall show forth my *praise.*" I Pet. 2:9, "But ye are a chosen generation, a royal priesthood, an holy nation, a peculiar people, *that ye should show forth the praises of him,* who hath called you out of darkness into his marvelous light."[39]

Isaac Watts in 1740 wrote of the Trinitarian structure of the image of God in man as first created in terms of his *Moral Image;* his *Natural Image,* which "consisted partly in his spiritual, intelligent and immortal Nature, and the various Faculties thereof; and his *political Image* (if I may so express it)[, which] consisted in his being made Lord and Governor over all the lower Creation."[40] The process of human recovery of

37. Quoted from the King James Version of the Bible [KJV], the prevailing translation in eighteenth-century America. Italics added for *dominion.* See Nathan O. Hatch and Mark A. Noll, eds., *The Bible in America: Essays in Cultural History* (New York: Oxford University Press, 1982): "The cadences of the Authorized Version [KJV] informed the writing of the elite and the speech of the humble" (p. 39).

38. Jonathan Edwards in *The Works of Jonathan Edwards,* vol. 8, *The Ethical Writings,* ed. Paul Ramsey (New Haven: Yale University Press, 1989), 491–92.

39. Ibid., 496. "The kingdom of God shall be taken from you, and given to a nation bringing forth the fruits thereof" (Matt. 21:43). Cf. Matt. 23:37, Rom. 9:30–33.

40. Isaac Watts, *The Ruin and Recovery of Mankind* (London: J. Brackstone, 1740), 7.

this true Image through rebirth as the New Man through the experience of spiritual conversion and subsequent quickening of the "Principle of true religion in the heart, is *created* by *God* after his Moral Image, wherein he created Man at first, *i.e.* with an holy Temper of Mind and Disposition to the ready Practice of all Righteousness as fast as Occasions and Opportunities arise."[41] John Wesley—himself politically a royalist who eventually opposed the Revolution and withdrew his missionaries, much to the consternation of American Methodists[42]—preached on "The New Birth" (John 3:7, "Ye must be born again") more than sixty times from 1740 onward. In the published version of the sermon (1771), which was a "distillate" of the oral presentations, Wesley adopted Watts's categories as just noticed after asking, "Why must we be born again?" The short answer is so as to restore the Image of God in man defaced by the Fall. Wesley explains that when God created Man,

> We read, "And God," the three-one God, "said, Let us make man in our image, after our likeness. So God created man in his own image, in the image of God created he him." Not barely in his *natural image*, a picture of his own immortality, a spiritual being endued with understanding, freedom of will, and various affections; nor merely in his *political image*, the governor of this lower world, having "dominion over the fishes of the sea, and over the fowl of the air, and over all the earth"; but chiefly in his *moral image*, which, according to the Apostle, is "righteousness and true holiness." In this image of God was man made. "God is love": accordingly man at his creation was full of love, which was the sole principle of all his tempers, thoughts, words, and actions. God is full of justice, mercy, and truth: so was man as he came from the hands of his Creator. God is spotless purity: and so man was in the beginning pure from every sinful blot. Otherwise God could not have pronounced *him* as well as all the other works of his hands, "very good."[43]

41. Ibid., 7n, glossing Eph. 4:24 and Col. 3:10.

42. Cf. John Wesley, *A Calm Address to Our American Colonies* (London, 1775), and the anonymous reply to it, titled *A Constitutional Answer to Mr. Wesley's Calm Address*, of the same year in *Political Sermons*, ed. Sandoz, 373–420; also John Wesley, "The Late Work of God in North America" [1778; elsewhere titled "A Wheel within a Wheel," based the text from Ezek. 1:16], sermon no. 113, in *The Works of John Wesley*, vol. 4, *Sermons IV*, ed. Albert C. Outler (Nashville: Abingdon Press, 1984), 594–608.

43. *Works of John Wesley*, vol. 2, *Sermons II*, ed. Outler, 34–70, 188; see Gen. 1: 26–28 and Ps. 8:6–8 on *dominion*. For other scriptural references consult the original.

But Adam sinned, and the Fall mutilated the divine image in man, which is now to be restored through grace in the faithful. It is at such a renewal and ascent toward Perfection that the evangelist's preaching aimed in proclaiming the Good News far and wide during his ministry and the "Revival" we call the Great Awakening.

The specifically political implications of this influential and subtle perspective can more fully be grasped from the following insightful analysis given by a contemporary theologian.

> [Wesley's] mode of thinking is vocational in that it is defined by the call of God to image the governing of God in the care of creation.... *Political image* keeps the focus of political institutions and their operations on God's political work, not on themselves.
>
> It follows ... that one does not grasp the true meaning of political institutions apart from faith in the clarifying, revelatory word of God.... How do [persons] fit into and serve the whole-making work of God, expressed in the Old Testament as *shalom* and in the New Testament as reconciliation? ... The framing of these questions, and the possibility of answering them rightly, depend ultimately on trinitarian theology, not on natural law or common agreement or practical experience. These dimensions of the political work of God shape the true meaning of political institutions.... They are fully consonant with John Wesley's transformationist theological language: his vision of the restoration of all

---

For related exposition in Wesley's *Sermons* see especially no. 60, "The General Deliverance," ibid., 2:436–50; also 2:284, 400, 409, 438, 474, 537; 3:75, 256; vol. 4: 63, 163, 292–93. Editor Albert C. Outler writes: "The recovery of the defaced Image of God is the axial theme of Wesley's soteriology"(2:185n). See also Albert C. Outler, ed., *John Wesley* (New York; Oxford University Press, 1964), 108, on mysticism and justification, quoting from Wesley's "On God's Vineyard" [1788]: "at the same time a man is justified, sanctification properly begins," and his conversion or new birth (Jn. 3:3, 6) is marked not by "an outward change only, as from drunkenness to sobriety, ... but an inward change from all unholy to all holy tempers, from pride to humility, from passionateness to meekness, from peevishness and discontent to patience and resignation; in a word from an earthly, sensual, devilish mind to the mind that was in Christ Jesus [cf. Phil. 2:5]." Also Outler, ed., *John Wesley,* 162, for Wesley's interest in Thomas à Kempis and publication of his own translation of *De imitatione Christi* as *The Christian Pattern* in 1735. Outler writes: "If Wesley's writings on perfection are to be read with understanding, his affirmative notion of 'holiness' *in the world* must be taken seriously—active holiness in *this* life—and it becomes intelligible only in the light of its indirect sources in early and Eastern spirituality" (*John Wesley,* 252; italics as in original).

things in the ultimate fulfillment of God's activity, and his evangelical call for the recovery of the moral image. In broad terms they conceptualize his vocation of peacemaking. They disclose the social meaning of "going on to perfection."

Theodore Weber further argues that the

> heart of John Wesley's evangelism is the message that God acts to restore the lost moral image, not for the few, but for the entire human race; not coercively, but through the empowerment of the Holy Spirit that enables the response to God's gracious gift. God opens our eyes to our condition of being without God in the world (prevenient grace), bestows forgiveness of sins (justifying grace), and encourages us lovingly to become more loving and to "have that mind which also was in Christ Jesus" ([Phil. 2:5] sanctifying grace, Christian perfection). Through this process, this grace-filled ordering of salvation, the moral image is restored, the "capacity for God" returns, true humanity is recovered, and the born-again creature comes to stand before God and to love other creatures in the holiness of grace. This is the good news. . . . It is the order of God's salvation for sinful humanity.[44]

Wesley's anthropology builds on the traditional Christian analysis and mysticism noticed earlier but is sharpened because of his emphasis

44. Quotations from Theodore R. Weber, *Politics in the Order of Salvation: New Directions in Wesleyan Political Ethics* (Nashville: Kingswood Books, Abingdon Press, 2001), 405–10. The original should be consulted for details of a rich analysis. The Great Awakening is considered from the present perspective in Sandoz, *GOL,* esp. 99, 147, 153, 230, and literature cited therein. Indispensable is Alan Heimert, *Religion and the American Mind: From the Great Awakening to the Revolution* (Cambridge, MA: Harvard University Press, 1966); also Heimert and Miller, eds., *Great Awakening.* The Anglo-American *Second Reformation* (as that term is used herein) and its political significance is fatefully contrasted with German pietistic experience by Eric Voegelin, "Democracy in the New Europe" and "Freedom and Responsibility in Economy and Democracy" in *CW* 11:8, 61–63. Voegelin writes: "Through the spreading of the Methodist Church and its influence on other churches, the second reformation, initiated by . . . John Wesley . . . became socially effective, with enormous consequences barely understood in their significance on the Continent. For in the critical period of the Industrial Revolution and the forming of the industrial proletariat, the second reformation carried Christendom in England to the people; it Christianized the working population and small middle class and thereby virtually immunized them against later ideological movements. A comparable phenomenon does not exist on the Continent, above all not in Germany" (72).

upon the vital experiential aspects of faith and of the grace-filled life, i.e., the experience of "a movement toward immediacy, toward direct communion with God through his Holy Spirit, in independence of all outward and creaturely aids."[45] Made in the image of God, like God man is spirit but designed to dwell on earth and so "lodged in an earthly tabernacle." His innate principle is *self-motion,* which distinguishes spirit from matter, and like his Creator he was endued with *understanding,* with "a *will,* exerting itself in various affections and passions; and lastly, with *liberty,* or freedom of choice, without which all the rest would have been in vain." It is in these attributes that "the natural image of God consisted."[46] Not only does Wesley stress that the nature of man is *spirit,* but he is at pains to reject the secularizing eighteenth-century Enlightenment's version of the idea that the *differentia specifica* separating human beings from brutes is reason. "It is not reason.... But it is *this: Man is capable of God; the inferior creatures are not.* We have no ground to believe that they are in any degree capable of knowing, loving, or obeying God. This is the specific difference between man and brute—the great gulf which they cannot pass over. And [before the Fall] a loving obedience to God was the perfection of men, [just as] a loving obedience to man was the perfection of brutes."[47] Through Christ and the New Birth the original image can be restored in those who experience it. The road to Perfection of faith-grace can thereby be found that ultimately leads, beginning if not consummated in the here and now, to eternal blessedness and eschatological fulfillment. "Here then we see ... what is real religion: a restoration of man, by him that bruises the serpent's head, to all that the old serpent deprived him of; a restoration not only to favor, but likewise to the image of God; implying not barely deliverance from sin but [to] being filled with the fullness of God.... [N]othing short of this is Christian religion."[48] The high standard, thus, is this, Wesley insisted: "None are

45. Geoffrey F. Nuttall, *The Holy Spirit in Puritan Faith and Experience,* 2nd ed. (Oxford: B. Blackwell, 1947), 91–92.

46. John Wesley, "The General Deliverance" [1782], sermon no. 60, in *The Works of John Wesley,* vol. 2, *Sermons II,* ed. Outler, 438–39. This sermon concludes with a vision of cosmic redemption as the climax of the eschatological transformation of man and the world in the end time, the universal deliverance.

47. Ibid., 441. Italics added.

48. John Wesley, "The End of Christ's Coming" [1781], sermon no. 62, ibid., 482–83.

[truly] Christians but they that have the mind which was in Christ, and walk as he walked."[49]

The political implications seem never to have been drawn by John Wesley himself, and in his personal politics (as mentioned) he was no republican but a Tory who broke with the American movement for independence prior to the Revolution and withdrew his missionaries.[50] Thus, his theology and his pragmatic politics must be distinguished. Nor was he, as a relentless itinerant evangelist, at all focused on politics but on the redemption of souls for eternity, as were the other leading figures in the Awakening. The republican—and one must say *democratic*—political implications would only emerge fully in the subsequent flowering of Methodism, begun to be sure in the eighteenth century but surging in the later frontier revivals, the rise of the "common man" in the Jacksonian period, into the moralistic effusions of the Abolitionist movement that culminated in the catastrophe of Civil War.[51] The result was that by 1850 the Methodist Church was the largest organization in the United States, apart from the federal government itself. These later Methodists brought a new religious vision, one only incipient in Wesley's own theology. They viewed the state itself "as a moral being and political action as a way to introduce God's kingdom."[52] Such attitudes and convictions about national community and personal identity, prefigured in Wesley himself, were shared with Baptists and other denominations, to be sure, and ultimately burst the boundaries of mere church affiliation. They gained such general prominence and power over time as palpably to endure into the present as major components of anything that can be called American civil theology. As prominent scholars have recently argued:

> The Christianization of the United States was neither a residue of Puritan hegemony nor a transplantation of a European sacred canopy. It was the striking achievement of nineteenth-century

49. John Wesley, "The Mystery of Iniquity" [1783], sermon no. 61, ibid., 467. Cf. Rom. 12:16; Phil. 1:27, 2:2–5: "Let this mind be in you, which was also in Christ Jesus [v. 5]."

50. See Wesley's *Calm Address to Our American Colonies*, in *Political Sermons*, ed. Sandoz, 409–20.

51. See Nathan O. Hatch and John H. Wigger, eds., *Methodism and the Shaping of American Culture* (Nashville: Kingswood Books, Abingdon Press, 2001).

52. Ibid., 20, 27.

activists. . . . Unlike Europe, American popular culture remained more religious than did high culture. David Martin has argued that Methodists, only a counterculture in England, succeeded in America in defining the core of democratic culture: "Arminian evangelical Protestantism provided the *differentia specifica* of the American religious and cultural ethos."[53]

The intellectual and spiritual groundwork was laid in the Great Awakening, and its aftermath, and in the Reformed theology articulate in John and Charles Wesley. The experiential power of Francis Asbury— in 1784 the first bishop ordained by John Wesley along with the "constitution of the Methodist Episcopal Church as an independent body"— and his "boiling hot religion"[54] clearly was present in the revival as preached by the Wesleys, George Whitefield, Jonathan Edwards, and other eighteenth-century evangelists.

A glance at the sources is evidence enough. Especially telling is the dry reportage of Whitefield, who, after preaching in the church of the great philosopher and preacher Jonathan Edwards, in Northampton, wrote: "Preached this morning, and good Mr. Edwards wept during the whole time of exercise. The people were equally affected; and, in the afternoon, the power increased yet more. Our Lord seemed to keep the good wine till the last."[55] Head and heart needed to be as one for *real* Christianity to flower in the man, and the evangelists sought to thread the needle between enthusiasm and formalism in stirring hearts and breaking the dry crust of doctrine and dogma through the power of the Word. The essential goal of them all, to repeat, was "a movement toward immediacy, toward direct communion with God through his Holy Spirit" *for every person*— "in independence of all outward and creaturely aids." The goal was to do so in a way neatly captured in the title of a 1750 book by the Edwardsian Joseph Bellamy: *True Religion delineated; or, Experimental Religion, as distinguished from Formality on the one Hand, and Enthusiasm on the other, set in a Scriptural and Rational Light.*[56]

53. Ibid., 37–38 (citing Martin's *Tongues of Fire* [Oxford: B. Blackwell, 1990,] 21).

54. Taves, *Fits, Trances, and Visions,* 84; Hatch and Wigger, eds., *Methodism,* 34. Cf. Noll, *America's God,* chaps. 9 and 16.

55. Iain Murray, ed., *George Whitefield's Journals* (Edinburgh: Banner of Truth Trust, 1960), 477. The entry is dated Sunday, October 19, 1740.

56. *Works of John Wesley,* vol. 18, *Journal and Diaries I,* ed. W. Reginald Ward and Richard P. Heitzenrater (Nashville: Abingdon Press, 1988), 10, quoting Nuttall, *The*

Religious apperceptive *experience* grounded in a spiritual *sensorium* of the psyche was understood to be an indelible mark of the image of God in the person, restored through grace in his life, the fruit of the blessed presence in a person of the Holy Spirit exceeding merely naturalistic powers and modes of perceptual experience.[57] Its discernment and privileged place in the anthropology powerfully armed the rise of a true individualism and a human dignity now solidly anchored in the person's participatory spiritual and intellectual capacities. Man was more than a natural being and participated in the divine. His individualism, inherent liberty, and accountability did not bottom on his animal nature or acquisitive propensities (as in Locke) but in his higher faculties as a gift or infusion of divine grace. Both Jonathan Edwards and John Wesley, in slightly different ways of no concern here, embraced *this* understanding of what it means to be a human being. It carried them and their publics philosophically and theologically far beyond the Lockean-Humean secularizing and naturalist models of experience and individualism. It was insistently and widely propagated and affirmed in the general population through the continuing revival where the stresses fell on each person's salvation or damnation, his ultimate answerability to God for his life and actions at the Judgment. Herein lies the root of the revolutionary conception of every individual person as both *king and priest,* as we have seen the Norman Anonymous long before proclaiming every baptized believer to be.[58]

Holy Spirit in Puritan Faith and Experience, 91–92; Taves, *Fits, Trances, and Visions,* 48. This was not unique to the Great Awakening, of course. "During the [English] Civil War testimonies of religious experience were published in great numbers, testimonies which took classic shape in Bunyan's *Grace Abounding*" (Editors' introduction, *Works of John Wesley,* 18:10).

57. "Wesley presupposed a 'whole theory of knowledge with its notion of a "spiritual sensorium" analogous to our physical senses and responsive to prior initiatives of the Holy Spirit'" (Taves, *Fits, Trances, and Visions,* 52, quoting Albert Outler's quotation of John Wesley). The term is of interest also because of Eric Voegelin's characterization of the soul as the *sensorium of transcendence* in man. Thus, Voegelin, *OH* I, *Israel and Revelation* (Baton Rouge: Louisiana State University Press, 1956), 235: "The leap in being, the experience of divine being as world-transcendent, is inseparable from the understanding of man as human. The personal soul as the sensorium of transcendence must develop parallel with the understanding of a transcendent God."

58. For the Norman Anonymous, see n29 above. The argument here is supported by the analyses of Colin Morris, *The Discovery of the Individual, 1050–1200* (New York: Harper & Row, 1972), and also by Louis Dumont, "A Modified View of Our

Against the British moral philosophers' movement toward a secu-
larized understanding of the affections grounded in an innate
"moral sense," Edwards grounded what he deemed to be specifically
religious, that is God-given "gracious" affections in a new "spiritual sense." ... [He] described the new spiritual sense using the
language of Paul's Letter to the Galatians. Arguing that the "spirit
of God" dwelt in true saints, he added that "Christ by his Spirit
not only is in them [the saints], but lives in them ... so that they
live by his life; so is his Spirit united to them as a principle of life
in them; they don't only drink living water, but this living water
becomes a well or fountain of water, in the soul." ... In other
words, this new spiritual sense was not a new thing perceived by
the senses, but an altogether new sense. It was not [merely as in
Locke's sense] a "new faculty of understanding, but ... a new
foundation laid in the nature of the soul." ... This new spiritual
sense thus provided the theoretical foundation for direct religious
experience.... While the Spirit of God operated *directly* through
its indwelling in the new spiritual sense of the saints, the Spirit,
"in all his operations upon the minds of natural men, only moves,
impresses, assists, improves, or some way acts upon natural principles.... Thus while the Spirit of God operated as a "first cause"
with respect to spiritual persons, the Spirit operated only as a
"second cause," that is through natural means, with respect to
[unconverted] natural persons.[59]

As with early Christianity, so under the revivalist thrust from the
Awakening onward, "to become a Christian was a deliberate personal
choice, involving both an interior change (repentance) and an exterior
one (baptism and acceptance of Christ as Lord)."[60] The puzzle in the

---

Origins: The Christian Beginnings of Modern Individualism," *Religion* 12 (1982): 1–
27. Cf. the discussion of *liber homo* in J. C. Holt, *Magna Carta*, 2nd ed. (New York:
Cambridge University Press, 1992), 2, 9–11, 276–80, 290–95.

59. Taves, *Fits, Trances, and Visions*, 38–39, citations omitted.

60. Morris, *Discovery of the Individual*, 24. The debt to "the classical as well as
Christian past" is stressed by Morris in his analysis of the twelfth-century develop-
ments, ibid., 159. A similar texture was present in eighteenth-century America, where
the Golden Age of the classics coincided with the Revolutionary period. Cf. Meyer
Reinhold, *Classica Americana: The Greek and Roman Heritage in the United States*
(Detroit: Wayne State University Press, 1984).

eighteenth century was how to draw the line between nature and the divine, but this was not novel either and had bedeviled Christian thought at least from the time of Aquinas (d. 1274). Is the "moral sense" (often designative of instinctive *storgé*)[61] of Francis Hutcheson and the eighteenth-century British Common Sense philosophers natural, or is it the light of the Lord infused by grace into the soul of his creature man?[62] Perhaps the decisive point is the acknowledgment of the *fact* of such a capacity in man—which immediately enlists the concurrence of Aristotle as well as Aquinas, not to mention Thomas Jefferson and John Adams—whatever the metaphysical differences. We may observe, however, that this is a false dichotomy to be set aside by recognition of the further facts that reason and passion are far from being opposites. Rather, they are reconcilable with and texture friendship *(philia)* as well as philosophy per se, understood (very much as Edwards himself ultimately understood it) as the love of wisdom through the love of Being as its source.[63] Also it is evidenced by noticing that

---

61. For the Greek *storgé* in this context, see the discussion in Norman Fiering, *Jonathan Edwards's Moral Thought and Its British Context* (Chapel Hill: University of North Carolina Press, 1981), of "permutations of self-love," 158–60. In G. W. von Leibniz's explanation: "nature gives to man and also to most of the animals affectionate and tender feelings for those of their species.... Besides the general instinct of *society*, ... there are some more particular forms of it, as the affection between the male and female, the love which father and mother bear toward the children, which the Greeks call *Storgé* and similar inclinations" (quoted ibid., 159).

62. The debate over "moral sense" and whether it was divine or natural was intense. "Edwards writes with indirect but obvious reference to Francis Hutcheson that 'unless we will be atheists, we must allow that true virtue does primarily and most essentially consist in a supreme love to God.' Wesley writes with direct reference to him that 'God has nothing to do with [Hutcheson's] scheme of virtue from beginning to end. So that to say the truth, his scheme of virtue is atheism all over'" (Richard B. Steele, *"Gracious Affection" and "True Virtue" According to Jonathan Edwards and John Wesley* [Metuchen, NJ: Scarecrow Press, 1994], 340).

63. These matters are addressed in Edwards's two works, *Some Thoughts Concerning the Revival of Religion* (1743) and *Treatise on the Religious Affections* (1746); see the discussion in Taves, *Fits, Trances, and Visions,* 36–41: "By locating the higher, spiritual passions in the soul and by postulating a new spiritual sense through which God could act directly on the soul, Edwards could provide separate explanations for the genesis of true and false religion" (40). Also, see esp. the first two chapters of Edwards's valedictory work, *The Nature of True Virtue* in *Works of Jonathan Edwards,* vol. 8, ed. Ramsey, 539–61. "By these things it appears that a truly virtuous mind, being as it were under the sovereign dominion of *love to God,* does above all things seek the

the love of God and neighbor supremely expresses in the *shema* of ancient Israel (Deut. 6:4; Lev. 19:18) as well as in the Great Commandment of the Gospel (Matt. 22:37) *both* noetic rationality and profoundest revelatory passion: Plato's erotic rise to the vision of *Agathon* and the Christian mystic's loving rise to the *Beatific Vision* are more alike than dissimilar and tend to obliterate the distinctions between reason and revelation in sharing a common joyful tension toward the mysterious transcendent ground of Being. The mutual interaction of noetic and pneumatic experiences perhaps reaches its apogee in the Johanine *amicitia* proclaimed in the First Epistle of John (4:16, 19: "God is love. . . . We love him because he first loved us"), which was so marvelously elaborated philosophically by Aquinas. Never mind that it was Aquinas himself who routinely also embraced the natural reason-supernatural revelation dichotomy that, with continuing dogmatic authority, thereby inconsistently pits rationality and feeling, head and heart against one another existentially.[64]

In sum: The adaptation of Platonism from multiple sources (whatever the terminological differences) structured the philosophical and moral theology of both Edwards and Wesley—from the meditative identification of *summum bonum* and highest Being alike with God-revealed-incarnate-in-Christ, to the understanding of morality-virtue in all its amplitude as *derivative* from loving communion with divine Being through the participatory faith-grace relationship as *fruitio dei* evinced in the individual person's pilgrimage through time toward blessedness from conversion and sanctification to Perfection.

The uneasy suspicion of anachronism in pointing to ancient and medieval sources and equivalences in the thought of such seminal eighteenth-century figures as Wesley and Edwards and their catholicity deserves a word of emphasis, so as to counter the prevalent false assump-

---

glory of God, and makes *this* his supreme, governing, and ultimate end. . . . And it may be asserted in general that nothing is of the nature of true virtue, in which God is not the *first* and the *last*" (559–60, italics as in original).

64. On the technical complexities of the general problem of the relationship of religious faith in pneumatic experience and noetic intuition in philosophical experience see Eric Voegelin, "The Beginning and the Beyond: A Meditation on Truth," in *CW* 28:173–232, esp. the epistemological considerations stated at 188–93, which have application to the present discussion.

tions Ralph Barton Perry identified as the "fallacy of difference."[65] The sources support the present line of interpretation, as I have tried to make clear even in this concise general account that is unable to do justice to the full complexities—which the reader is free to explore to his own satisfaction by looking for himself at the sources cited herein. On the chief point, for instance, in considering Jonathan Edwards's substantial agreement with Thomas Aquinas on the Beatific Vision, Paul Ramsey explains that the "contention that beatitude cannot consist in the vision of God because such an object absolutely surpasses human capacities is ruled out by Aquinas on theological and philosophical grounds." Ramsey continues:

> It is contrary to faith: since we are assured by faith that God is our ultimate good, we must suppose that our ultimate happiness will consist in a vision of the essence of God which will completely fulfill our highest human capacities as spiritual being, intellect and will. To deny this destiny is also contrary to what we can know about human nature: if the rational creature is incapable of attaining knowledge of the first cause of things, then its natural tendency to know the causes of things would in the end be doomed to frustration. It is true that God transcends all creaturely knowledge, but this rules out creaturely *comprehension*, not *vision*, of his essence. . . . [T]he human mind must receive an infusion of the grace of glory to permit the human being to enjoy the vision of God. . . . Nothing short of this vision can render human beings ultimately happy. . . . Edwards would agree, including . . . that there is need for an infusion of grace or divine love in the heart.[66]

Grappling more technically with the issues philosophically, Edwards no less than Wesley, both anchored in mystical experiences of transcendent truth, resolutely refuses to concede either reason or faith to the new Philistines, even in the face of a civilization-wide onslaught against both. Their common ground (and that of the emerging American community) is comprehensible in terms of *experience*—not dogmatics or

65. Discussion and citations in Sandoz, *GOL*, 98–99.
66. "Appendix III: Heaven is a Progressive State," in *Works of Jonathan Edwards*, vol. 8, ed. Ramsey, 706–38, at 722.

doctrines or mere verbalism as matters indifferent. Indeed, only that can be the ultimate basis both of social *homonoia* and of the saving doubt that make civility in politics and toleration in religion and matters of conscience at all possible.[67] One scholar in comparing Edwards and Wesley writes of their commonality and its consequences as follows:

> [T]he truth of every "Scripture doctrine" is supposed to be manifest in the moral virtues and religious affections of those who profess it. Both epistemologically and theologically, cognition, volition, and emotion are existentially inseparable, even if they may be heuristically distinguishable. Knowledge of, obedience to, and delight in God all presuppose, reinforce, and interpenetrate one another. One who claims to know God without obeying him is an antinomian ... to know God without loving him, a rationalist ... to obey God without loving him, a Pharisee ... to love God without obeying him, a hypocrite ... to love or obey God without knowing the Scriptures in which he is revealed, an illuminist. Experimental theology, as it was worked out by Edwards and Wesley, attempted to combat all these aberrations, to hold the profession of orthodox doctrine, the practice of "true virtue," and the experience of "gracious affection" in a creative and dynamic equipoise.[68]

In the immediate horizon of our discussion the debate in context turned (as it still does) on the meaning of *experience,* with a monopoly of acceptability and authenticity increasingly being claimed (following Lockean-Humean epistemology) for "external" experience, with "internal" experience being darkly suspected of irrationality or as being the realm of demonism manifesting itself in enthusiasm and personal and social disorder. Never mind that all experience is *internal* to the experiencing *consciousness* of a concrete human personality. This onslaught by Enlightenment rationalism—deeply and rightly suspected of error and of the theoretical reductionism so grotesquely exhibited in the cadaverous stick-figure "Man" of positivism proffered in subsequent times into our own era—was rejected and resisted as deficient and vigorously

---

67. This fundamental prerequisite of religious liberty and toleration is expounded in John Wesley's "Catholic Spirit," sermon no. 39, in *Works of John Wesley,* vol. 2, *Sermons II,* ed. Outler, 79–96.

68. Steele, *"Gracious Affection" and "True Virtue,"* 365.

fought by both Jonathan Edwards and John Wesley. Full analysis of the complex issues lies beyond present purposes, but the points of their agreement have been summarized as follows:

> First, both Edwards and Wesley defined true religion in opposition to both formalism and enthusiasm. Second, they both equated true religion with vital or heart religion as manifest in conversion and a continuing process or sanctification. Third, they both defended the possibility of a direct or immediate experience of the Spirit of God, and they both argued that authentic experience must be tried and tested in practice. They differed somewhat in their terminology, with Edwards preferring the phrase "experimental religion" and the "indwelling of the Spirit of God" and Wesley "true Christian experience" and the "witness of the Spirit of God."[69]

The aim of it all, however, is the same in both men: "inward holiness," "the union of the soul with God," "true living faith" and not merely works, so as to become "partakers of the divine nature" (2 Pet. 1:4). Drawing from various meditative traditions of holiness and mysticism, including Thomas à Kempis, Michael Molinos, and especially "Macarius the Egyptian," Albert Outler writes that Wesley's distinctive notion of "perfection" or " 'holiness' *in the world* must be taken seriously—active holiness in *this* life." This is the understanding of perfection as a process rather than a state. "Thus it was that the ancient and Eastern tradition of holiness as *disciplined* love became fused in Wesley's mind with his own Anglican tradition of holiness as *aspiring* love" and came to be what he regarded as his most distinctive teaching.[70] In

---

69. Taves, *Fits, Trances, and Visions,* 48.

70. Quotations from Outler, ed., *John Wesley,* 63, 65, 66, 252, 9–10, respectively. His third publication, a recent edition of Wesley's English edition of Thomas à Kempis's (d. 1471) classic of *devotio moderna, The Imitation of Christ,* is John Wesley, *The Christian's Pattern; or An Extract of The Imitation of Christ* (Nashville: Abingdon Press, n.d.). The original—an Augustinian search of the disciple's soul for union with God—is abbreviated and recast as a dialogue between Christ and the Christian. The anthropology (which echoes in Wesley's *Sermons*) is especially to be found in bk. 3, chap. 38 (chap. 60 in the original) as it opens with the Christian's supplication: "O lord, my God, who hast created me after thy image and likeness, grant me this grace which thou hast showed to be so great and necessary to salvation, that I may overcome my wicked nature which draweth me to sin and to perdition" (97).

Wesley's exposition the pilgrim's progress in holiness moves by degrees, mounting upward from the faith of the *servant,* who obeys out of fear (the beginning of Wisdom) but who is exhorted not to stop there but to press on until he obeys out of love, as is the privilege of the children of God. "Exhort him to press on by all possible means, till he passes 'from faith to faith'; from the faith of a *servant* to the faith of a *son;* from the spirit of bondage unto fear, to the spirit of childlike love. He will then have 'Christ in his heart'[2 Cor. 4:6; Eph. 3:17]." From here the ascending way of holiness lies open to accept the Apostle Paul's invitation to leave those "'first principles of the doctrine of Christ' (namely repentance and faith) '[to] go on to perfection....' 'To love the Lord your God with all your heart, and with all your soul.' These are they to whom the Apostle John gives the venerable title of *'fathers,'* who 'have known him that is from the beginning,' [1 Jn. 2:13, 14] the eternal Three-One God." Wesley adds: "And those who are fathers in Christ generally (though I believe not always) enjoy the *plerophory* or 'full assurance of hope' [Heb. 6:11]; having no more doubt of reigning with him in glory than if they already saw him coming in the clouds of heaven. But this does not prevent their continually increasing in the knowledge and love of God."[71] The mystic state is distinguished by this: "in the mystic state, God is not satisfied merely to help us think *about* him.... He gives us an experimental, intellectual knowledge of his presence."[72]

Insight into the full range of spiritual experience (briefly hinted in the foregoing) as understood by Wesley and his contemporaries is important in itself but also for its implications for an adequate conception of authentic human existence. There are obvious implications for stewardship and for the latent *political* dimension of theology as involving godliness in man as well as in citizen. Action toward righteousnesss and justice by the faithful arises from this core experience as dimensions of the human vocation historically manifest in Methodism and in American culture more generally. Thus, at the heart of spiritual individualism lay the *experience* (however accounted for) of the creature's communion with the Creator. Edwards attributed this capacity in the

71. Quoting from Wesley, "On the Discoveries of Faith" [1788], sermon no. 117, in *Works of John Wesley,* vol. 4, *Sermons IV,* ed. Outler, 35–37.
72. Ibid., 37n80.

human being to his *spiritual sense* and emphatically argued against an array of critics at the time who espoused the new philosophy in various forms that God had no need for secondary or intermediate means for communicating spiritual knowledge. Norman Fiering writes: "Edwards meant by spiritual sense not only a new capacity for being affected by the things of God, but also a new inclination or a new will directed toward those things. The new sense of the heart brought about by the working of grace is also a new disposition or an infused habit that is identical to holy love or holiness." "[God] imparts this Knowledge immediately, not making use of intermediate natural Causes." He states the key point: "Edwards believed that converting grace was a physical influence on the will that changed the will's delectation from self to God. This 'fact' cannot be broken down into simpler elements."[73] There is nothing very novel in this. It in spirit reaches back to classical and medieval traditions, especially as formed by Platonic *noesis* ("intuitionism") and Augustinian voluntarism, and to Scholastic philosophy and mysticism. We should try not to resent too deeply the fact that the likes of Wesley, Edwards, and the founding generation itself were more profoundly mindful of the Western heritage that is our birthright than are most educated people today. As one writer concisely elogized the abiding insights at hand:

> We are taught in metaphysicks [*sic*], that being, truth and goodness, are really one. How sweet a rest now doth the spirit, with its understanding, and its will, find to it self [*sic*] in every being, in every truth, in every state or motion of being, in every form of truth. When it hath a *sense* of the highest love, which is the same with the highest goodness, designing, disposing, working all in all, even all conceptions in all understandings, all motions, in every will, human, angelical, divine? With what a joy and complacency unexpressible doth the will, the understanding, the whole spirit now lie down to rest everywhere, as upon a bed of love, as in the bosom of goodness it self?[74]

Fiering writes: "For Edwards, true virtue is the spontaneous overflowing of a purified soul.... Love to being in general ... is the essence of

---

73. Fiering, *Jonathan Edwards's Moral Thought*, 126, 128n51.

74. Ibid., 125, quoting Peter Sterry, *Discourse of the Freedom of the Will* (1675), Fiering's italics and editing. Cf. Augustine, *Confessions* 13.37.52, *City of God* 11.10.

true virtue, and this internal habit or disposition produces an enormous superfluity of love, out of which, subordinately, love for the particular being in the creation will flow."[75]

The aesthetic dimensions of experience are prominently stressed as beauty, goodness, and justice beckon the devout soul, especially in Edwards's work, in keeping with his mystical Platonism. And it has been well-said that Methodism was born in song, often sung to poetry written by Charles Wesley. The hymns communicated and by rote taught the theology as it lifted the hearts of the faithful. The recondite insights of metaphysics and epistemology were thereby democratized and made lucid in the spiritual convictions of everyman: Christ came for all, not merely for the elite. The Wesleys' 1780 *Collection of Hymns for the use of the People called Methodists* was a cornerstone of evangelism in the founding period. John Wesley stated in the preface that the "'hymns are not carelessly jumbled together, but carefully ranged under proper heads, according to the experience of real Christians.' The witness of the Spirit, the idea upon which Wesley built his theological understanding of real Christian experience, was central to the hymn-book and . . . comprised the heart of the distinctively Methodist message."[76] From this hymnal, for instance, congregations sang (hymn 93) about enlightenment through the witness of the Holy Spirit:

> We by his Spirit *prove*
> And *know* the things of God;
>
> . . . .

---

75. Fiering, *Jonathan Edwards's Moral Thought*, 350. "For Edwards, as for [Nicolas] Malebranche earlier, God is being. He who is, He whose essence is to exist, and He who is absolutely self-sufficient. God is also properly designated 'being in general,' because God's being is itself the cause of all created essences. All existence, all being, derives from God, who is the one self-sufficient being. It seems clear that Edwards meant by 'being in general' the transcendent God *plus* his ordered creation. Similarly, St. Thomas had said that God is not contained in *ens commune* (being in general), but transcends it. Edwards's concept of being in general included all of what is now called 'nature' as well as God, who is above nature" (ibid., 326). Edwards's *The Nature of True Virtue*, the basis of these analytical remarks, was written in 1755 but first published (along with *Concerning the End for which God created the World* as *Two Dissertations*) posthumously in 1765. Edwards died in 1758. Cf. *Works of Jonathan Edwards*, vol. 8, ed. Ramsey, 400.

76. Taves, *Fits, Trances, and Visions*, 50.

His Spirit to us he gave,
And dwells in us, we know
The witness in ourselves we have,
And all his fruits we show.[77]

The milestone sermon by John Wesley, "Free Grace," where he for the first time fully expounded his conviction that *all* may hope for eternal salvation through Christ and for a universal deliverance at the end of time (the "Arminian" defection from strict Calvinist predestination that aroused a furor and provoked the breach with George Whitefield in 1740), concludes with one of several poems titled "Universal Redemption." It begins and ends as follows:

Hear, holy, holy, holy, Lord,
Father of all mankind,
Spirit of love, eternal Word,
In mystic union join'd.
Hear, and inspire, my stammering tongue,
Exalt my abject thought,
Speak from my mouth a sacred song,
Who spak'st the world from nought.
* * * *
A power to choose, a will to obey,
Freely his grace restores;
We all may find the Living Way,
And call the Saviour ours.
* * * *
Shine in our hearts, Father of light;
Jesu, thy beams impart;
Spirit of truth, our minds unite,
And make us one in heart.
Then, only then, our eyes shall see
Thy promised kingdom come;
And every heart by grace set free,
Shall make the Saviour room
Thee every tongue shall then confess,

77. Quoted from ibid., 56.

> And every knee shall bow.
> Come quickly, Lord, we wait thy grace,
> We long to meet thee now.[78]

The youthful Eric Voegelin admiringly saw in Jonathan Edwards's thought the "independence of the American history of ideas from that of Europe" and, moreover, regarded him as a "pantheistic" mystic who had left far behind merely dogmatic Calvinism. As Voegelin expounds Edwards's posthumous work, "The divine being is being in general, encompassing universal existence. . . . The goal of world history is an ever more perfect emanation of God in the world, by his making it ever more like himself. 'The heart is drawn nearer and nearer to God, and the union with him becomes more firm and close: and, at the same time, the creature becomes more and more conformed to God.'" Instead of tending, as in Humean skepticism, toward the *closed* self that emerged and continued in English philosophy after Thomas Reid and the Scottish school, in Edwards and later on in "[America] the same ideas did not follow any skeptical tradition but worked with the 'openness' of the self; the naïve juxtaposition of God and man remains intact. The theory of knowledge does not suffer from dialectics."[79] The impetus toward understanding *openness* as the very essence of the human being, evident in Edwards (and in Wesley, as we have seen), was carried forward as a general American social characteristic. In American philosophy it can be traced in Charles Peirce and William James and even George Santayana—and, we would add, exceptionally in Europe in Henri Bergson's late work, *Two Sources of Morality and Religion.*[80]

---

78. Appended to "Free Grace," sermon no. 110, in *Works of John Wesley,* vol. 3, *Sermons III,* ed. Outler, 559–63. This text was set to music and published as a hymn in *Hymns and Sacred Poems* (1740). Whether John Wesley or his brother Charles Wesley composed it is uncertain.

79. Eric Voegelin, *CW* 1, chap. 3, "A Formal Relationship with Puritan Mysticism," 126–43, at 140–42. The original of this book, *Über die Form des americanischen Geistes,* his *Habilitationsschrift* at the University of Vienna, was published in 1928 when the author was twenty-seven years old, after he had spent two years in the United States studying and traveling.

80. Ibid. Bergson, *Les deux sources de la morale et de la religion* (1932), English translation published in 1935 by Henry Holt. The *open soul* and society, and the *closed soul* and society, are key terms of Bergson's analysis—but cannot be the source of Voegelin's terminology here, since his book was published four years earlier than Bergson's.

Of his first experience in America Voegelin more than four decades later remarked: "I began to sense that American society had a *philosophical background* far superior in range and existential substance... to anything that I found represented in the methodological environment in which I had grown up [in Vienna]."[81]

§6. Revolution and Religion

At the *commonsense* level—conceived as a generally held residual substratum of understanding anchoring the contemplative experiences and philosophizing we have been considering—ordinary pragmatic moral and result-oriented political *action* will be demanded of statesmen. The utilitarian perspective disdained by Wesley and Edwards, as evangelists intent not on this world but on saving souls for the next, will fade into the background, and one consequence will be the kind of outlook captured in Davy Crockett's motto (which echoed Benjamin Franklin's maxim): "Be sure you're right, then go ahead!" The hierarchy of being—the layered structure of existence familiar from ordinary experience—is matched by a hierarchy of modes of response to experiences of reality's truth. Human affairs of a political order, with life and death held in the balance, cannot be conducted like a mystic's meditation or a philosophy seminar, but at best merely in light of understanding and conviction grounded in highest truth—and even that is often only faintly present or missing entirely. Thus, at the political and military (pragmatic) levels of action where the brute facts count and concrete actions must be taken, the resolute attitude formulated by Crockett was evidenced after 1765 in the movement increasingly fueling opposition to perceived tyranny and in favor of liberty and (ultimately) independence leading to the founding—as it must ever be in practical human affairs, if we are true to ourselves. Crockett's attitude is still patently exemplified in American political policy and action.[82]

81. Quoted from Eric Voegelin, *AR*, 29. Italics added. The original text dates from 1973.

82. Quoted from D. H. Meyer, *The Instructed Conscience: The Shaping of the American National Ethic* (Philadelphia: University of Pennsylvania Press, 1972), 110. Meyer points out the analogous sentiment in Benjamin Franklin's maxim: "Resolve to perform what you ought; perform without fail what you resolve" (ibid., 186n2).

The debt to loftier considerations and moralism may be present but is not necessarily an unmixed blessing. If we take social and political morality to be only private morality writ large, we run into problems that have bedeviled American policy-makers from the beginning of the republic, through the presidencies of Lincoln and Woodrow Wilson, until today. This often consists in some variety of suspended judgment or utopian hopefulness (metastatic faith) that ignores the delimitation on rational action in the world concisely signaled for all time in the Gospel's "My kingdom is not of this world" (Jn. 18:36): for familiar instance, fighting a war to end war, or one to rid the world of evil. As one writer formulates the poignant practical dilemma that still plagues us and flaws such thinking: "It was inconceivable that we can be morally obliged to do what we ought not do."[83] The abiding structure of reality is not so malleable as ideologues, optimists, and well-intentioned millenarians compulsively suppose. At the surface, the watchword here is as old as Aristotle's dismissive critique of Plato's community of women, children, and property proposed by Socrates in the *Republic*, and it is sagely exemplified during the founding era nowhere better than in John Dickinson's famous comments in the Constitutional Convention of 1787: "Experience must be our only guide. Reason may mislead us!"[84] Dickinson had primarily the *philosophes* and their defective brand of "rationalism" in mind.[85] The root in both

83. Ibid., 118, with reference to slavery and Francis Wayland's *The Limitation of Human Responsibility* (1838).

84. Reported in *Madison's Debates,* in *Records of the Federal Convention of 1787,* ed. Max Farrand (1911; repr., New Haven: Yale University Press, 1966), 2:278; see the discussion in Sandoz, *GOL,* 220–22. For Aristotle see *Politics* 2.1260b37–1265b18.

85. What this usage of the term *rationalism* specifically means in modern political theory has been explored by Michael Oakeshott in his *Rationalism in Politics, and Other Essays,* new and expanded ed., foreword by Timothy Fuller (1962; repr., Indianapolis: Liberty Fund, 1991), who speaks of "the disease of Rationalism" and shows it to involve "an identifiable error, a misconception with regard to the nature of human knowledge, which amounts to a corruption of the mind" (37). John Adams (and some of his colleagues) perfectly understood all the essentials of this already at the time, even before the dawn of behaviorism in psychology and behavioralism in the social sciences, and without benefit of Oakeshott's masterful analysis. Thus, at his acerbic best, Adams wrote in his marginalia: "It is to Ideology, to that obscure metaphysics, which searching with subtlety after first causes, wishes to found upon them the legislation of nations, instead of adapting their laws to the knowledge of the human heart and to the lessons of history, that we are to attribute all the calamities

instances is a failure to observe the autonomy of the different strata of reality, especially as here those identified as spiritual and noetic reality on one hand and the political reality of statesmen on the other, and to distinguish between them. Human life is a unity; but it is a complex unity, one not susceptible of simplistic treatment without courting disaster through inadvertent perversion. Thus, on further reflection, Aristotle was both right and wrong, as was also John Dickinson. The former ignored the noetic character of the argument setting forth the contours of the paradigmatic *polis* of the Idea in the *Republic* in favor of a kind of literalist fundamentalism—a move bordering on what we might call a cheap shot, one that Aristotle must have recognized as such as a connoisseur of Plato's thought. The latter tacitly acknowledged the deformed rationality (i.e., irrational rationalism: already fully diagnosed by John Adams) of the intellectuals' prevailing climate of opinion. He spoke to the problem at hand in those terms, but all the while in so speaking he restored the fullness of rationality to his own discourse and thereby tacitly appealed to that same amplitude in his auditors. As experienced men of affairs themselves, the other framers were largely uncorrupted by trendy Enlightenment fashions and, therefore, intuitively responded to Dickinson's caveat.

The American Revolution itself, of course, had been preached as a revival and had the astonishing result of succeeding, Perry Miller once remarked, and we have seen evidence that he was right in that judgment. The theology of the evangelists varied considerably, of course, but substantively it lay close to that of John Wesley and Jonathan Edwards as just glimpsed. Their differences over free will, election, predestination, free grace, universal reconciliation, and other burning theological issues provide a backdrop of importance as between especially John Wesley and Whitefield. But first things first. In George Whitefield's blunt statement: "Let a man go to the grammar school of faith and repentance, before he goes to the university of election and

---

that our beloved France has experienced. . . . The political and literary world are much indebted for the invention of the new word IDEOLOGY [*sic*]. Our English words Ideocy, or Ideotism [*sic*], express not the force or meaning of it. It is presumed its proper definition is the science of ideocy" (quoted from Zoltán Haraszti, *John Adams & the Prophets of Progress: A Study in the Intellectual and Political History of the Eighteenth Century* [1952; repr., New York: Grossett & Dunlap, 1964], 167).

predestination. A bare head-knowledge of sound words availeth nothing. I am quite tired of Christless talkers."[86]

An intimate connection between civic action and the holy work of redemption through faith and grace was widely assumed and manifested, whatever the details and precise rationale. As Ezra Stiles said in invoking a favorite biblical metaphor for providential favor, "[I]t is truly important that his vine, which God hath planted with a mighty hand in this American wilderness, should be cultivated into confirmed maturity."[87] The matter cannot be stressed too much and is surely of central importance. Indicative is the fact that Congress declared at least sixteen national days of prayer, humiliation, and thanksgiving between 1776 and 1783; and Presidents Washington and Adams continued the practice under the Constitution.[88] The onset of the so-called Second Great Awakening conventionally is dated from around 1790, but in fact it seems to have begun earlier. New Side and New Light evangelism stirring personal spiritual experience continued throughout the period, and the political sermons often were extraordinary in power and substance. Religious services were routinely held in the newly completed Capitol itself in Washington, in the House and Senate chambers as these became available. President Thomas Jefferson and his cabinet attended, along with the members of Congress and their families, inaugurating a practice that continued until after the Civil War. The newly formed United States Marine Corps band supplied

---

86. Murray, ed., *George Whitefield's Journals*, 491. The thorny issues at stake can be seen from "A Letter to the Rev. Mr. John Wesley in Answer to his Sermon entitled *Free Grace*," ibid., appendix 2. For the offending sermon itself (signaling the great "Arminian" split from orthodox Calvinism in the Awakening), see sermon no. 110, in *Works of John Wesley*, vol. 3, *Sermons III*, ed. Outler, 542–63.

87. Ezra Stiles, "A Discourse on the Christian Union [1761]," in *Great Awakening*, ed. Heimert and Miller, selection 51, 605. Cf. Ps. 80:15.

88. On the national days of prayer, fasting, and thanksgiving in the founding period, see Derek H. Davis, *Religion and the Continental Congress, 1774–1789: Contributions to Original Intent* (Oxford and New York: Oxford University Press, 2000), chap. 5, esp. 83–91, and his further remark that "all of the presidents since Jackson have issued prayer proclamations, either annually or in connection with important or critical events, such as American entries into war. Moreover, in 1952 the Congress passed a law providing for a National Day of Prayer, observed annually since, and which from 1988 has been observed on the first Thursday in May" (90). See also Sandoz, *GOL*, chap. 5, "Reflections on Spiritual Aspects of the American Founding," for texts and commentary.

the music for holy services at President Jefferson's instigation, we are told. When the playing of sacred music fell short of expectations, the president suggested recruitment of some professional Italian musicians to help out, and eighteen were in fact enlisted as Marines and brought from Italy for the purpose—where they found, to their dismay, the mud streets and "log huts" of the young nation's new capital.[89] One authority has cogently argued that there was, indeed, a *Revolutionary revival* in America: "Far from suffering decline, religion experienced vigorous growth and luxuriant development during the Revolutionary period. In a host of ways, both practical and intellectual, the church served as a school for politics."[90]

Swarms of witnesses might be called in support of the present line of analysis, but I shall mention only three as representative. Thomas Paine in *Common Sense* (1776) argued the biblical foundations of republican liberty. Thus he wrote: "Near three thousand years passed away from the Mosaic account of the creation, till the Jews under a national delusion requested a king. Till then their form of government... was a kind of republic administered by a judge and the elders of the tribes. Kings they had none, and it was held sinful to acknowledge any being under that title but the Lord of Hosts."[91] Benjamin Rush, signatory of the Declaration of Independence, fervently urged (1786) the schools of Pennsylvania to adopt the Bible as the basic textbook, writing: "The only foundation for a useful education in a republic is to be laid in RELIGION. Without this, there can be no virtue, and without virtue there can be no liberty, and liberty is the object and life of all republican governments.... The religion I mean to recommend in this place is the religion of JESUS CHRIST.... A Christian cannot fail of being a republican."[92] Last, we hear the aged John Adams, in the marvelous correspondence with Thomas Jefferson, identifying the two principal springs of their original revolutionary republicanism and

---

89. Helen Cripe, *Thomas Jefferson and Music* (Charlottesville: University Press of Virginia, 1974), 24–26.

90. Stephen Marini, "Religion, Politics, and Ratification," in *Religion in a Revolutionary Age,* ed. Ronald Hoffman and Peter J. Albert (Charlottesville: University Press of Virginia, 1994), 193. Cf. the related discussion in Sandoz, *Politics of Truth,* chap. 4, "Philosophical and Religious Dimensions of the American Founding."

91. *Common Sense... and other Essential Writings of Thomas Paine,* ed. Sidney Hook (New York: New American Library, 1969), 30.

92. Quoted from Sandoz, *GOL,* 132.

the community that undergirded it as *Whig Liberty* and *Christianity*. Adams movingly wrote (1813): "Now I will avow, that I then believed, and now believe, that those general Principles of Christianity, are as eternal and immutable, as the existence and attributes of God; and those Principles of Liberty are as unalterable as human Nature and our terrestrial, mundane System."[93]

These sentiments did not die with the original founders. In the middle of the nineteenth century and a time of great crisis, Abraham Lincoln borrowed Paul's symbol of *corpus mysticum* from 1 Corinthians 12 and applied it to the America evoked through the Declaration of Independence:

> We have besides these men—descended by blood from our an-
> cestors—among us perhaps half our people who are not descen-
> dants at all of these men, they are men who came from Europe—
> German, Irish, French and Scandinavian.... [T]hey cannot carry
> themselves back into that glorious epoch and make themselves
> feel that they are parts of us, but when they look through that
> old Declaration of Independence they find those old men say
> that "We hold these truths to be self-evident that all men are cre-
> ated equal," and then they feel that moral sentiment taught in
> that day evidences their relation to these men, that it is the father
> of all moral principle in them, and that they have a right to claim it
> as though they were blood of blood and flesh of flesh of the men
> who wrote that Declaration, and so they are. That is the electric
> cord in that Declaration that links the hearts of patriotic and
> liberty-loving men together, that will link those patriotic hearts as
> long as the love of freedom exists in the minds of men through-
> out the world.[94]

§7. Eschatology and Experience

As a study in contrast, Girolamo Savonarola and his community reestab-
lished the Florentine republic at the end of the fifteenth century as a

---

93. Quoted from Sandoz, *Politics of Truth*, 68.
94. Abraham Lincoln quoted from Joseph R. Fornieri, *Abraham Lincoln's Political Faith* (DeKalb: Northern Illinois University Press, 2003), 154–55, citing *The Collected Works of Abraham Lincoln*, ed. Roy P. Basler, 8 vols. (New Brunswick, NJ: Rutgers University Press, 1953–55), 2:499–500.

"civil and political government," one observed by Machiavelli, who gained immortality partly as theorist of classical republicanism.[95] For his trouble Fra Girolamo and two principal associates were at length excommunicated and burnt together as heretics in 1498 in the central marketplace of the city, where a plaque in the pavement still marks the spot. He was graciously spared the worst torments of this horrendous death by first being strangled, since he was an old friend of Pope Alexander VI, and friends in high places should count for something. In the history of republicanism the Machiavellian Moment might with almost equal warrant be known as the Savonarolan Moment: Modern free popular republican government was off to its rocky start after a scant four years of existence. Savonarola's was preached as a republic of virtue and godliness, one thirsting for revival and aimed at purifying and reforming not only corruption in the church but the evil world itself—the beginning of an eschatological and holy *sacrum imperium* with Florence the New Jerusalem of a chosen people, an Elect protected by the Holy Ghost, apocalyptically envisaged as *perhaps* leading

95. Donald Weinstein, *Savonarola and Florence: Prophecy and Patriotism in the Renaissance* (Princeton: Princeton University Press, 1970), 308. Also Lorenzo Polizzotto, *The Elect Nation: The Savonarolan Movement in Florence, 1494–1545* (Oxford: Clarendon Press, 1994), *passim*. "Savonarola took seriously many of Saint Paul's teachings. [He] indicated that he sought to please God, not men, 'because the Apostle says, "if I should still please men, I would not be a servant of Christ."'... It was never in Savonarola's vision to please men. He believed in the wisdom of Saint Paul's words: 'To those [who think they are wise] I shall say, together with the Apostle: "We are fools for Christ: you, however, are the wise [cf. 1 Cor. 3:18–19]"'" (Marion Leathers Kuntz, *The Anointment of Dionisio: Prophecy and Politics in Renaissance Italy* [University Park: Pennsylvania State University Press, 2001], 234–35). For Savonarola's vision, see his *Treatise on the Constitution and Government of the City of Florence*, in *Humanism and Liberty: Writings on Freedom from Fifteenth-Century Florence*, trans. and ed. Renée Neu Watkins (Columbia: University of South Carolina Press, 1978), 231–60: "This government is made more by God than by men, and those citizens who, for the glory of God and for the common good, obey our instructions and strive to make it perfect, will enjoy earthly happiness, spiritual happiness, and eternal happiness" (256). William Penn's perspective is brought to mind in this regard: "Now, what is this Kingdom of God, but God's Government? And where is this Kingdom and Government to be set up, but in Man? So Christ tells us, *Behold the Kingdom of God is within you. . . .* We are taught to pray for it, . . . *Thy Kingdom come, thy Will be done.*" See *The Political Writings of William Penn*, intro. and annotations by Andrew R. Murphy (Indianapolis: Liberty Fund, 2002), 190–91, quoting Luke 17:21 and 11:2.

mankind's transition into the Millennium and the final Eighth Day of eternal Sabbath ending history.

An array of comparable chiliastic and millenarian sentiments was well represented in America during the Revolutionary period and potently influenced the political theology of the fledgling nation as perhaps destined to be the new Israel or chosen people and even the site of the inauguration of the thousand-year reign of God's saints on earth. Since Christianity still plays a large role in America, echoes of these sentiments can be heard to this very day.[96] But "enthusiasm" already was restrained in Milton's work with *reason* the centerpiece, and the validity of traditional authority was readily embraced unless in conflict with scripture.[97] Now muted were the earlier radical expectations of the *Parousia,* or imminent divine intervention, when God "shall come skipping over the mountains and over difficulties" and Christ "shall reign upon earth, here in this world" with His saints.[98] Wesleyan theology served as a moderating force in this respect. In his great election

96. See Stephen A. Marini, "Uncertain Dawn: Millennialism and Political Theology," in *Anglo-American Millennialism from Milton to the Millerites,* ed. Richard Connor and Andrew C. Gow (Leiden: Brill, 2004), 159–76 and the literature cited therein. Also Wald, *Religion and Politics in the United States,* chap. 3; and Richard M. Gamble, *The War for Righteousness: Progressive Christianity, the Great War, and the Rise of the Messianic Nation* (Wilmington, DE: ISI Books, 2003): "America's anointment as the world's political messiah did not end . . . in 1919. . . . Transcending party politics and most ideological boundaries, nearly all of the language of universality and emancipation, of the 'city on a hill' and the world's rebirth, of light and dark, Messiah and Armageddon, reverberates down to the present moment" (22). Further, a German scholar writes: "With respect to the religious underpinning of cultural life, the U.S. is a non-secularized modern society. . . . Wilsonianism became the synonym for the moralism, liberal or conservative American foreign policies of the twentieth century. It merged national interest and the American Creed and proclaimed America custodian of a new world order. The rise to global world leadership . . . confirmed the notion of an 'Almost Chosen People' engaged in war against evil . . . under the benevolent guidance of the American God" (Jürgen Gebhardt, "Conservatism and Religion in the United States," in *Conservative Parties and Right Wing Politics in North America,* ed. Rainer Olaf Schultze and Roland Sturm [Opladen: Leske & Budrich, 2003], 152, 159).

97. Cf. Milton, *Areopagitica and Other Political Writings,* ed. Alvis, 172, 238, 425–29, 435. But "libertie hath a sharp and double edge fitt onelie to be handl'd by just and virtuous men" (453).

98. Quoted from a 1641 tract entitled *A Glimpse of Sion's Glory,* in *Puritanism and Liberty: Being the Army Debates (1647–9) . . . ,* ed. with an intro. by A. S. P. Woodhouse, foreword by D. Lindsay (Chicago: University of Chicago Press, 1951), 233–41, at 240, 236.

sermon of 1783 at the war's end, Ezra Stiles (president of Yale College) cautiously found "reason to hope, and . . . to expect that God [might] . . . make us high among nations in praise, and in name, and in honor."[99] In 1790 Samuel Adams replied to cousin John Adams's startling (perhaps ironic, perhaps not) inquiry: "You ask what the World is about to become? And, Is the Millennium commencing?" Samuel Adams cautiously continued:

> The Love of Liberty is interwoven in the soul of Man, and can never be totally extinguished. . . . What then is to be done?—Let Divines, and Philosophers, Statesmen and Patriots unite their endeavors to renovate the Age, by . . . inculcating in the Minds of youth the fear, and Love of the Deity, and universal Phylanthropy; and in subordination to these great principles, the Love of their Country—of instructing them in the Art of *self* government, . . . in short of leading them in the Study, and Practice of the exalted Virtues of the Christian system, which will happily tend to subdue the turbulent passions of Men, and introduce that Golden Age beautifully described in figurative language [Isa. 11:6–9]; when the Wolf shall dwell with the Lamb, and the Leopard lie down with the Kid—the Cow, and the bear shall feed; their young ones shall lie down together, and the Lyon shall eat straw like the Ox—none shall then hurt, or destroy; for the Earth shall be full of the Knowledge of the Lord. When this *Millennium* shall commence, if there shall be any need of Civil Government, indulge me in the fancy that it will be in the republican form, or something *better.*[100]

Within this rich context of faith and common sense, American republicanism, as it came from the hands of the founders in 1787 and 1791, provided a redefinition of the concept. It took on sobriety and a substantially different aspect. It retained covenantal form as a newly conceived compound representative republic, one federally organized. But it became more emphatically a republic for sinners rather than saints— for a people at best hopeful under divine Providence of salvation

99. Ezra Stiles, *The United States Elevated to Glory and Honor,* in *Pulpit of the American Revolution. . . . ,* ed. John Wingate Thornton (1860; repr., New York: Burt Franklin, 1970), 438–39.

100. Samuel Adams to John Adams, Oct. 4, 1790, in *The Writings of Samuel Adams,* ed. Harry A. Cushing, 4 vols. (New York: Octagon Books, 1968), 4:340–43.

through faith and divine grace—rather than for the wholly virtuous or perfect (Matt. 5:48).[101] Above all else, American statesmen were both realists and men of faith who relied on experience and common sense, who profoundly understood the history and operations of the sophisticated constitutional order of which they were heirs and adapters.

These attributes are reflected in John Adams's *Defence of the Constitutions* (1787), written in response to Turgot's criticisms of America's early state constitutions. There Adams stressed the rationality of his countrymen's statesmanship and their reliance on "the simple principles of nature," and insisted that it should "never be pretended that any persons employed in that service had interviews with the gods, or were in any degree under the inspiration of Heaven."[102] But lest it be inferred that atheism and rationalism suddenly had triumphed in America (as is sometimes done) Adams goes on to clarify his meaning in so denouncing enthusiasm and bigotry. Tyranny and superstition in the form of popery remained the enemies of liberty of an enlightened American people. "Thirteen governments thus founded on the natural authority of the people alone, without a pretence of miracle or mystery ['even the pious mystery of holy oil had no more influence than that other one of holy water'] . . . are a great point gained in favor of the rights of mankind. The experiment is made, and has completely succeeded; it can no longer be called in question, whether authority in magistrates and obedience in citizens can be grounded on reason, morality, and the *Christian religion,* without the monkery of priests, or the knavery of politicians."[103]

101. Cf. esp. *The Federalist Papers* Nos. 9–10, 39, 47–51, 55.

102. *A Defence of the Constitutions of Government of the United States of America, Against the attack of M. Turgot . . . Vol. 1,* in *The Works of John Adams, Second President of the United States . . . ,* 10 vols., ed. Charles Francis Adams (Boston: Little and Brown, 1850–56), 4:292.

103. Ibid., 293, italics added. On Adams's dim view of the Middle Ages as a conspiracy of monarchs and priests to keep the people "ignorant of everything but the tools of agriculture and war" and the Reformation as the dawn of liberty, see Adams's *Dissertation on the Canon and Feudal Law* (1765), ibid., 3:450–51 and *passim;* see also the discussion in John R. Howe Jr., *The Changing Political Thought of John Adams* (Princeton: Princeton University Press, 1966), 40–45, 133–55; and Zoltán Haraszti, *John Adams and the Prophets of Progress* (1952; repr., New York: Grosset & Dunlap, 1964), 139–64, on Turgot and the *Defence.* The fatal flaw of philosophers, and especially of French *philosophes* such as Condorcet, is this, Adams writes: "Not

§8. Conclusion: *A True Map of Man*

While the American founders relied on Aristotle and Cicero and cited Montesquieu, they understood with Saint Paul that "all have sinned, and come short of the glory of God" (Rom 3:23; cf. 1 Tim. 1:15). They, therefore, accepted the corollary drawn by the judicious Hooker that laws can rightly be made only by assuming men so depraved as to be hardly better than wild beasts[104]—even though they are created little lower than the angels and beloved of God their Creator (Psalm 8).

To generalize and simplify, but not to argue perfect homogeneity: From the Anglo-Norman Anonymous and John Wyclif to John Wesley, Jonathan Edwards, John Adams, and Abraham Lincoln's evocation of "government of the people, by the people, and for the people," lines of religious development undergirded and fostered a shared sense of the sanctity of the individual human being living in immediacy to

---

one of them takes human nature as it is for his foundation"—as Americans had in fact done (*Works of John Adams*, 4:258).

104. Cf. *Federalist* No. 6. Thus, Hooker, *Of the Laws of Ecclesiastical Polity [1593],* ed. McGrade, bk. 1.10.l, pp. 87–88: "Laws politic, ordained for external order and regiment amongst men, are never framed as they should be, unless presuming the will of man to be inwardly obstinate, rebellious, and averse from all obedience unto the sacred laws of his nature; in a word, unless presuming man to be in regard of his depraved mind little better than a wild beast, they do accordingly provide notwithstanding so to frame his outward actions, that they be no hindrance unto the common good for which societies are instituted: unless they do this, they are not perfect." Similarly Machiavelli: "All writers on politics have pointed out . . . that in constituting and legislating for a commonwealth it must needs be taken for granted that all men are wicked and that they will always give vent to malignity that is in their minds when opportunity offers" (*The Discourses* 1.3, ed. Bernard Crick [Harmondsworth: Penguin Books, 1974], 112). Indeed, the tension between the reason of the law and the passion of the human being is fundamental to the philosophical anthropology underlying the whole conception of rule of law and of a government of laws and not of men, from Aristotle onward. Cf. the *locus classicus:* "He who asks law [*nomos*] to rule is asking God and intelligence [reason, *nous*] alone to rule; while he who asks for the rule of a human being is importing a wild beast too; for desire is like a wild beast, and anger perverts rulers and the very best of men. Hence the law is intelligence without appetition" (Aristotle *Politics* 3.16, 1287a23–31, trans. T. A. Sinclair, rev. Trevor J. Saunders [Harmondsworth: Penguin Books, 1981], 226). In sum, as stated elsewhere: "In fact, my axiom of politics (a minor contribution to the science) is this: *Human beings are virtually ungovernable.* After all, human beings in addition to possessing reason and gifts of conscience are material, corporeal, passionate, self-serving, devious, obstreperous, ornery, unreliable, imperfect, fallible, and prone to sin if not outright depraved. And we have some bad qualities besides" (Sandoz, *Politics of Truth*, 39).

God and associated the Christian calling to imitate God in their lives with political duty, capacity for self government based on consent, *salus populi,* and the ethic of aspiration through a reciprocal love of God. From this fertile ground emerged the institutions of civil society and republicanism so admirably devised in the American founding.

Among other things, the framers—faced with the weighty challenge of how to make free government work—banked the fires of zealotry and political millenarianism in favor of latitudinarian faith and a quasi-Augustinian understanding of the two cities. They humbly bowed before the inscrutable mystery of history and the human condition with its suffering and imperfection and accepted watchful waiting for fulfillment of the hoped-for providential destiny known only to God—whose "kingdom is not of this world" (Jn. 18:36). But as we have seen—in addition to understanding government as a necessary coercive restraint on the sinful creature—they reflected a faith that political practice in perfecting the image of God in every man through just dominion was *itself* a blessed vocation and the calling of free men: It was stewardship in imitation of God's care for his freely created and sustained world, one enabled solely by the grace bestowed on individuals in a favored community. They embraced freedom of conscience as quintessential liberty for a citizenry of free men and women, as had John Milton long before, who exclaimed in *Areopagitica:* "Give me the liberty to know, to utter, and to argue freely according to conscience, above all liberties." And, for better or worse, they followed Milton (as well as Roger Williams and John Locke) in heeding his plea "to leave the church to itself" and "not suffer the two powers, the ecclesiastical and the civil, which are so totally distinct, to commit whoredom together."[105] The correlate was religious toleration within limits, as necessary for the peaceful existence of a flourishing civil society whose free

105. Milton, *Areopagitica and Other Political Writings,* ed. Alvis, 44, 406. Cf. John Locke, *Writings on Religion,* ed. Victor Nuovo (Oxford: Clarendon Press, 2002), 73–82; also Edwin S. Gaustad, *Liberty of Conscience: Roger Williams in America* (Grand Rapids: Eerdmans, 1991), who writes at 219: "In the past half-century, American society has become noisily and notoriously pluralistic. This has made Roger Williams more relevant, for he had strong opinions about what government should do about religious pluralism: leave it alone. Turks, Jews, infidels, papists: leave them alone.... Religion has the power to persuade, never the power to compel. Government does have the power to compel, but that government is wisest and best which offers to liberty of conscience its widest possible range."

operations minimized tampering with religious institutions or dogmas. Yet the historically affirmed vocation of a special people under God still could be pursued through active devotion to public good, liberty, and justice solidly grounded in Judaeo-Christian transcendentalism. Citizens were at the same time self-consciously also pilgrims aware that this world is not their home, that they were merely sojourners passing through this mysterious process of historical existence in the attitude of *homo viator,* since nothing better than hope through faith avails them. It is this ever-present balanced living tension with the divine Ground above all else, perhaps, that has made the United States so nearly immune politically to the ideological and eschatological maladies that have ravaged the modern world, such as fascism and Marxism and now Islamism.

Like all of politics, the founders' solutions were compromises, offensive to utopians and all other flaming idealists. But this may be no detraction from their work, since despite all national vicissitudes, we still today strive to keep our republic—under the world's oldest existing constitution. Moreover, there has yet to appear an American dictator after more than two centuries of independent national existence; and the United States, at grievous cost in lives and treasure, has steadfastly stood in wars of global reach as the champion of human freedom in the face of raging despotisms of every description.

To conclude then: Let us not overlook the great secret that a *sound map of human nature* (as John Adams insisted) uniquely lies at the heart of the Constitution of the United States and its elaborate institutional arrangements. Men are not angels, and government, admittedly, is the greatest of all reflections on human nature: The *demos* ever tends to become the *ochlos*—even if there could be a population of philosophers and saints—and constantly threatens majoritarian tyranny. Merely mortal magistrates, no less than self-serving factions, riven by *superbia,* avarice, and *libido dominandi,* must be restrained artfully by a vast net of adversarial devices if just government is to have any chance whatever of prevailing over self-serving human passions while still nurturing the liberty of free men. To attain these noble ends in what is called a government of laws and not of men, it was daringly thought, perhaps ambition could effectively counteract ambition and, as one more *felix culpa,* therewith supply the defect of better motives. This is most dramatically achieved, at least in theory, through the routine operations of the central mechanisms of divided and separated powers and of checks and balances that display the genius of the Constitution and serve as the well-known hallmark of America's republican experiment itself. *All of this would have been quite inconceivable without a Christian anthropology, enriched by classical political theory and the common law tradition, as uniquely embedded in the habits of the American people at the time of the founding and nurtured thereafter.* On this ground an extended commercial republic flourished where love of God and love of mammon somehow sweetly kissed, and America became a light to the nations. Alexis de Tocqueville noticed this incongruity in the 1830s and wrote: "'I know of no country, indeed, where the love of money has taken a stronger hold on the affections of men.'" One scholar attributes this striking alliance to the prevalent form taken by American Christianity, in "a society awash in religion and in making money—and confident of divine favor upon both endeavors. American Methodism was the prototype of a religious organization taking on market form."[106]

As is evident, a true map of man is vital and so are the principles of what the founders termed the "divine science of politics." Love of liberty and even love of God, vital as both assuredly are, of themselves clearly are not enough in politics. Thus, representative of the many cautions on this head by John Adams is this one: "John Milton was as honest a man as his nation ever bred, and as great a friend of liberty; but his greatness most certainly did not consist in the knowledge of the nature of man and of government." All philosophers ancient and modern had missed the mark and for one basic reason, he thought: "Not one of them takes human nature as it is for his foundation."[107] The true *political* anthropology, divine science of politics, and the principles of government Adams had in view and helped to formulate were later refined for our compound constitutional republic and collected in a book written for forensic purposes and entitled *The Federalist Papers.*[108]

106. Nathan O. Hatch in *Methodism,* ed. Hatch and Wigger, 38, including the quotation from Tocqueville. Cf. the conclusion of Calvin's role in this by Dumont, "A Modified View of Our Origins," 23.

107. *Works of John Adams,* ed. C. F. Adams, 4:466; and Haraszti, *John Adams and the Prophets of Progress,* 258.

108. On *forensics,* in this sense, and *forensic history,* see John Phillip Reid, *The Ancient Constitution and the Origins of Anglo-American Liberty* (DeKalb: Northern Illinois University Press, 2005), chap. 1.

This does not mean that Adams substituted his political faith for his religious faith, of course, as he explained to Jefferson in 1818:

> I believe in God and in his Wisdom and Benevolence: and I cannot conceive that such a Being could make such a Species as the human merely to live and die on this Earth. If I did not believe in a future State I should believe in no God. This Universe, this all, this *to pan* would appear with all its swelling Pomp, a boyish Fire Work. And if there be a future State Why should the Almighty dissolve forever all the tender ties which unite us so delightfully in this world and forbid us to see each other in the next?[109]

Nagging questions remain: Can a political order ultimately grounded in the tension toward transcendent divine Being, memorably proclaimed in the Declaration of Independence and solidly informed by biblical revelation and philosophy, indefinitely endure—resilient though it may be—in the face of nihilistic assault on this vital spiritual tension by every means, including by the very institutions of liberty themselves? Perhaps these are only growing pains that afflict us, rather than the symptoms of the disintegration of our civilization. The positivist, scientistic, and Marxist climate of opinion is so pervasive and intellectually debilitating in the public arena and universities as often to make philosophical and religious discourse incomprehensible oddities whose meaning is lost to consciousness amid the din of deformation and deculturation. And the damage to common sense itself, and to the middling range of publicly effective prudential understanding basic to the science of human affairs—first elaborated by Aristotle and adapted for our republic by the American founders' divine science of politics—by neglect, miseducation, and deculturation is incalculable. For instance,

109. John Adams to Thomas Jefferson, Dec. 8, 1818, in *Adams-Jefferson Letters: The Complete Correspondence between Thomas Jefferson and Abigail and John Adams,* ed. Lester J. Cappon, 2 vols. in 1 (1959; repr., New York: Simon & Schuster/Clarion Books, 1971), 530. Cf. David L. Holmes, *The Religion of the Founding Fathers* (Charlottesville, VA: Ash Lawn–Highland, and Ann Arbor: Clements Library, University of Michigan, 2003), who concludes as follows: "The six Founding Fathers surveyed in this study appear to have been neither wholehearted Deists nor orthodox Christians.... In the spirit of their times, they appeared less devout than they were—which seems a reversal from modern politics" (130–31). See also John Witte Jr., "Facts and Fictions about the History of Separation of Church and State," *Journal of Church and State* 48 (Winter 2006): 15–45.

the "walls of separation between these two [church and state] must forever be upheld," Richard Hooker wrote in contemptuously characterizing religious zealots of his distant time. By way of Thomas Jefferson's famous 1801 letter and the U.S. Supreme Court more recently, that metaphor now lives on as the shibboleth of strange new fanatics of our own day, including those sometimes identified as atheist humanists.[110] The abiding truths of politics and of faith atrophy together before our eyes, even as we weigh their distinctiveness and autonomy as independent spheres of human knowledge and action. But like every other consideration, this one too becomes a meaningless gesture to clever reductionists and nihilists in our midst who find no truth worth living for, preserving, or, for that matter, worrying about.

Even as religious revival today enlivens American spirituality, we observe the strong countercurrents of intellectual, moral, and social disarray of the republic—and not of the American republic alone. We test our faith that the truth shall prevail and look for hopeful signs on the horizon. But this is not new either. Perhaps we remember and take heart from the epochal images of Elijah on Horeb and of Socrates in the Heliaia, to recall that revealed truth and philosophical reason ever have been nurtured by resolute *individuals'* resistance to apostasy, injustice, and corruption. Those called to be representatives of truth play their modest parts in the drama of history. At time's decree, they pass the mantle to younger hands, thereby vivifying through the generations some adventitious saving remnant that perseveres and, against all odds, may help illumine the darkness encompassing our mysterious existence.

110. Hooker, *Laws of Ecclesiastical Polity*, bk. 8.1.2, p. 131; *Everson v. United States*, 330 U.S. 1 (1947) at 15–16; cf. the classic study by Henri de Lubac, *The Drama of Atheist Humanism*, trans. E. M. Riley (London: Sheed & Ward, 1949).

2

Foundations of American Liberty and Rule of Law

They constantly try to escape
From the darkness outside and within
By dreaming of systems so perfect that no one will need to
* be good.*
But the man that is will shadow
The man that pretends to be.

"Choruses From 'The Rock' (VI)"
T. S. Eliot

The argument I wish to offer regarding the foundations of American liberty and rule of law (or *constitutionalism,* a word invented by Americans at the time) stresses the debt of the founders to their civilizational past.[1] Whether, or to what degree, the Anglo-American constitutional and philosophical past was and is unique is largely a matter for another day. And I must confess my prejudice in favor of American *exceptionalism,* as the historians call it: i.e., for all the debts to the general legacy of Western civilization, and to Graeco-Roman civilization and to Israel, American constitutional democracy is unique.[2] So, I will have it both

---

Epigraph quoted from T. S. Eliot, *The Complete Poems and Plays, 1909–1950* (New York: Harcourt, Brace & World, 1952), 106. Copyright © 1971 by Esme Valerie Eliot. Quoted with permission.

1. See Harold J. Berman, *Law and Revolution: The Formation of the Western Legal Tradition* (Cambridge, MA: Harvard University Press, 1983), 9, 395–96.

2. See Jack P. Greene, *The Intellectual Construction of America: Exceptionalism and Identity from 1492 to 1800* (Chapel Hill: University of North Carolina Press,

ways: It is a product of a common European, even Mediterranean, past; and it is something startlingly different from anything else that has ever happened in the history of the world.

Critics will doubtless take pleasure in exploiting the contradiction. For how can one and the same thing be both profoundly old and profoundly new at one and the same time? Elementary logic has something forceful to say about that. I shall seek to find some answers to this most reasonable question in the next few pages. But at the outset it should be noticed that our subject involves complex series of events and arrays of symbolisms scattered over millennia, and not merely a discrete entity nor even a single series. Rather, it forms a texture of polyphonic intricacy. Moreover, I am shamelessly ready, if truth demands it and when all else fails, to take refuge behind Ralph Waldo Emerson's defiant maxim, heedless of the prescribed stature: "A foolish consistency is the hobgoblin of little minds, adored by little statesmen and philosophers and divines. With consistency a great soul has simply nothing to do. He may as well concern himself with his shadow on the wall. Speak what you think now in hard words and tomorrow speak what tomorrow thinks in hard words again, though it contradict every thing you said today."[3] But perhaps a synthesis will emerge as the discussion proceeds.

I will address three principal questions: What is old, what new, about American liberty and constitutionalism? What maladies most threaten liberty and aspirations to rule of law regimes, in America and elsewhere?[4]

1993); Anthony Molho and Gordon S. Wood, eds., *Imagined Histories: American Historians Interpret the Past* (Princeton: Princeton University Press, 1998); Charles Lockhart, *The Roots of American Exceptionalism: History, Institutions, and Culture* (New York: Palgrave Macmillan, 2003); Seymour Martin Lipset, *American Exceptionalism: A Double-Edged Sword* (New York: W. W. Norton, 1996), from a large and burgeoning literature.

3. Ralph Waldo Emerson, *Self-Reliance,* in *The Complete Essays and Other Writings of Ralph Waldo Emerson,* ed. Brooks Atkinson (New York: Modern Library, 1940), 152.

4. The argument here extends and partly summarizes lines of analysis detailed in the author's recent work: *A Government of Laws: Political Theory, Religion, and the American Founding* (1990; rev. ed., Columbia: University of Missouri Press, 2001), *Political Sermons of the American Founding Era, 1730–1805* (Indianapolis: Liberty Fund, 1991), and *The Roots of Liberty: Magna Carta, Ancient Constitution, and the Anglo-American Tradition of Rule of Law* (Columbia: University of Missouri Press,

§1.

The radical break with the past, characteristic of the French Revolution, was not overtly part of the American Revolution and its rhetorical justification. The contrasts can most forcefully be seen from a brilliant page in Edmund Burke's 1796 *Letters on a Regicide Peace* where he identifies *Regicide, Jacobinism,* and *Atheism* as the hallmarks of the former. By this he meant: (1) sanctioning the murder of the king merely because kingship is by definition usurpation, this being done with impunity in the name of Democracy as the sole legitimate form of government; (2) wholesale confiscation of private property from its owners who might freely be killed whether they struggled against the taking or not, in the name of Liberty; and (3) rejection and unrelenting persecution of Christianity and its ministers, along with the defacement and destruction of its churches, as matters of public policy done in the name of Reason.[5] However one might wish to qualify Burke's analysis, the intent of the French revolutionaries of 1789 to wipe the slate clean and effect a total destruction of the hated *ancien régime* of their country so as to establish a new order of their own devising seems beyond debate.

In short, then, neither in spirit nor in substance was American Whig liberty at all the same as French Jacobin liberty.[6] The American founding generation's resistance to tyranny and claim to liberty as free men echoed themes as old as the civilization itself and constantly recurred to that tradition. Coming during the Golden Age of the classics, the American appeal was grounded in philosophy as expressed in Aristotle, Cicero, Aquinas, Harrington, Locke, and Thomas Reid; in Protestant Christianity in the form of a political theology that mingled religious revival, keeping the faith and fighting the good fight, providential

---

1993)—the latter two being edited volumes. For the "maladies," see also my *Politics of Truth and Other Untimely Essays: The Crisis of Civic Consciousness* (Columbia: University of Missouri Press, 1999), esp. chap. 8.

5. Edmund Burke, *Letters on a Regicide Peace (I),* in *The Writings and Speeches of Edmund Burke,* 12 vols. (Boston: Little, Brown, 1901), 5:308–10. This "Book Lover's Limited Edition" apparently reprints the standard American edition, i.e., *The Works of the Right Honorable Edmund Burke,* published by Little, Brown, 1865–67.

6. Cf. Hannah Arendt, *On Revolution* (1963; repr., New York: Penguin Books, 1990).

purpose, and a palpable sense of special favor or choseness; and in a constitutionalism that recapitulated all of the arguments seventeenth-century Englishmen had thought valid in resisting the tyranny of Stuart kings by invoking common law liberty back to Magna Carta and the ancient constitution, especially as this tradition had been authoritatively propounded by Sir Edward Coke (d. 1634) in his eleven volumes of *Reports* (1601–1615) and four volumes of *Institutes* (1628–1644). Coke's books formed the legal and constitutional mind of America down to the 1770s, when Sir William Blackstone's *Commentaries* (four volumes, 1765–1769) supplanted them as the basis of legal education on both sides of the Atlantic. As Thomas Jefferson wrote James Madison in one of his last letters:

> You will recollect that before the Revolution, Coke Littleton was the universal elementary book of law students, and a sounder Whig never wrote, nor of profounder learning in the orthodox doctrines of the British constitution, or in what were called English liberties. You remember also that our lawyers were then all Whigs. But when his black-letter text, and uncouth but cunning learning got out of fashion, and the honeyed Mansfieldism of Blackstone became the students' hornbook, from that moment, that profession (the nursery of our Congress) began to slide into toryism, and nearly all of the young brood of lawyers now are of that hue. They suppose themselves, indeed, to be Whigs, because they no longer know what Whigism or republicanism means.[7]

In sum, John Locke (read as a Christian philosopher, even as an Aristotelian in his political theory), the Bible, and Coke's version of the Lancastrian constitution of England formed the heart of the political, theological, and constitutional theory pervasive in America during the founding era.

What does this come down to? The brief answer is that American founders—revolutionaries and constitution-makers alike—laid claim to their heritage out of a profound veneration for it instilled from many quarters. "*In a sentence, the founding was the rearticulation of Western*

---

7. Thomas Jefferson to James Madison, Feb. 17, 1826, in *The Life and Writings of Thomas Jefferson*, ed. A. Koch and W. Peden (New York: Modern Library, 1944), 726. Jefferson (and, remarkably, John Adams as well) died on July 4, 1826.

civilization in its Anglo-American mode."[8] Emphases shifted, to be sure, even gyrated wildly, as the several stages of the founding unfolded from the Declaration of Independence (1776), to the Articles of Confederation (1781), the conclusion of the war (1783), the framing of the Constitution (1787), and the ratification of the Bill of Rights (1791)—to mention some of the principal landmarks. Undergirding all of the "events" lay a concerted education of the general populace of America in the political theory and jurisprudence of liberty and rule of law that created the *civic consciousness* of citizenship essential to the formation of civil community or society and to the foundation of the nation. It seems likely to me that the origins of a national American community with a special destiny in world history lay in the work of George Whitefield and other itinerant preachers who crisscrossed the country for decades, bringing the Great Awakening to America from 1739 onward, sporadically right into the Revolutionary and constitutional periods. Religious and political corruption were readily viewed as two sides of the same coin, whether decried as sin and apostasy or as corruption and Robinarchy. By 1783, in the flush of triumph over Britain, President Ezra Stiles of Yale College could preach a nearly apocalyptic election sermon, entitled "The United States Elevated to Glory and Honor," proclaiming the rise of American Zion. "We have reason to hope," Stiles said, "that God has still greater blessings in store for this vine which his own right hand hath planted, to make us high among the nations in praise, and in name, and in honor."[9]

A historical jurisprudence as well as a natural law jurisprudence were basic in America, unlike England. The political and constitutional preoccupation had begun in earnest in the early 1760s soon after the succession of George III to the throne. It reached fever-pitch with enactment of the Declaratory Act of 1766, by which parliament laid claim to a power over the colonies "to bind [them] in all matters whatsoever." The contrast between rule *of* law and rule *by* law—announced by Hobbes and basic to the legal positivism of the modern *Rechtsstaat*—comes to view in this connection. By the former, there is an appeal to a higher

---

8. Sandoz, *GOL,* 151. Italics added.

9. Ezra Stiles, "The United States Elevated to Glory and Honor," in *Pulpit of the American Revolution,* ed. John Wingate Thornton (1860; repr., New York: Burt Franklin, 1970), 397–520, at 438–39.

standard of law and justice than the merely mortal or, at the least, than the enacted law of merely contemporary rulers. It is tempting to summarize by saying that the constitutional split between Britain and America at the time of the Revolution is explainable in considerable degree in terms of a *preposition*. Law must be just and reasonable as arising from a source superior to the state.[10]

Thus, law does not rest merely on *will*, even if it be the will of a duly constituted authority or sovereign, whether a sovereign king or a sovereign parliament; as Coke had said earlier, *sovereignty* is no parliamentary word. From the common law perspective of Coke and his American disciples, the argument is from immemorial usage of the prescriptive ancient constitution and the liberties of free men. In the words of Magna Carta of 1225 (cap. 1), which became through Edward I's statutory confirmation in 1297 the first English statute, "all the freemen of our realm [omnibus liberis hominibus regni nostri]" are granted "forever, all of the underwritten liberties." According to Coke's famous dictum in *Doctor Bonham's Case* (1610), "when an act of parliament is against common right and reason, or repugnant, or impossible to be performed, the common law will controul it and adjudge such act to be void."[11] Herein lies the root of judicial review and the remarkable empowerment of the federal judiciary in the United States after *Marbury v. Madison* (1803). But in the America of the founding period, the appeal went equally to higher law, to the "Laws of Nature and of Nature's God," as the Declaration of Independence averred. The classical and medieval conceptions endured as commonplace: Human law must conform with higher law; for as Augustine had written over a millennium before (and Aristotle had implied still earlier), an unjust law is no law at all. While English jurisprudence shied away from entangling common law and natural law, it was a legitimate inheritance from Sir John Fortescue and Coke nonetheless, as can be seen from the latter's report

---

10. For the distinctions drawn, see Harold J. Berman, "The Rule of Law and the Law-Based State (*Rechtsstaat*) (with Special Reference to Developments in the Soviet Union)," *Harriman Institute Forum* 4 (May 1991): 1–3. It may be stressed that Hobbes's "sovereign" is above all law in the commonwealth as its exclusive source, so that while rule is by laws, they do not bind him.

11. 8 *Coke's Reports* 107a (1610), 2 *Brownl.* 225 (1610), quoted from Edward S. Corwin, *The "Higher Law" Background of American Constitutional Law* (1928–29; repr., Ithaca: Cornell University Press, 1955), 44.

of *Calvin's Case* (1610), where he wrote in summary: "[The] law of nature is part of the laws of England . . . the law of nature was before any judicial or municipal law in the world...the law of nature is immutable, and cannot be changed." Coke then quaintly explained that the

> law of nature is that which God at the time of creation of the nature of man infused into his heart, for his preservation and direction; and this is *Lex aeterna,* the moral law, called also the law of nature. And by this law, written with the finger of God in the heart of man, were the people of God a long time governed before the law was written by Moses, who was the first reporter or writer of law in the world. . . . And Aristotle, nature's Secretary Lib. 5. *Aethic.* [7.1.1334b20] saith that *jus naturale est, quod apud omnes homines eandem habet potentiam* [natural justice is that which everywhere has the same force and does not exist by people's thinking this or that]. And herewith doth agree Bracton lib. 1. cap. 5. and Fortescue cap. 8. 12. 13. and 16. *Doctor and Student* cap. 2. and 4.[12]

Americans of the time would readily have embraced Aquinas's teaching that, if positive or human law departs from the law of nature, it is no longer law but perversion of law.[13] The flavor is captured in James Otis's *Rights of British Colonies Asserted and Proved* (1764) where he echoes Cicero:

> The law of nature was not of man's making, nor is it in his power to mend it or alter its course. He can only perform and keep or disobey and break it. The last is never done with impunity, even in this life, if it is any punishment for a man to feel himself

---

12. 7 *Coke's Reports* 12a–12b. Corwin notes that Bacon's argument in this case invoked the law of nature. Corwin, *"Higher Law" Background of American Constitutional Law,* 46. On the mingling of natural law and common law in America, in contrast to England where they "had been inimical," see J. C. Holt, *Magna Carta,* 2nd ed. (Cambridge: Cambridge University Press, 1992), 16–18. Of major importance for linking English jurisprudence with Thomas Aquinas is Fortescue, *A Treatise Concerning the Nature of the Law of Nature,* pt. 1, in *The Works of Sir John Fortescue, Knight . . . ,* ed. Sir Thomas (Fortescue) Lord Clermont (London, 1869), esp. 194, 205–6, 215–16, 219–22, and *passim.* See Sandoz, *Politics of Truth,* chap. 6, "Fortescue as Political Philosopher."

13. Cf. Augustine *De lib. arb.* 1.5, in Thomas Aquinas, *Summa theologiae* 1–2.95.2; Aristotle, *Rhetoric* 1.15.1375a27 et seq.

depraved, to find himself degraded by his own folly and wicked-
ness from the rank of a virtuous and good *man* to that of a brute,
or to be transformed from the friend, perhaps father, of his country to a devouring lion or tiger.[14]

What comes to view in the foregoing paragraphs is the Great Chain
or hierarchy of being with man's place in it an intermediary one between
God and brute, obliged to obey natural and divine law, to be obedient
to human authority as divinely ordained unless to do so violates God's
law, in which circumstance at least passive resistance is demanded if not
an appeal to heaven that may end in the deposition of the tyrant. Government, so conceived, rests on the consent of free men. In fact, *liberty* in one of its principal meanings during the founding meant to live
under laws consented to by the people either directly or through their
representatives, whence the term *free government*.[15] The stress comes
much earlier, however. Thus, the hallmark of English rule (as Fortescue in the fifteenth century insisted and Coke and American Whigs
subsequently believed), is not merely regal (as in France) but political
and regal *(dominium politicum et regale)*. By this is especially meant that
the king legislates, not solely by his own will, but only with the consent of the realm as given through parliament: "a king of this sort is
obliged to protect the law, the subjects, and their bodies and goods,
and he has power for this end issuing from the people, so that it is not
permissible for him to rule his people with any other power."[16] The
close approach to the later notion of popular sovereignty is to be
observed. In Richard Hooker's elegant summation: "Laws they are not
therefore which public approbation hath not made so."[17] But this was
so at least as early as *De laudibus* (ca. 1470) when Fortescue laid it
down that royal power in England (in sharp contrast to the *lex regia* of
Roman law as institutionalized as *dominium tantum regale* in the France

14. James Otis, *Rights of British Colonies Asserted and Proved* (Boston, 1764),
quoted from Sandoz, *GOL*, 202. Cf. Cicero, *De re pub.* 3.22; Lactantius *Inst.* 6.8.6–9.
15. This is extensively documented in John Phillip Reid, *The Concept of Liberty
in the Age of the American Revolution* (Chicago: University of Chicago Press, 1988),
79–82, 111, and *passim*.
16. Sir John Fortescue, *De Laudibus Leges Angliae*, chap. 13, quoted from Sandoz,
ed., *The Roots of Liberty*, 10.
17. Richard Hooker, *Of the Laws of Ecclesiastical Polity* 1.10.8, quoted by John
Locke, *Second Treatise of Government*, sec. 134n; cf. Sandoz, *GOL*, 118–19.

of Louis XI) is limited by law and that law could neither be made nor altered without consent of parliament, perhaps the first direct assertion of parliamentary authority as a constitutional limit on the king's power. Thus, England as a *mixed monarchy of double majesty* found articulation. Behind the words lay also the political tradition (capable of being revived over centuries as crises demanded) of an independent baronage with power to confront the king and insist upon his observing the limits imposed through covenant and law upon his great office—as had in fact been done on that memorable June 15 in 1215 at Runnymede when Magna Carta was signed by King John. Four hundred years later, by the time of the crisis leading to the Petition of Right (1628), Coke found that Magna Carta had been confirmed no less than thirty-two times by English monarchs.

That "princes are bound by and shall live according to their laws" as a matter of natural law was concluded by the Bolognese monk Gratian in about 1140, in his great work entitled *A Concordance of Discordant Canons (Decretum);* this had been asserted earlier by Ivo (1040–1115) but was not to be found in Roman or German law.[18] The principle took on new life, however, with Henry de Bracton (d. 1268) in *De legibus,* written in the wake of the signing of Magna Carta and the Great Charter's having been confirmed four times by Henry III (in 1216, 1217, 1225, and 1251). Bracton's words were aptly recalled at a climactic moment in the great seventeenth-century struggle between crown and parliament that had been led at earlier stages by Coke and John Selden before civil war ensued. In 1649, John Bradshaw, the Puritan parliamentary prosecutor, addressed "Charles Stuart," after the court had condemned him for murder, arbitrary rule, and tyranny but before the sentence of death by beheading was pronounced, as follows: "The king has a superior, namely, God. Also the law by which he is made king. Also his *curia,* namely, the earls and barons, because if he is without bridle, that is without law, they ought to put the bridle on him." Bradshaw explained the political theory in his own words: "This we learn: the end of having kings, or any other governors, it is for the enjoying of justice; that is the end. Now, Sir, if so be the king will go

18. Gratian, *Decretum,* in *Corpus Iuris Canonici,* ed. Emil Friedberg, vol. 1 (1879; repr., Graz: Akademische Druck und Verlagsanstalt, 1959), dist. 9, c. 2. Quoted and cited from Berman, *Law and Revolution,* 145, 585.

contrary to the end of his government, Sir, he must understand that he is but an officer in trust, and he ought to discharge that trust; and they are to take order for the punishment of such an offending governor. This is not law of yesterday, Sir, but it is law of old."[19]

§2.

With the old medieval representative assemblies of France and Spain gone under before the rising tide of absolutism, Britain alone among the major nations avoided absolute kingship—the vanguard of modernity whereby political rulers claim to be mortal gods entitled to exercise dominion without restraint. By this reading royal absolutism prefigures Bonapartism, proclamation of the *Übermensch,* and totalitarianism as quintessential modernity. That absolutism was avoided in Britain, and that supremacy of the law in its medieval guise came to be applied to modern states—the legacy claimed by eighteenth-century Americans as their birthright—was no accident. As the premier historian of English legal history wrote: "It is largely owing to the influence of [Coke's] writings that these medieval conceptions have become part of our modern law. . . . *They preserved for England and the world the constitutional doctrine of rule of law.*" They formed "the turning-point in English constitutional history."[20]

Constitutionalism, or rule of law (to use the terms as equivalents), means that the power of rulers is limited and that the limits can be enforced through established procedures. It means government that is, at once, devoted both to the public good of the entire community and to the preservation of the liberties of individual persons as far as that is consistent with public good. In John Selden's formulation during the Petition of Right debate, *salus populi suprema lex, et libertas popula summa salus populi* [the welfare of the people is the supreme law and

19. Henry de Bracton, *De legibus et consuetudinibus Angliae,* ed. S. E. Thorne, 4 vols. (Cambridge, MA: Harvard University Press, 1968), 2:110; cf. 33, 305; [Ed. anon.], *Trials of Charles the First, and of Some of the Regicides: With Biographies of Bradshaw, Ireton, Harrison, and others* (London, 1832), 81. Cf. Sandoz, *GOL,* 232–35.

20. Sir William Holdsworth, *A History of English Law,* 13 vols., variously revised by volume (London: Methuen, 1923–66), 5:493; 6 (2nd ed. rev.):66, 70. Italics added.

the liberty of the people the greatest welfare of the people].[21] Because the most precious liberties of free men are preserved in law conceived to be just, reasonable, and immemorial as the fundamental law or law of the land (Magna Carta's *lex terrae*), Coke gives the primary meaning of *libertates* as used in Magna Carta as "the Laws of the Realme, in which respect this Charter is called, *Charta libertatum.*"[22]

This understanding of *liberty* is akin to the philosophical one that only the man whose reason governs base passions, therewith to live justly, is truly free and, thus, capable of happiness conceived as a life lived in accordance with virtue. The opposite type is the banausic or materialistic man who is routinely governed by his desires and, in extreme cases, by *libido* with such compulsion that reason becomes merely instrumental as the means of finding ways to gratification: So to be enslaved by passion is to be radically unfree. Aristotle's "slave by nature" approximates Thomas Hobbes's typical man who, devoid of sensitivity for *summum bonum,* is consumed by self-love (*amor sui,* in the Augustinian sense).[23] Pride in such men can only be broken by the complete therapy prescribed in *Leviathan,* a work perhaps ironically intended by its author. Liberty is experienced in its primary sense only through willing acceptance of truth or reason's dictates as a matter of free choice, which rises in maturity into becoming an eager seeking after the transcendental Good for its actualizing attractiveness. This aspect blends philosophical and biblical teachings as symbolized by New Testament statements: "Ye shall know the truth, and the truth shall make you free" (Jn. 8:32); and, by verses dear to Americans during

---

21. Quoted from Paul Christianson, "Ancient Constitutions in the Age of Coke and Selden," in *The Roots of Liberty,* ed. Sandoz, 120. The second clause of the quotation is Selden's quip during debate in the House of Commons (March 28, 1628), augmenting the maxim given in Coke's *Tenth Reports (La Dixme Part des Reports* [London, 1614], f. 139). See Robert C. Johnson et al., eds., *Proceedings in Parliament 1628,* 6 vols. (New Haven: Yale University Press, 1977–78, 1983), 2:171–85.

22. Sir Edward Coke, *The Second Part of the Institutes of the Laws of England* ([1641]; London, 1642), 47. On the development of *lex terrae* as due process and to include trial by jury by the fourteenth century, see J. C. Holt, "The Ancient Constitution in Medieval England," in *Roots of Liberty,* ed. Sandoz, 45.

23. Cf. Thomas Hobbes, *Leviathan; or the Matter, Forme and Power of a Commonwealth Ecclesiasticall and Civil,* ed. Michael Oakeshott (Oxford: Blackwell, n.d.), 39, 63–65, 99, 101, 104–120; Augustine, *City of God* 14.28.

the Revolution: "So, then, brethren, we are not children of the bond-woman, but of the free. Stand fast therefore in the liberty wherewith Christ hath made us free, and be not entangled again with the yoke of bondage" (Gal. 4:31–5:1).[24]

In other words, *liberty* and *license* were clearly distinguished by Americans of the period, even if this may no longer be the case. And there are two other vital dimensions of liberty to be noticed: *liberty and private property* and *freedom of conscience*. With a Revolution fought whose motto (if it had one) was "No taxation without representation," the connection of freedom and property deserves emphasis. John Witherspoon, president of the College of New Jersey at Princeton—and, as the teacher there of eight of the fifty-five eventual participants in the Constitutional Convention of 1787 (including James Madison), probably the most influential professor in American history—stressed the indissoluble link between personal and property rights as part of the divine, natural, and civic order. "If we take tradition or Revelation for our guide," Witherspoon wrote, "the matter is plain, that God made man lord of works of his hands, and puts under him all the other creatures. . . . Private property is every particular person's having a confessed and exclusive right to a certain portion of the goods which serve for the support and conveniency of life." And in the face of the depredations of the British ministry, Witherspoon asserted in the Continental Congress that "[t]here is not a single instance in history in which civil liberty was lost, and religious liberty preserved entire. If therefore we yield up our temporal property, we at the same time deliver the conscience into bondage."[25] In his mighty last-ditch appeal of March 1775 to avoid war, Edmund Burke in the House of Commons reminded members that

> the people of the colonies are descendants of Englishmen. England, Sir, is a nation which still, I hope, respects, and formerly

24. For example, see the 1778 Massachusetts election sermon by the Reverend Phillips Payson, in *Pulpit of the American Revolution*, ed. Thornton, 329–30.

25. John Witherspoon, *An Annotated Edition of Lectures on Moral Philosophy*, ed. Jack Scott (Newark: University of Delaware Press, 1982), 126–27; Witherspoon, *Works of the Reverend John Witherspoon*, [ed. anon.], 4 vols. (Philadelphia, 1800–1801), 3:37.

adored her freedom. The colonists . . . are therefore not only devoted to liberty, but to liberty according to English ideas and on
English principles. Abstract liberty, like other mere abstractions,
is not to be found. Liberty inheres in some sensible object. . . .
[T]he great contests for freedom in this country were from the
earliest times chiefly upon the question of taxing. . . . On this point
of taxes the ablest pens and most eloquent tongues have been exercised, the greatest spirits have acted and suffered. . . . They took
infinite pains to inculcate, as a fundamental principle, that in all
monarchies the people must in effect themselves, mediately or
immediately, possess the power of granting their own money, or no
shadow of liberty could subsist. . . . [I]n order to prove that the
Americans have no right to their liberties, we are every day
endeavoring to subvert the maxims which preserve the whole spirit
of our own. . . . As long as you have the wisdom to keep the sovereign authority of this country as the sanctuary of liberty, the sacred
temple consecrated to our common faith, wherever the chosen
race and sons of England worship freedom, they will turn their
faces toward you. . . . Slavery they can have anywhere. It is a weed
that grows in every soil.[26]

§3.

With freedom of conscience we may sidle in the direction of what is
new in American liberty and rule of law. The line is hard to draw.
Burke in the place just quoted has much to say about the fierce American devotion to liberty and the centrality of their dissenting Protestant
beliefs to that cast of mind. Alexis de Tocqueville in the 1830s would
remind his readers that it should never be forgotten that religion gave
birth to America, that Christianity was as ubiquitous as the air we
breathe, and he saw Anglo-American civilization as the "product" of
two elements most often at war with one another elsewhere but here
to be found "forming a marvelous combination. I mean the *spirit of
religion* and the *spirit of freedom.*" The "main reason" for this happy state

---

26. Edmund Burke, *Speech on Moving His Resolutions for Conciliation with the
Colonies, March 22, 1775,* in *Edmund Burke: Selected Writings and Speeches,* ed. Peter J.
Stanlis (Chicago: Regnery Gateway Editions, 1963), 158–59, 164, 184.

of affairs, Tocqueville concluded, and "for the quiet sway of religion over their country was the complete separation of church and state."[27]

Freedom of religion in America at the time under discussion was overwhelmingly a *freedom to be religious* according to one's own lights. As the conflict with Britain intensified from the 1760s onward the terror swept the colonies that a bishop would be sent to America to secure conformity of worship and submission to the Church of England. George Whitefield himself sounded the alarm as early as 1764 when he warned two New Hampshire ministers: "There is a deep laid plot against both your civil and religious liberties, and they will be lost. Your golden days are at an end."[28] The Methodists were buoyed when John Wesley in 1774 supported the colonial cause, but the satisfaction turned to horror when Wesley changed sides a year later and chose to explain himself in a pamphlet partly plagiarized from Samuel Johnson. This went through nineteen printings and was widely circulated by the British government but seized and burnt by American Methodists wherever they could find copies, trying to keep them out of the country where they and Wesley were vilified.[29] Reverend James Madison, cousin of the statesman and an Anglican priest who became the first American Episcopal bishop in 1790, as president of William and Mary became captain of militia and led his students in battle during the Revolution. As mentioned earlier, he was said to have been so intense in his patriotism as to emend the Lord's Prayer, on occasion, by intoning "Thy Republic come."[30] And we have noticed that Americans during the Revolution were called to their houses of worship for public days of prayer, fasting, humiliation (or thanksgiving, as suited) many times by formal Proclamation of the Continental Congress, a practice that continued during the early administrations under the Constitution, of which the modern observance of Thanksgiving Day is a relic, and the practice was revived by President George W. Bush in 2001. With completion of

27. Alexis de Tocqueville, *Democracy in America*, ed. J. P. Mayer, trans. George Lawrence, 2 vols. in 1 (Garden City, NY: Doubleday Anchor Books, 1969), 46–47, 295, 432.

28. Quoted from Carl Bridenbaugh, *Spirit of '76: The Growth of American Patriotism before Independence, 1607–1776* (New York: Oxford University Press, 1975), 117–19.

29. Cf. Sandoz, ed., *Political Sermons*, 409–40, which reprints Wesley's pamphlet *A Calm Address to Our American Colonies* (London, 1775).

30. Ibid., 1305–20.

the new Capitol in the District of Columbia, church services regularly were held for the Congress and officials of government, including the president and cabinet members, in the House of Representatives chamber on Sundays, a practice that continued until well after the Civil War.[31] Thus, even the institutional separation between church and state was never so absolute as Tocqueville may have supposed. Clearly, much of the moral basis of the Revolution came from the religious communities, with the preachers playing a vital, perhaps decisive role in forming the resolve of the country for independence and in sustaining courage to see the war through to the end.[32]

The role of the dissenting religious communities—Baptists, Presbyterians, Lutherans, Quakers, plus Jews and Catholics—was equally vital in arriving at the unique American solution to the vexed problems of religious conflict and persecution so admired by Tocqueville and, indeed, so worthy of admiration. For the solution turned on the matter of disestablishment, so that public money was not devoted to religious entities, thereby favoring one sect over another; and side-by-side with this was the requirement that freedom of religion not be tampered with by public officials. The major victory on these grounds was won in Virginia shortly before the calling of the Federal Convention and prefigured the form to be taken in the initial clauses of the First Amendment, which read: "Congress shall make no law respecting an establishment of religion, or prohibiting the free exercise thereof." The leadership in both instances came from James Madison, whose interest in matters religious was profound. He personally defended jailed Baptist ministers at the beginning of a public career that next saw him helping to frame the Virginia Declaration of Rights, defending his state against the advocates of religious establishment through authorship of the Memorial and Remonstrance Against Religious Assessments, securing passage of Thomas Jefferson's long dormant Bill/Statute for Religious Freedom (January 1786), leading the drafting and passage of the federal Bill of Rights in the First Congress under the Constitution, enforcing it as president, and never deviating throughout his lifetime in devotion to

---

31. Cf. Anson P. Stokes, *Church and State in the United States,* 3 vols. (New York: Harper, 1950), 1:499–507; Sandoz, *GOL,* 136–41; Sandoz, ed., *Political Sermons,* 1571–96. For President Bush's proclamations, see the White House Web site. See chap. 4 n8 for the text of President George W. Bush's January 2001 proclamation.

32. Cf. Sandoz, *GOL,* 111.

liberty of conscience. He regarded securing the enactment of the Virginia Act Establishing Religious Freedom as his most gratifying legislative achievement. "We now give full credit to the contribution of James Madison, mediating with consummate skill among Baptists, Presbyterians, and liberal Anglicans, putting through the Statute while Jefferson was in Paris," Henry F. May writes. "The troops were Baptists and Presbyterians and the tactics were Madison's, but the words . . . were Jefferson's. These were and are wholly representative of the Revolutionary Enlightenment."[33]

A hallmark of American liberty, the Bill of Rights deserves further special comment at this juncture.[34] The Bill of Rights of the United States Constitution consists of the first ten amendments taken together, especially the first eight of these, which identify specific individual rights. These were proposed in 1789 by Representative James Madison, who was solidly backed by President George Washington during the First Congress. Ten of the twelve congressionally approved amendments were ratified by ten states so as to take effect on December 15, 1791. Their general tenor is to protect individual personal, political, and religious liberties against infringement by government, principally by the national government in the original conception and down to 1925 when a process of "nationalization" gradually began that has brought protection against invasion by the states of most of the rights listed and of a number only implied by (or "penumbral" to) the rights specified. The philosophical foundation of the Bill of Rights is set forth in the Declaration of Independence's first sentences, especially the announcement of "certain unalienable rights" grounded in the "laws of nature and nature's God." The effectiveness of the provisions of the Bill of Rights in protecting fundamental personal liberties through American law is uniquely dependent upon the power of judicial review as exercised by the federal judiciary, with a last resort in the Supreme Court

33. Henry F. May, *Divided Heart: Essays on Protestantism and the Enlightenment in America* (New York: Oxford University Press, 1991), 172. See the discussion in Ralph Ketcham, *James Madison: A Biography* (New York: Macmillan, 1971), esp. 165–68.

34. The following paragraphs quote from Ellis Sandoz, "Bill of Rights," in *The Oxford Companion to the Politics of the World*, ed. Joel Krieger et al. (New York: Oxford University Press, 1993), 79–81. Copyright © 1993 by Oxford University Press. Used by permission.

of the United States. The judiciary determines with finality, on a case-by-case adversary basis, the meaning and force of laws under the Constitution considered as the Supreme Law of the Land (Art. VI).

The origins of the liberties protected and general theory of rights undergirding that protection are of great antiquity and grounded in immemorial usage (or *prescription*) and natural right, although meaning and importance were sharpened by the debate leading to American independence and revolution and gained impetus from the eighteenth-century Enlightenment with its emphasis upon reason and the individual. It remains generally true, however, that the rights protected substantively were part and parcel of an inherited tradition of common law liberty and rule of law that emerged in medieval England from the time of King Edward the Confessor (d. 1066), last of the Saxon kings, to Magna Carta as developed in the jurisprudence of Henry de Bracton, refined in the Lancastrian constitutional jurisprudence of Sir John Fortescue (lord chief justice and lord chancellor under Henry VI, d. 1479?). This tradition was recovered, vivified, and perfected in seventeenth-century England especially by Sir Edward Coke (1584–1634) in the House of Commons during the long contest between parliament and the Stuart kings memorialized in the Petition of Right (1628), the beheading of Charles I (1649), and eventuating in the Glorious Revolution of 1688, Settlement of 1689, and parliamentary enactment of the Declaration of Rights as the English Bill of Rights of the same year, thus giving its name to the genre. The constitutional form authoritative at the time of the American founding was powerfully shaped by Coke, former attorney general and lord chief justice of England, who led a successful resistance against extension of the royal prerogative and the attendant establishment of absolutism and rule by divine right that saved rule of law and constitutionalism for England and the modern world, as Sir William Holdsworth emphasized. Decisive for the continuity of this vision of liberty through law and limited government was the education of subsequent generations of lawyers, including the American revolutionary generation and beyond, by Coke's *Institutes* and *Reports.* There is, thus, this international or ecumenic dimension, that while the bill-of-rights concept may be primarily American, the liberties protected, and institutional modes devised for their protection, are deeply moored in Anglo-American political and constitutional history, especially in those passages of it in which the absolutism was narrowly averted that swept over almost all of Western civilization in the seventeenth century with consequences into the present. Indeed, the securing of personal liberty and free government through rule of law is a legacy quite self-consciously reaching back to distant antiquity, to Cicero in Rome and Aristotle in Hellas.

Well before 1789 when, under heavy political pressure from the Antifederalists and public sentiment fearful that personal liberties might be imperiled by the new Constitution, Madison proposed his amendments, virtually *all* of the rights to be included in the federal Bill of Rights already had been set out in bills of rights ratified by eleven of the original thirteen states plus Vermont. The inventory of such rights already adopted by one or another of the new American states, thus, included the following: no establishment of religion, free exercise of religion, free speech, free press, assembly, petition, right to bear arms, no quartering of soldiers, searches and seizures protection, requirement of grand jury indictment, protection against double jeopardy and self-incrimination, guarantee of due process of law, just compensation, a public trial, jury trial, accusation and confrontation, witnesses, guarantee of counsel, protection against excessive bail, fines, and punishment. The only major provision not found in the earlier state documents is the retained rights provision of the Ninth Amendment. The Massachusetts Declaration of Rights (1780), drafted by John Adams, even included a reserved powers clause (Art. IV) analogous to the Tenth Amendment's provision. The Massachusetts document also had the merit of partly replacing the admonitory language of *ought* used by George Mason in drafting the 1776 Virginia Declaration of Rights (the model for eight other states' bills of rights), with the imperative *shall* of legal command found (along with *shall not*) in Madison's Bill of Rights.

With a glance at developments since the founding, it can be noted that there was virtually no judicial construction of the meaning of the various provisions of the Bill of Rights until well after adoption of the Civil War amendments, numbers thirteen, fourteen, and fifteen. A voluminous litigatory process variously termed "absorption," "selective incorporation," and identification of liberties occupying a "preferred position" (First Amendment rights), or as being "fundamental rights," has accelerated, however, since the *Adamson* case in 1947, which results in applying the Bill of Rights to state governments and even private actions, no less than to actions of the federal government. Today the liberty protected against invasion by the states under the Due Process Clause of the Fourteenth Amendment embraces all provisions of the First Amendment and nearly all provisions of the Fourth, Fifth, Sixth, Seventh, and Eighth Amendments. The principal exceptions are the Fifth Amendment's right to a grand jury indictment in criminal cases and the Seventh Amendment's guarantee of a jury trial in civil cases. In addition, there is a substantial expanse of additional personal liberty, especially race-related "civil rights," protected by the Equal Protection Clause, and strictly extra-constitutional rights (such as privacy and the right to travel) that an activist judiciary has discovered in "penumbras" of the express rights or has construed as being included in the Retained Rights Clause of the Ninth Amendment and, perhaps, even in the "blessings of liberty" phrase of the Preamble to the Constitution.[35]

§4.

Much remains that is new and remarkable about the American founding, but the occasion does not allow for a fuller statement. The most noteworthy structures of the Constitution—the *separation* of powers and attendant system of checks and balances organizing the central branches of the national government, and the *division* of powers between the national government and the several states in the intricate web constitutive of the federal system—especially deserve mention, of course. I would be remiss if I did not stress that the theory of human nature that underlies the separation of powers and checks and balances mechanism is its secret. True enough, it is an old secret, one going back to Aristotle's *Politics* where the philosopher weighs the argument

---

35. *Adamson v. California*, 332 U.S. 46 (1947). Of the vast literature on the Bill of Rights and relied on in the foregoing summary, see especially: Sir William Holdsworth, *Some Makers of English Law: Tagore Lectures of 1937–38* (Cambridge: Cambridge University Press, 1938); Robert A. Rutland, *The Birth of the Bill of Rights, 1776–1791* (Chapel Hill: University of North Carolina Press, 1955); Bernard Schwartz, ed., *The Bill of Rights: A Documentary History*, 2 vols. (New York: McGraw-Hill, 1971); Bernard Schwartz, *The Great Rights of Mankind: A History of the American Bill of Rights* (New York: Oxford University Press, 1977); Ellis Sandoz, *Conceived in Liberty: American Individual Rights Today* (North Scituate, MA: Duxbury Press, 1978); Helen E. Veit, Kenneth R. Bowling, and Charlene Bangs Bickford, eds., *Creating the Bill of Rights: The Documentary Record from the First Federal Congress* (Baltimore: Johns Hopkins University Press, 1991); and Sandoz, *GOL*, 163–217.

that "the rule of law... is preferable to that of any individual.... Therefore he who bids the law rule may be deemed to bid God and Reason
alone rule, but he who bids the man rule adds an element of the beast;
for desire is a wild beast and passion perverts the minds of rulers, even
when they are the best of men. The law is reason unaffected by desire....
[A] man may be a safer ruler than the written law, but not safer than
the customary law."[36]

As we have considered in the previous chapter, the *question* so strik-
ingly answered by the American founders was how to arrive at a government of laws and not of men when there were only men available to rule.
Their estimate of human nature was as well informed as was Aristotle's,
and they understood what Acton would later express in the maxim
that "power corrupts and absolute power corrupts absolutely." Publius
in *The Federalist Papers* writes of the fallibility of men, of their tendency
to favor their own causes, and in a famous passage asks:

> What is government itself but the greatest of all reflections on
> human nature? If men were angels, no government would be
> necessary. If angels were to govern men, neither external nor in-
> ternal controls on government would be necessary. In framing a
> government which is to be administered by men over men, the
> great difficulty lies in this: you must first enable the government
> to control the governed; and in the next place oblige it to control
> itself. A dependence on the people is, no doubt, the primary con-
> trol on the government; but experience has taught mankind the
> necessity of auxiliary precautions.[37]

Primary reliance is upon a virtuous and civic-minded people—but
"prudence" requires something more than this, Publius wrote. The
"system" is not so perfect that no one will have to be good; the system
is a backup, expressly an "auxiliary" precaution. No utopian expectations
here! Its mechanism takes seriously the understanding of human nature
as it comes from the classic philosophers and is enriched with Christian
teaching about the willful selfishness of human beings in their fallen,
sinful state. Man is viewed as capable of virtue but inclined to vice and

36. Aristotle *Politics* 3.16.1287a19 et seq., trans. B. Jowett.
37. Jacob E. Cooke, ed., *The Federalist* (Middletown, CT: Wesleyan University
Press, 1961), 349 (No. 51).

to favoring his own cause whenever he has the opportunity to do so.[38] The mechanism addresses just this fallible human material, by pitting rival ambition against rival ambition in persons occupying each of the three major branches of government, which overlap: legislative, executive, and judicial. This major innovation is an entirely new conception of separation of powers. It is one directly to be contrasted to that found in the French Constitution of 1791, where the separation is adopted without the checks and balances, thereby making the legislature supreme (rule *by* law) and cutting off the possibility of judicial review as it developed in America as a key to rule *of* law as a practical matter.[39] Under our Constitution, the ambitiously striving persons, then, are given the constitutional means in each instance of resisting encroachments that overweening ambition is inclined to seek on others' authority. It is in the interest of each to repel encroachment or suffer the diminishment of one's own power and authority: thereby, "the private interest of every individual [becomes] a sentinel over the public rights." Through these checks of ambition counteracting ambition, a three-way cancellation process is effected in the normal operations of the machinery of government. The "rival interests," Publius wrote, supply the "defect of better motives." Especially ambition (John Adams called it the desire for *emulation*) drives political man, and this lends vigor to the institutions of government, but control is requisite.[40] Because of the ingenuity of institutional design channeling adversarial interplay, a noble residue of reason and justice is the outcome of normal operations. Passion is sufficiently blunted that a government of laws under moderately favorable circumstances becomes a realistic possibility. The constitutional equilibrium achieved by the mixed constitution of rival estates in Britain is supplanted in potentially egalitarian America by a new set of equivalences that function to similar purpose. In Edward S. Corwin's words, the "opposition . . . between the desire of the human governor

38. Ibid., 59, 378, 538 (Nos. 10, 55, 80, respectively).
39. Berman, "The Rule of Law and the Law-Based State," 3, 10, citing André Hauriou, Jean Gicquel, and Patrice Gélard, *Droit constitutionnel et institutions politiques*, 6th ed. (Paris: Montchrestien, 1975), 195–97, and Joseph LaPolombara, *Politics within Nations* (Englewood Cliffs, NJ: Prentice-Hall, 1974), 106.
40. Cf. Charles Francis Adams, ed., *The Works of John Adams, Second President of the United States . . .*, 10 vols. (Boston: Little, Brown, 1850–56), 4:391, 408, 410, 436, 5:10, 40, 273, 6:234, 246–48, 252, 271–72, 279, 284, and *passim*.

and the reason of the law lies, indeed, at the foundation of the American interpretation of the doctrine of separation of powers and so of the entire system of constitutional law."[41]

Born of a philosophically sound "map of man," society, and history that maintained a clear vision of the tension structuring reality toward transcendent divine Being, the civic consciousness whose long experience in self-government and robust common sense made possible the American founding seems, in many respects, a unique growth. And it is both fragile and perishable, as was known from the beginning. We have a republic, but can we keep it?—to recall the question asked Benjamin Franklin as he left the Convention after its work finally was done.

Urgent questions impose themselves, expressive of deep-seated maladies afflicting historically constituted free government. Is the American founders' political vision so exceptional (as we hear argued today) as to be impossible to sustain in the modern world or to propagate in alien soil—even in a world paradoxically hungry for the blessings of liberty, free enterprise, and rule of law but bafflingly plagued by both irreligion and by religious animosities, by a nihilistic disdain for the hard-won insights of faith, history, and reason?[42] Will Jacobinism, expressive of the revolution of the miserable, in Hannah Arendt's phrase, yet carry the day? Will the war against Islamist terrorism take such a toll on devotion to liberty under law in America as to force a substantive change in the constitutional order itself? Have virulent secularism and social amnesia at long last so overwhelmed the mind of the country as to make it forgetful of its very self to the point of the disintegration of the community? The blunt question a Czech friend asked more than a decade ago must still give us pause: "Are you going to win the Cold War and lose your own country?"

41. Corwin, *"Higher Law" Background of American Constitutional Law*, 9.
42. Cf. *American Exceptionalism and Human Rights*, ed. Michael Ignatieff (Princeton: Princeton University Press, 2005), esp. pt. 3.

3

Education and the American Founding

While virtually everyone has agreed that the American founding and the generation that achieved it were extraordinary, of towering significance and formative importance in modern history, what besides blind good luck and raw talent in able men somehow disposed to collaborate and to act at a propitious moment lay behind the achievement? Thus, in looking for at least a few explanatory clues, I propose to approach this large subject by raising a further (no doubt preliminary) question: *What spiritual and intellectual resources enabled the founding generation to achieve what it did?* That question, in turn, requires a brief recollection of their achievement, the founding itself. This I would venture to summarize roughly as follows.

The founding was the rearticulation of Western civilization in its Anglo-American mode.[1] It was essentially anti-modernist in resisting absolutism in the form of perceived parliamentary exercise of unlimited arbitrary or tyrannical power. It thus stands substantially in line with the great seventeenth-century struggle against the Stuart kings whose monuments are the Petition of Right and the Glorious Revolution understood as Burke understood it—as a revolution not so much made

---

1. The summary given here is indebted to the author's previously published work, esp. Ellis Sandoz, *A Government of Laws: Political Theory, Religion, and the American Founding,* 2nd ed. (1990; rev. ed., Columbia: University of Missouri Press, 2001), 151–56 and *passim;* also Ellis Sandoz, ed., *The Roots of Liberty: Magna Carta, Ancient Constitution, and the Anglo-American Tradition of Rule of Law* (Columbia: University of Missouri Press, 1993), 1–21; and Ellis Sandoz, ed., *Political Sermons of the American Founding Era, 1730–1805,* 2 vols., 2nd ed. (1991; repr., Indianapolis: Liberty Fund, 1998); and Ellis Sandoz, *The Politics of Truth and Other Untimely Essays: The Crisis of Civic Consciousness* (Columbia: University of Missouri Press, 1999).

as one avoided, thus resting on an appeal to the prescriptive Ancient Constitution.

Primary characteristics of self-consciousness or identity include: constitutionalism or rule of law, consent, limited powers of government, popular sovereignty, individual dignity and liberty, metaphysical equality of all men with political consequences, a Creator-creaturely understanding of the compass of reality, the source of human law and rights in the experienced human tension toward the transcendent Ground of being as the core of human participation in reality, a historic as well as a natural jurisprudence, and a sense of being a particular community that yet embodied and served universal truth and justice under divine Providence—an exceptional, favored, perhaps chosen people (e.g., Benjamin Franklin, Samuel Adams, and Ezra Stiles).

The pertinent "education question," then, is: *How did Americans get that way?* The manifold of reason and experience contributed, and the question is a larger one than can adequately be answered here, but a number of elements can be noted as especially important. To begin with, there is direct instruction by tutors (often clergymen) in schools and colleges. Then, of cardinal importance, creation of the *civic consciousness* from a long history of independent or quasi-independent self-government, capped by a great political and existential debate during the fifteen-year struggle against tyranny leading to independence. James Madison in old age recalled the wisdom of his countryman in seeing the hand of tyranny in the 3 pence per pound tax on tea levied by the Townshend Duties of 1767, which eventually led to the Boston Tea Party of 1773. Young Madison was at Princeton in 1770 when the Boston Massacre occurred, a founding member of the American Whig Society, and heard James Witherspoon (President John Witherspoon's son) argue the affirmative side of a debate in Latin on the thesis "Subjects are bound and obliged by the law of nature, to resist their king, if he treats them cruelly or ignores the law of the state, and to defend their liberty."[2]

The general context of religious influences, political praxis, and constitutional understanding from Mayflower Compact onward forms essential background, along with self-government flourishing during

2. Irving Brant, *James Madison: The Virginia Revolutionist* (Indianapolis: Bobbs-Merrill, 1941), 80–85, 94.

salutary neglect, thus allowing the development of independence of mind, spirit, and institutional order. The general effects of Enlightenment thought are significant, with its heightening of the sense of individual autonomy and an egalitarianism corrosive of social hierarchy. Of substantial importance is the general character of the American community itself as delineated by John Jay, who found that "Providence has been pleased to give this one connected country, to one united people, a people descended from the same ancestors, speaking the same language, professing the same religion, attached to the same principles of government, very similar in their manners and customs, and who, by their joint counsels, arms and efforts, fighting side by side through a long and bloody war, have nobly established their general Liberty and Independence. This country and this people seem to have been made for each other."[3] In addition, the fact of the relative homogeneity of American elites during the period of the founding makes meaningful generalization plausible: "The Founding Fathers were so similar to the broader elite of Revolutionary executive officeholders as to be indistinguishable from them."[4]

In sum: The principal educational sources may be identified as the Bible and Protestant Christianity as the fundamental matrix of the society; a schooling in the Latin and Greek classics as the foundation of all education; a political and constitutional preoccupation that tended to dominate public discourse from the 1760s on as nurtured especially by Coke, Locke, Montesquieu, and later Blackstone; and an enlightened sense of individual capacity and responsibility under God as created *imago dei* and accountable for stewardship, for serving truth and

3. *Federalist* No. 2 as in *The Federalist,* ed. Jacob E. Cooke (Middletown, CT: Wesleyan University Press, 1961), 9.

4. Richard D. Brown, "Founding Fathers of 1776 and 1787: A Collective View," *William and Mary Quarterly,* 3rd ser., 33 (1976): 465–80, at 466. The educational ideas of the founders and founding period are explored in many places, and especially the following may be mentioned: Bernard Bailyn, *Education in the Forming of American Society: Needs and Opportunities for Study* (Chapel Hill: University of North Carolina Press, 1960); Robert Middlekauff, "A Persistent Tradition: The Classical Curriculum in Eighteenth-Century New England," *William and Mary Quarterly,* 3rd ser., 18 (1961): 54–67; Eugene F. Miller, "On the American Founders' Defense of Liberal Education in a Republic," *Review of Politics* 46 (1984): 65–90; and Lorraine Smith Pangle and Thomas L. Pangle, *The Learning of Liberty: The Educational Ideas of the American Founders* (Lawrence: University Press of Kansas, 1993).

justice, and for resisting by every means corruption and evil. The latter factors were nurtured by a range of influences generally to form American civic consciousness.

The strategy to be followed herein is one of illustrative analysis with more and less famous examples taken from the lives of representative personalities to include James Madison, John Adams, Thomas Jefferson, Benjamin Rush, Joseph Story, James Kent, Noah Webster, and David Ramsay. Illustrations will bear mainly on the Bible and Christianity, the classics, and legal and political education. Some repetition of material cited in the foregoing chapters will be unavoidable if the analysis here is to stand solidly on the most pertinent sources.

In staking out the ground to be covered, one scholar wrote: "Both historians and the general reader have agreed that the classical heritage of Greece and Rome played a large part in the ideas and activities of Colonial America, with a climax of interest at the end of the eighteenth century. The evidence is so convincing that the case may be stated rather than defended. Careful investigation has proved that the classical tradition was, *next to the Bible and the Common Law,* a vital factor in provincial life and thought."[5]

§1. Bible and Christianity

If the Moral Majority, the so-called Christian Right, and evangelicals can be major forces in contemporary American politics, why should it be to *anyone's* surprise that religion was a major factor in the period of the founding? From a variety of motives, dogmatic rejection seems to be a principal part of the answer. The fact of the matter is that the best recent scholarship supports the proposition that the Christian perspective was alive, well, and flourishing in the period and that it was central to many of its major events.

Bible reading was ubiquitous in America throughout the period formally identified as "the founding," which benefited from the Great Awakening's revitalization of faith and coincided with the onset of the Second Great Awakening that carried well into the nineteenth century.

---

5. Richard M. Gummere, *Seven Wise Men of Colonial America* (Cambridge, MA: Harvard University Press, 1967), v. Italics added.

Perry Miller remarked a generation ago, as previously noticed, that a cool rationalism such as Jefferson's might have declared the independence of such folk but could never have persuaded them to fight for it. Edmund Burke, speaking in the Commons on the eve of the Revolution (1775), stressed that the Americans' love of liberty on English principles was powerfully informed by their faith as Christians (mainly in dissenting traditions), which is fundamental to their perspective.

David Ramsay, in his contemporary (1789) *History of the American Revolution,* echoed Burke by writing:

> The religion of the colonists also nurtured a love for liberty. They were chiefly Protestants, and all Protestantism is founded on a strong claim to natural liberty, and the right of private judgement. A majority of them were of that class of men, who, in England, are called Dissenters. Their tenets, being the Protestantism of the protestant religion, are hostile to all interference of authority, in matters of opinion, and predispose to a jealousy for civil liberty. They who belonged to the Church of England were for the most part independents, as far as church government and hierarchy, were concerned. They used the liturgy of that church, but were without Bishops, and were strangers to those systems, which make religion an engine of state. That policy, which unites the lowest curate with the greatest metropolitan, and connects both with the sovereign, was unknown among the colonists. Their religion was their own, and neither imposed by authority, nor made subservient to political purposes. Though there was a variety of sects, they all agreed in the communion of liberty, and all reprobated the courtly doctrines of passive obedience, and non-resistance.[6]

One modern scholar has turned empirical analysis to good use in discovering that a full one-third of all citations in the enormous pamphlet literature of the period were to texts in the Bible, far more than to any other single source.[7] George Trevelyan comments that "the effect of the continual domestic study of the [Bible] upon the national character, imagination, and intelligence for three centuries—was greater than

6. David Ramsay, *The History of the American Revolution* [Philadelphia, 1789], ed. Lester H. Cohen, 2 vols. (Indianapolis: Liberty Classics, 1990), 1:26–27.

7. Donald S. Lutz, "Relative Influence of European Writers on Late Eighteenth-Century American Political Thought," *American Political Science Review* 78 (1984): 189–97.

that of any literary movement in the annals, or any religious movement since St. Augustine."[8]

Everybody's favorite authority, Alexis de Tocqueville (writing in 1835, the year of John Marshall's death and the year before that of James Madison, last of the Founding Fathers), elaborately stressed the centrality of Christianity in America. For example he wrote: "For the Americans the ideas of Christianity and liberty are so completely mingled that it is almost impossible to get them to conceive of the one without the other." "The religious atmosphere of the country was the first thing that struck me on arrival in the United States." And he described the frontiersman of the 1830s as "a very civilized man prepared for a time to face life in the forest, plunging into the wildernesses of the New World with his Bible, ax, and newspapers."[9] In the second volume of his famous work, Tocqueville had not changed his mind and wrote in 1840, in chapter one: "It was religion that gave birth to the English colonies in America. One must never forget that. In the United States religion is mingled with all the national customs and all those feelings which the word fatherland evokes. . . . Christianity has kept a strong hold over the minds of Americans . . . [I]ts power is . . . that of a religion believed in without discussion. . . . Christianity itself is an established and irresistible fact which no one seeks to attack or to defend. Since the Americans have accepted the main dogmas of the Christian religion without examination, they are bound to receive in like manner a great number of moral truths derived therefrom and attached thereto."[10] But we somehow manage to forget or explain it away with an ease reminiscent of the oblivion hole of Orwell's Ingsoc.[11] Facts and truth are pesky, inconvenient things for those whose agendas cannot stand the light of day.

8. Quoted by H. Richard Niebuhr, "The Idea of Covenant and American Democracy," *Church History* 22 (1954): 130.

9. Alexis de Tocqueville, *Democracy in America*, ed. J. P. Mayer, trans. George Lawrence, 2 vols. in 1 (Garden City, NY: Doubleday Anchor Books, 1969), 293, 295, 303.

10. Ibid., 432.

11. Cf. George Orwell, *1984* (1949; repr., New York: New American Library, Signet Classics, 1961), "Appendix: The Principles of Newspeak": "The purpose of Newspeak was not only to provide a medium of expression for the world-view and mental habits proper to the devotees of Ingsoc, but to make all other modes of thought impossible" (246).

John Adams writing to Thomas Jefferson in their old age found the heart of the revolutionary American community to lie in the universally accepted "*general principles* of Christianity" shared by all, by which he chiefly meant the Ten Commandments and the Sermon on the Mount, and in the "general principles of English and American Liberty, in which all those young men united [who fought the Revolution], and which had united all parties in America, in majorities sufficient to assert and maintain her Independence. Now I will avow [Adams continued], that I then believed, and now believe, that those general Principles of Christianity are as eternal and immutable as the Existence and attributes of God; and those principles of liberty are as unalterable as human nature and our terrestrial, mundane system."[12] Jefferson elsewhere explained that the latter were set forth in the Declaration of Independence, upon which all Whigs at the time had agreed.

When some inkling of Jefferson's deep if heterodox religious convictions leaked out with discovery of his work on the New Testament (*The Philosophy of Jesus* and *The Life and Morals of Jesus,* in which he excerpted and studied the Gospels in the various ancient and modern languages),[13] his resolute study of the Bible, biblical scholarship, church fathers, and other theological literature in Greek, Latin, French, and English, he was urged to make his convictions known to the public, to publish his religious sentiments. In 1824 (two years before his death) Jefferson declined in a letter to George Thatcher and wrote: "But have they not the Gospel? If they hear not that, and the charities it teacheth, neither will they be persuaded though one rose from the dead."[14]

Stoutly upholding liberty of conscience and separation of church and state did not and does not equate with lack of religious faith. James Madison apparently considered the ministry as a young man

12. John Adams to Thomas Jefferson, June 28, 1813, in *The Adams-Jefferson Letters: The Complete Correspondence between Thomas Jefferson and Abigail and John Adams,* ed. Lester J. Cappon, 2 vols. in 1 (1959; repr., New York: Simon & Schuster/ Clarion Books, 1971), 1:339–340. Some emendation of punctuation and capitalization from the original text.

13. Collected and annotated along with all other relevant sources pertaining to Jefferson's religious views in Dixon W. Adams, ed., *Jefferson's Extracts from the Gospels: "The Philosophy of Jesus" and "The Life and Morals of Jesus"* (Princeton: Princeton University Press, 1983).

14. Quoted from Sandoz, *GOL,* 149.

and decided against it partly because of his poor speaking voice.[15] But he stayed on an extra half-year at the College of New Jersey in Princeton to study moral philosophy and Hebrew with his great mentor, President John Witherspoon, a Scottish Presbyterian and the only clergyman to sign the Declaration of Independence. When time came to select theology books for the library at the University of Virginia that he and Jefferson founded in their old age and served as the first two rectors, it was to Madison that Jefferson turned because of his expertise in the field.[16] In his retirement years at Montpellier after his presidency, James Madison and his wife, Dolly, regularly drove the four miles on Sundays to attend services "at the quaint old brick church in the center of Orange Court House."[17]

Such may not have been Jefferson's practice in his later years, but he had regularly attended Bruton Church in Williamsburg as a student at William and Mary and afterward.[18] Moreover, as president of the United States residing in the new capital of Washington he began a practice, mentioned earlier, one that endured until well after the Civil War, of holding church services regularly in the Capitol. This was done at first in the Senate chamber and, after construction was completed, in the House of Representatives' chamber. The president frequently was present, often with the cabinet as well as members of Congress and the general public in attendance. On occasion, worship services were conducted simultaneously in both chambers with overflow crowds present. To be invited to preach there was, of course, a great honor for the various ministers, such as Jefferson's fiery Baptist admirer the Elder John Leland (1802) of "mammoth Cheese" fame who (along with George Eve) had been a formidable force in James Madison's Virginia House constituency when the Bill of Rights was at issue in 1789.[19] In his old age Jefferson looked forward to eternal life and to reunion with

15. Brant, *James Madison: The Virginia Revolutionist,* 118 and chap. 6 *passim.*

16. Ibid., 120; Gaillard Hunt, ed., *The Writings of James Madison,* 9 vols. (New York: G. Putnam's Sons, 1900–10), 9:203–207.

17. Maud Wilder Goodwin, *Dolly Madison* (New York: Charles Scribner, 1896), 275–76.

18. Dumas Malone, *Jefferson and His Time,* vol. 1, *Jefferson the Virginian* (Boston: Little, Brown, 1948), 52; cf. pp. 274–85.

19. Cf. Anson P. Stokes, *Church and State in the United States,* 3 vols. (New York: Harper, 1950), 1:499–507; see Helen Cripe, *Thomas Jefferson and Music* (Charlottesville: University Press of Virginia, 1974), 24–26.

those other stalwarts of the American cause already departed. He believed he was a Christian in the only sense that Jesus would have recognized, and he sought to return to the primitive purity and simplicity of the Gospel. Basic was his unswerving commitment to the existence of God, the creator and sustainer of the world and ultimate ground of being, and he lavishly praised Jesus for making God worthy of human worship. Thus, the unity of God, the moral teachings of Jesus as the most sublime in the history of the world, and the expectation of personal immortality formed his Christianity.[20]

Dr. Benjamin Rush, the famous patriot scientist-physician, signatory of the Declaration of Independence, medical pioneer, and professor of Philadelphia, urged that the Bible be the primary textbook of the public schools following the Revolution and replace instruction in Latin and Greek as being more republican. Rush wrote in 1786: "The only foundation for a useful education in a republic is to be laid in RELIGION. Without this, there can be no virtue, and without virtue there can be no liberty, and liberty is the object and life of all republican governments. . . . The religion I mean to recommend in this place is the religion of JESUS CHRIST. . . . A Christian cannot fail of being a republican."[21] Rush maintained that "Man is as necessarily a praying as he is a sociable, domestic, or religious animal. As 'no man liveth and sinneth not,' so no man liveth and prayeth not. . . . Prayer is an instinct of nature in man, as much so as his love of society." When his son James was departing for Edinburgh to follow his father's footsteps in the study of medicine, the elder Rush instructed him to "[c]ommit yourself and all that you are interested in daily to the protection of your Maker, Preserver, and bountiful Benefactor." He also urged James to follow his own practice of setting everything else aside and "[a]ttend public worship . . . on Sundays" and "[r]ead the Bible only on Sundays."[22]

---

20. For sources and discussion see Sandoz, *GOL*, 148 and *passim*.

21. Benjamin Rush, *A Plan for the Establishment of Public Schools and the Diffusion of Knowledge in Pennsylvania; to Which Are Added, Thoughts upon the Mode of Education, Proper in a Republic* (Philadelphia, 1786), repr. in *American Political Writing during the Founding Era, 1760–1805*, ed. Charles S. Hyneman and Donald S. Lutz, 2 vols. (Indianapolis: Liberty Fund, 1983), 1:675–92, at 681.

22. George W. Corner, ed., *The Autobiography of Benjamin Rush; His "Travels Through Life," together with his* Commonplace Book *for 1789–1813* (Princeton: Princeton University Press, 1948), 339, 280–81. In the internal quote Rush paraphrases Ecclesiastes 7:20.

Noah Webster is famed for his blue-backed speller, *The American Spelling Book* (1783: more than 100 million sold by the twentieth century), and as a great lexicographer whose *American Dictionary of the American Language* (1828) rested on an unprecedented philological apparatus involving more than twenty languages and was the most monumental work produced in America up until that time. In fact, Webster was the most prolific American author of the age, and his published bibliography runs more than six hundred pages. Having proposed a revision of the general government in May 1785 in *Sketches of Public Policy*, which he gave to Washington, he and Alexander Hamilton were among the first persons to anticipate the need for something like the Federal Convention of 1787.[23] Webster agreed with Rush on the centrality of the Holy Bible for education, regarding it as the source of all true wisdom.[24] He revised the King James Version (1611) and published an American edition of the Bible (1833). In its preface Webster wrote: "The Bible is the chief moral cause of all that is *good*, and the best corrector of all that is *evil*, in human society; the *best* book for regulating the temporal concerns of men, and the *only book* that can serve as an infallible guide to future felicity." Webster believed that duty to God was superior to any earthly obligation and toward the end of his life adopted the jeremiad style traditional with preachers throughout the Revolutionary period in judging America flawed, sinful, and depraved. "We are an erring nation ... we deserve all our public evils." "*We have forsaken God, and he has forsaken us,*" he wrote in 1838.[25]

George Washington regularly attended church and was a vestryman in the Episcopal Church. He gave great stress to religion in his Farewell Address (1796), calling "religion and morality" indispensable to political prosperity and patriotism and writing: "Let us with caution indulge

23. Harry R. Warfel, ed., *Letters of Noah Webster* (New York: Library Pubs., 1953), 256, 260, 528n; Emily E. F. Skeel, ed., *A Bibliography of the Writings of Noah Webster* (New York: New York Public Library, 1958). On the role of Hamilton, see the personal recollections of Chancellor James Kent in William Kent, *Memoirs and Letters of James Kent* (Boston: Little, Brown, 1898), "Appendix: Chancellor Kent's Memories of Alexander Hamilton," 279–331. Hereinafter cited as *Memoirs of Chancellor Kent*.

24. Richard M. Rollins, ed., *The Autobiographies of Noah Webster: From the Letters and Essays, Memoir, and Diary* (Columbia: University of South Carolina Press, 1989), 34.

25. *The Webster Bible* (1833; repr., Grand Rapids, MI: Baker Book House, 1987), v; Rollins, ed., *Autobiographies of Noah Webster*, 56.

the supposition, that morality can be maintained without religion." David Ramsay had anticipated the judgment in 1789. He summed up the lessons of the Revolutionary experience with these words: "Remember that there can be no political happiness without liberty; that there can be no liberty without morality; and that there can be no morality without religion."[26]

To stress that these religious convictions were no monopoly of New Englanders (a hangover from their original Puritanism), a summary of the political aspects of religious convictions of the time may be cited. Alice Baldwin writes: "Southern Presbyterian ministers based their political concepts upon the Bible. The idea of a fundamental constitution based on law, of inalienable rights which were God-given and therefore natural, of government as a binding compact made between rulers and peoples, of the right of the people to hold their rulers to account and to defend their rights against all oppression, these seem to have been doctrines taught by them all . . . [I]n the South as in New England, the clergy helped in making familiar to the common people the basic principles on which the revolution was fought, our constitutional conventions held, our Bills of Rights written and our state and national constitutions founded."[27]

Confronted with this and the mountain of related evidence, one modern scholar exclaims of the Americans of 1776: "Who can deny that for them the very core of existence was their relation to God?"[28] A great many people of various motivations deny it, of course, one of whom (a fellow historian) serenely writes that while "Jefferson and Madison along with George Washington, John Adams, Benjamin Franklin, and nearly all of the Founding Fathers claimed to be Christians hardly any of them was."[29] Presumably all politicians are pathological liars or don't know their own minds, even including founding Fathers.

26. Ramsay, *History of the American Revolution*, 2:667, last page. See also Michael Novak and Jane Novak, *Washington's God: Religion, Liberty, and the Father of Our Country* (New York: Basic Books, 2006).

27. Alice Baldwin, "Sowers of Sedition," *William and Mary Quarterly*, 3rd ser., 5 (1948): 76.

28. Carl Bridenbaugh, *The Spirit of '76: The Growth of American Patriotism before Independence, 1607–1776* (New York: Oxford University Press, 1975), 118.

29. John M. Murrin, "Religion and Politics in America from the First Settlements to the Civil War," in *Religion and American Politics: From the Colonial Period to the 1980s*, ed. Mark A. Noll (New York: Oxford University Press, 1990), 19–43, at

A final word on this subject can be given to the great jurist and legal philosopher Joseph Story (1779–1845), a member of the United States Supreme Court of John Marshall and Roger B. Taney, and longtime Dane Professor of Law at Harvard whose great work entitled *Commentaries on the Constitution of the United States* was first published in three volumes in Boston in 1833. Story therein states the following:

> Now there will probably be found few persons in this or any other Christian country, who would deliberately contend that it was unreasonable, or unjust to foster and encourage the Christian religion generally, as a matter of sound policy, as well as of revealed truth.... Indeed, in a republic, there would seem to be a peculiar propriety in viewing the Christian religion as the great basis, on which it must rest for its support and permanence, if it be what it has ever been deemed by its truest friends to be, the religion of liberty. Montesquieu has remarked, that the Christian religion is a stranger to mere despotic power.... Probably at the adoption of the constitution, and of the [First] amendment to it, ... the general, if not the universal sentiment in America was, that Christianity ought to receive encouragement from the state, so far as was not incompatible with the private rights of conscience, and the freedom of religious worship. An attempt to level all religions, and to make it a matter of state policy to hold all in utter indifference, would have created universal disapprobation if not universal indignation.
>
> It yet remains a problem to be solved in human affairs, whether any free government can be permanent, where the public worship of God, and the support of religion, constitute no part of the policy or duty of the state in any assignable shape. The future experience of Christendom, and chiefly of the American states, must settle this problem, as yet anew in the history of the world.[30]

29, 35; see also David L. Holmes, *The Religion of the Founding Fathers* (Charlottesville, VA: Ash Lawn–Highland, and Ann Arbor: Clements Library, University of Michigan, 2003), 131: "The Founding Fathers of the United States were remarkable, even noble men.... In the spirit of their times, they appeared less devout than they were—which seems a reversal from modern politics."

30. Joseph Story, *Commentaries on the Constitution of the United States: With a Preliminary Review of the Constitutional History of the Colonies and States, Before the Adoption of the Constitution*, ed. Edward W. Bennett, 3rd ed., 2 vols. (Boston: Little,

Because of decades of increasing secularization of American society, among other factors, the problem to which Story alludes may be more acute in the early twenty-first century than ever before in the history of the republic.

§2. Classics

Because for nearly two hundred years in America the Greek and Latin classics formed the foundation of education, the thought of antiquity was second nature to Americans of the founding era. That was the golden era of the classics, as Meyer Reinhold has said, and especially Cicero was central—a happy circumstance, since Cicero digested and transmitted the substance of Greek political philosophy from the perspective of a great lawyer.[31] Reinhold writes:

> The Founding Fathers, with a common core of knowledge from the obligatory traditional classical curriculum and from omnivorous adult reading, venerated the ancient commonwealths, statesmen, and the classical virtues as models of republicanism. In Revolutionary America love of liberty and political expertise were associated with classical learning.... There is perhaps no better epitome of the Revolutionary generation's commitment to classical learning than John Adams' exhortation to his son John Quincy in 1781: "In Company with Sallust, Cicero, Tacitus and Livy you

---

Brown, 1858), 2:662–63 (bk. 3, chap. 44, pars. 1873, 1874, 1875). For analysis, see James McClellan, *Joseph Story and the American Constitution* (Norman: University of Oklahoma Press, 1971), chap. 3, "Christianity and the Common Law."

31. "Cicero's ideas on [the mixed constitution] run like a stream underground through colonial writings" (Richard M. Gummere, *The Colonial Mind and the Classical Tradition: Essays in Comparative Culture* [Cambridge, MA: Harvard University Press, 1963], 176). Cicero also was the mediator between ancient Greek and early Christian civilization, as Augustine suggests, and also between classical antiquity and the Renaissance. "Cicero, who was originally read above all because of his style and then was prized because of the content of his work, especially *De natura deorum...* plays an important role in transmitting material from antiquity" (Henning Graf Reventlow, *The Authority of the Bible and the Rise of the Modern World*, trans. John Bowden [Philadelphia: Fortress Press, 1985], 420n53). The statement applies also to America, where Cicero served similar functions.

will learn Wisdom and Virtue. . . . You will ever remember that
all the End of Study is to make you a good Man and a useful
Citizen."[32]

As hinted, the entering college student came to one of the nine pre-
Revolutionary colleges with a standardized preparation in which the
Greek and Latin languages were the passwords for admission and
progress toward the bachelor's degree. Preparation was arduous and
typically began at age eight, whether in private tutorials or in grammar
schools. Pupils commonly studied classics from eight until eleven every
morning and from one until dark in the afternoon. There was widespread prohibition against using English translations. The experience
was not always a happy one. Discipline was strict and sometimes severe,
as with the perhaps unusually stern Master Sawney at the Boston Latin
School who found student Bangs unprepared. Rufus Dawes recounts
the episode from 1811:

> "Well!" continues Sawney, switching the air with his cane, "well,
> muttonhead, what does an active verb express?"
> After a little delay—"I'll tell you what it expresses," he resumes,
> bringing the stick down upon the boy's haunches with decided
> emphasis, "it expresses an action and necessarily supposes an agent
> (flourishing the cane, which descends again as before) and an object
> acted upon, as [in] *castigo te,* I chastise thee; do you understand?"
> "Yes, sir! Yes, sir!" replies the boy, doing his best to get out of
> the way of the rattan. But Sawney is not disposed to let him off so.
> "Now tell me when an active verb is transitive."
> "I don't know, sir," drawls Bangs doggedly.
> "Don't you?" follows Sawney. "Then I'll inform you. An active
> verb is called transitive when the action passeth over (whack,
> whack) to the object. You (whack) are the object. I am (whack)
> the agent. Now take care how you go home and say that I never
> taught you anything. Do you hear? (whack)"[33]

32. Meyer Reinhold, *Classica Americana: The Greek and Roman Heritage in the United States* (Detroit: Wayne State University Press, 1984), 174.
33. Quoted from Carl J. Richard, *The Founders and the Classics: Greece, Rome, and the American Enlightenment* (Cambridge, MA: Harvard University Press, 1994), 15–16.

While whipping was common, there were many schoolmasters of exceptional skill and ability. For example, Donald Robertson's boarding school at Dunkirk, Virginia, in the 1760s had such students as James Madison, John Taylor of Caroline, John Tyler (father of the president), and George Rogers Clark. He provided them with a rigorous classical education, teaching Greek, Latin, and French in a Scottish brogue. Madison at age eleven entered and over a four-year period read selections from Virgil, Horace, Justinian's *Institutes,* Cornelius Nepos, Julius Caesar, Tacitus, Lucretius, Eutropius, Phaedrus, Herodotus, Thucydides, and Plato before returning home in 1767 for another two years of study with Reverend Thomas Martin. Carl Richard writes that "Madison's early training was so thorough that although he arrived at the College of New Jersey in 1769 only two weeks before final examinations in Greek, Latin, the New Testament, English, and mathematics, he passed them all."[34]

When John Jay applied to King's College (Columbia) in 1760 he was required to give a rational account of Greek and Latin grammar, demonstrate ability to read three orations of Cicero and three books from the *Aeneid,* and convert the first ten chapters of the Gospel of John into Latin, and to be proficient in mathematics as far as the Rule of Reduction. Requirements a half century later at Brown were similar, and under the examination by the president and tutors the candidate had to read, explain, and parse Cicero, the Greek Testament, and Virgil, write true Latin prose, know the rules of prosody and "vulgar arithmetic," and submit evidence of a blameless life and conversation. Similarly when Jefferson was planning the entrance requirements for the University of Virginia after 1818, he agreed with Dr. Thomas Cooper's statement:

> It should be scrupulously insisted on that no youth can be admitted to the university unless he can read with facility Virgil, Horace, Xenophon, and Homer: unless he is able to convert a page of English at sight into Latin: unless he can demonstrate any proposition at sight in the first six books of Euclid, and show an acquaintance with cubic and quadratic equations.

34. Ibid., 18.

Jefferson concurred that to require less than this would make the proposed university "a mere grammar school."[35] Cooper had translated Justinian's *Institutes* and published it in Philadelphia in 1812, and he was Jefferson's choice for the position of professor of law but was rejected by the university's board. It was recalled of Jefferson as a student at William and Mary in the 1760s that "he studied 15 hours per day and carried his Greek grammar with him wherever he went." Fondness for the classics never left him, and when he died in 1826 three items lay on his reading table at Monticello: a French political pamphlet, a volume of Seneca, and Aristotle's *Politics*.[36]

Such classical background figured in those prominent in founding the country. Thus, twenty-seven college men out of fifty-six in Congress signed the Declaration of Independence (including eight from Harvard), while twenty-three out of the thirty-nine who signed the Constitution in 1787 were college men, nine from Princeton, eight of them including James Madison educated by John Witherspoon—surely the most influential professor in American history. The framers did not merely echo or superficially quote the classical sources but applied them by adapting their insights into the tasks at hand, especially those of Aristotle, Cicero, and Polybius.[37] Witherspoon's name should not pass without also a mention of his key role in introducing Scottish Common Sense philosophy (especially of Thomas Reid and Francis Hutcheson) into America, a dominant intellectual force that endured into the late nineteenth century and seems to be reviving today in such works as James Q. Wilson's *Moral Sense*.[38]

35. Gummere, *The Colonial Mind and the Classical Tradition*, 56–57; Richard, *The Founders and the Classics*, 34–35. On Jefferson's own education as a youth see Malone, *Jefferson and His Time*, vol. 1, *Jefferson the Virginian*, 40–48 and chap. 4, "At the College, 1760–1762."

36. Richard, *The Founders and the Classics*, 22, 276n21; Malone, *Jefferson the Virginian*, 56.

37. Malone, *Jefferson the Virginian*, 66, 173.

38. Sandoz, *GOL*, 179–89. Cf. John Witherspoon, *An Annotated Edition of Lectures on Moral Philosophy*, ed. Jack Scott (Newark: University of Delaware Press, 1982), 50: "In terms of Scottish Common Sense philosophy, Witherspoon's thought is neither original nor profound. Rather, his real significance is in making Princeton a citadel of Scottish realism—a citadel that, in turn, dominated philosophical thought in American higher education for many decades.... Appropriately, the last great champion of Scottish realism in America was Princeton President James McCosh (1868–88), another imported Scot who arrived in America exactly one hundred years

The influences from the classics bore fundamentally on American prudential and political theory as embodied in the whole civic life of the country, but especially in the Constitution and constitution-making of the states. Central elements include: the theory of human nature, the conception of the mixed and balanced government, federalism, the Ciceronion and generally Stoic conception of political virtue, and the notion of the rule of law as embodying reason in contrast to the rule of men. The latter, as Aristotle and Madison teach, involve passions in inevitably distorting and self-serving ways. The rule of law of Aristotle's *Politics,* as reinforced by the government of laws of James Harrington's *Oceana* (1656), found its way into the Massachusetts Constitution of 1780 (in which John Adams played a large part), thence into American constitutional law in Chief Justice John Marshall's opinion in *Marbury v. Madison* (1803). The Virgilian farmer and classical pastoral ideal make a major and enduring appearance with the Jeffersonian republicans' yeoman farmer as the American paradigm. There is, of course, republicanism itself as well as the great Federalist and Antifederalist debates over its true meaning. Political virtue classically understood as enlightened service to the common good was common coin of the founding; and the Roman virtues of frugality, simplicity, temperance, fortitude, selflessness, honor, and love of liberty were purposely inculcated as traits of character by George Washington and others of his age. They were not generally thought to contradict Christian virtues.[39] Washington himself as "the father of the Country" received the benefits of a classical metaphor originally applied by Cato to Cicero.[40] Then there is that wonderful ornament of American literature and of classical learning exhibited in the post-1812 correspondence between those two old Argonauts of the founding, John Adams and Thomas Jefferson, who

---

after Witherspoon." Scott also notes that, out of 469 Princeton graduates during President Witherspoon's tenure of twenty-five years (1768–94), "six were members of the Continental Congress, twenty-one were United States Senators, thirty-nine were Representatives, three were Justices of the Supreme Court, and one became President" (*Lectures on Moral Philosophy,* 15–16). James Q. Wilson's *The Moral Sense* was published in New York in 1993. Cf. the discussion of "moral sense" in chap. 1, §5, herein. Cf. Scott P. Segrest, "Common Sense Philosophy and Politics in America: John Witherspoon, James McCosh, and William James" (Ph.D. diss., Louisiana State University, December 2005), 269.

39. Richard, *The Founders and the Classics,* 147, 184–85.
40. Ibid., 69.

still were debating the meaning of the Greek texts of Hesiod and of Theognis of Megara on *aristoi,* or natural aristocracy, as well as on moral sense, conscience, intuition, reason—in short, on learning ancient and modern at large throughout their twilight years in letters back and forth between Monticello and Quincy—until the end at last came for them both on July 4, 1826, the fiftieth anniversary of independence.[41]

The special case of Benjamin Rush may again be mentioned. Typically for the time, he was educated between his eighth and fourteenth years at boarding school by the Reverend Samuel Finley, a New Side (Whitefield) Scottish Presbyterian minister, who later became president of the College of New Jersey. Young Rush studied Latin and Greek, arts and sciences, English, public address, and the Bible, and memorized the Shorter Catechism of the Church of Scotland, which was repeated every Sunday evening, when the boys also were examined over the content of the sermon heard earlier in the day. He entered Princeton at age fifteen in 1759 as a junior, being so well prepared that he graduated in the following year with the bachelor of arts degree. He received his M.D. from Edinburgh in 1768.[42]

After the Revolution, however, he argued against the overemphasis in the grammar schools on Greek and Latin as immoral, pagan, monkish, and for many other reasons "all wrong"—especially in a Christian republic.[43] Decades later in 1810 and old age, he and John Adams renewed the controversy in a bantering, mock-serious way. Thus Adams writes: "I do most cordially hate you for writing against Latin, Greek, and Hebrew. I never will forgive you until you repent, retract, and reform. No never! It is impossible."

To this Rush replies:

> Hate on, and call upon all the pedagogues in Massachusetts to assist you with their hatred of me, and I will after all continue to say that it is folly and madness to spend four or five years in teaching boys the Latin and Greek languages. I admit a knowledge of the Hebrew to be useful to divines, also as much of the Greek as will enable them to read the Greek testament, but the

41. This correspondence is collected as the second volume of Cappon, ed., *The Adams-Jefferson Letters,* 283–614.

42. Corner, ed., *The Autobiography of Benjamin Rush,* 30–32, cf. 345 f.

43. Ibid., 345–46.

Latin is useless and even hurtful to young men in the manner in which it is now taught.... Were every Greek and Latin book (the New Testament excepted) consumed in a bonfire, the world would be the better for it.... "Delenda, delenda est lingua Romana" should be the voice of reason and liberty and humanity in every part of the world.

Adams:

Hobbes calumniated the classics because they filled young men's heads with ideas of liberty and excited them to rebellion against Leviathan [chap. 21]. Suppose we should agree to study the oriental languages, especially the Arabic, instead of Greek and Latin. This would...gratify Hobbes much better.... Where can you find in any Greek or Roman writer...sentiment[s] so sublime and edifying for George and Napoleon.... I would put you into your own tranquilizer until I cured you of your fanaticism against Greek and Latin.... My friend, you will labor in vain. As the love of science and taste for the fine arts increases in the world, the admiration of Greek and Roman science and literature will increase. Both are increasing very fast. Your labors will be as useless as those of Tom Paine against the Bible, which are already fallen dead and almost forgotten.[44]

A further illustration of the centrality of classics to the American mind can be seen in James Kent (1763–1847), chancellor of the State of New York and author of the celebrated work of jurisprudence entitled *Kent's Commentaries on American Law,* which appeared in four volumes (1824–1830). Based on his lectures as professor of law at Columbia, the *Commentaries* went through a number of editions. In his review of it, George Bancroft stated: "Now we know what American law is."[45]

Young James began his education at age five and the study of Latin at age nine, then with the Reverend Ebenezer Baldwin, the distinguished preacher at Danbury. By age thirteen Kent had read Eutropius,

44. John A. Schutz and Douglass Adair, eds., *The Spur of Fame: Dialogues of John Adams and Benjamin Rush, 1805–1813* (San Marino, CA: Huntington Library, 1980), 168–71, quoted from correspondence dated in September and October 1810.

45. Quoted from Bancroft's 1827 review in Charles Warren, *A History of the American Bar* (Boston: Little, Brown, 1911), 543.

Justin, Cornelius Nepos, and Virgil. He entered the New Haven College (Yale) of Ezra Stiles at fourteen, received the bachelor of arts degree in 1781 and the master's in 1784. The classics provided the backbone of instruction with Virgil, Cicero, and Horace in Latin and the New Testament, Homer, and Xenophon in Greek.[46]

This, however, was only the beginning. Kent continued his reading of the classics throughout his life of eighty-four years. As he later wrote in his *Diary:*

> At the June circuit, in 1786, I saw Edward Livingston (afterwards the codifier for Louisiana), and he had a pocket Horace and read some passages to me, and pointed out their beauties, assuming that I well understood Horace. I said nothing, but was stung with shame and mortification. I purchased immediately Horace and Virgil, a dictionary and grammar, and a Greek lexicon and grammar, and the Testament, and formed my resolution, promptly and decidedly, to recover the lost languages. I studied in my little cottage mornings, and devoted an hour to Greek and another to Latin daily. I soon increased it to two for each tongue in the twenty-four hours. My acquaintance with the languages increased rapidly.
>
> After I had read Horace and Virgil, I ventured upon Livy for the first time in my life; and, after I had construed the Greek Testament, I took up the Iliad, and I can hardly describe at this day [1839] the enthusiasm with which I perseveringly read and studied, in the originals, Livy and the Iliad. It gave me inspiration. I purchased a French dictionary and grammar, and began French, and gave an hour to that language daily. I appropriated the business part of the day to law, and read Coke on Littleton and made copious notes. I devoted evenings to English literature in company with my wife.[47]

Kent was appointed to the New York Supreme Court at age thirty-five by Governor John Jay and became chief justice six years later (1804), but his reading continued. As he wrote to his brother, Moss Kent, in 1799: "It is only by becoming thoroughly master of Greek and Roman learning, —

46. Kent, *Memoirs of Chancellor Kent,* 1–14.
47. Ibid., 24–25.

> 'Of all the ancient sages thought,
> The ancient bards sublimely taught,' —

and also a profound acquaintance with English classics and with the sages of the law, that a man can attain to distinction and dignity and impart to the mind all its energies and all its grandeur."[48] A Washington-Hamilton Federalist who disliked John Adams's supposed tendency to elevate monarchy and detested Thomas Jefferson and James Madison for their perceived Jacobinism, Kent wrote this estimate of the first president: "The patriotism, firmness, wisdom, prudence, enterprise, and matchless simplicity, integrity, and industry of General Washington... are beyond precedent. The United States is indebted for its independence to him, more than to all Congress united."[49]

In sum, with respect to the founders and the classics, "so skillfully were the classical, Whig and American traditions interwoven that the founders considered them one and the same: 'the tradition of Liberty.'" For his part John Adams wrote: "Whig principles were the principles of Aristotle and Plato, of Livy and Cicero, and Sidney, Harrington, and Locke."[50]

§3. Legal Education

In the famous final letter by Jefferson to Madison (February 17, 1826) that concludes with "Take care of me when dead, and be assured that I shall leave with you my last affections," the primary concern is with legal education and selection of a law professor for the University of Virginia. Eager to allow diversity of religious beliefs, Jefferson and Madison saw no anomaly in fostering orthodoxy of political belief, if that could be managed. Their university was to be an engine designed for the very purpose. Thus Jefferson wrote:

> In the selection of our Law Professor, we must be rigorously attentive to his political principles. You will recollect that before the Revolution, *Coke Littleton* was the universal elementary book of

---

48. Ibid., 143–44.
49. Ibid., 249.
50. Richard, *The Founders and the Classics*, 83.

law students, and a sounder Whig never wrote, nor of profounder learning in the orthodox doctrines of the British constitution, or in what were called English liberties. You remember also that our lawyers were then all Whigs. But when his black-letter text, and uncouth but cunning learning got out of fashion, and the honeyed Mansfieldism of Blackstone became the students' hornbook, from that moment, that profession (the nursery of our Congress) began to slide into Toryism, and nearly all of the young brood of lawyers now are of that hue. They suppose themselves, indeed, to be Whigs, because they no longer know what Whigism or republicanism means. It is in our seminary that this vestal flame is to be kept alive; it is thence it is to spread anew over our own and the sister States. If we are true and vigilant in our trust, within a dozen or twenty years a majority of our own legislature will be from one school, and many disciples will have carried its doctrines home with them to their several States, and will have leavened thus the whole mass.

Jefferson then movingly alludes to the philosophy of government he and Madison have devoted their lives to and which he hopes to see nurtured by the university:

The friendship which has subsisted between us, now half a century, and the harmony of our political principles and pursuits, have been sources of constant happiness to me through that long period.... It has ... been a great solace to me, to believe that you are engaged in vindicating to posterity the course we have pursued for preserving to them, in all their purity, the blessings of self-government, which we had assisted too in acquiring for them. If ever the earth has beheld a system of administration conducted with a single and steadfast eye to the general interest and happiness of those committed to it, one which protected by truth, can never know reproach, it is that to which our lives have been devoted. To myself you have been a pillar of support through life.[51]

The great constitutional debate that preceded the Revolution continued in transformed terms as the marriage of liberty and law that

51. Thomas Jefferson to James Madison, Feb. 17, 1826, in *The Life and Selected Writings of Thomas Jefferson*, ed. Adrienne Koch and William Peden (New York: Modern Library, 1935), 726–28.

was consummated by the ratification of the Constitution and Bill of Rights in later decades. The founding was conducted in significant part by lawyers. As the aged Jefferson implied, if Lord Coke had saved English liberties and constitutionalism for the world once in the seventeenth century, it is hardly too much to say that he did it twice with the success of the American cause after independence in the eighteenth century. Coke's four volumes of *Institutes* and eleven volumes of *Reports* were the cornerstone and much of the edifice of legal education in eighteenth-century America. The publication of Sir William Blackstone's *Commentaries on the Laws of England* (in four volumes, 1765–1769) and eager reception in America were not altogether unmixed blessings, as at least Jefferson thought.

There were few books of law available to the colonial student.[52] Only thirty-three law books were printed in America prior to 1776, and eight of those were different editions of the same work. A number of these, however, bore on jury trial, individual liberties, and constitutional questions back to Magna Carta. But there was no American reprint of Coke prior to 1776 or of any standard English law writer except Blackstone; nor were any English law reports reprinted. Editions of colonial laws were scarce or unobtainable. What existed were to be found mostly in the libraries of richer lawyers. Many of these were Tories, and they took their books with them when they fled the country at the outbreak of war. There were no college law lectures before 1780 and no law schools before 1784.

The situation faced by James Kent when he was appointed to the New York Supreme Court as its youngest member in 1798 may be taken as typical for the time of circuit-riding justice in America. "I never dreamed of volumes of reports and written opinions. Such things were not then thought of. . . . When I came to the Bench there were no reports or State precedents. The opinions from the Bench were delivered *ore tenus* [by word of mouth]. We had no law of our own, and nobody knew what it was. I first introduced a thorough examination of cases and written opinions. . . . This was the commencement of a new plan, and then was laid the first stone in the subsequently erected temple of our jurisprudence."[53]

---

52. I follow here Warren, *A History of the American Bar,* esp. chap. 8.
53. Kent, *Memoirs of Chancellor Kent,* 116–17.

Law was learned either through private study (Patrick Henry followed this route, being admitted to the bar after six weeks in solitude with *Coke on Littleton* in 1760), while clerking or serving as a copyist for some court and reading whatever books one could borrow (principally *Coke on Littleton,* the first volume of Coke's *Institutes*), or apprenticeship in a law office, for which the student paid a fee that ranged from $100 to $500. Bushrod Washington was so apprenticed to James Wilson in 1782, and uncle George Washington signed the note for his nephew in the amount of 100 guineas as fee.

When John Adams began the study of law in the offices of Jeremiah Gridley in Boston he was told: "A lawyer in this country must study common law and civil law and natural law and admiralty law and must do the duty of a counsellor, a lawyer, an attorney, a solicitor and even of a scrivener; so that the difficulties of the profession are much greater here than in England."[54] John Adams read Coke, Bracton, Britton, Fleta, Glanville, Fortescue, Justinian's *Institutes,* St. Germain's *Doctor and Student,* and a number of other titles after two years, but, he wrote, "Wood's *Institutes of Common Law* I never read but once, and my Lord Coke's *Commentary on Littleton* I never read but once. These two authors I must get and read over and over again. And I will get them and *break through,* as Mr. Gridley expresses it, all obstructions. Besides, I am but a novice in natural law. There are multitudes of excellent authors on natural law that I have never read; and indeed I never read any part of the best authors *Puffendorf* and *Grotius.*"[55] Young Adams promised himself to do better during the next two years.

When James Kent undertook the study of law with Attorney General Egbert Benson in 1781 in Poughkeepsie he was, by his own account,

> the most modest, steady, industrious student that such a place ever saw. I read, the following winter, Grotius and Puffendorf, in huge folios, and made copious extracts.... I was free from all dissipations; I had never danced, played cards, or sported with a gun, or drunk anything but water. In 1782 I read Smollett's History of England, and procured at a farmer's house where I boarded, Rapin's History [of England], and read it through; and I found

54. Warren, *History of the American Bar,* 83.
55. Quoted from ibid., 172.

during the course of the last summer, among my papers, my MS.
abridgment of Rapin's dissertation on the laws and customs of
the Anglo-Saxons. I abridged Hale's "History of the Common
Laws," and the old Books of Practice, and read parts of Blackstone again and again. The same year I procured Hume's History,
and his profound reflections and admirable eloquence struck most
deeply on my youthful mind. I extracted the most admired parts,
and made several volumes of MSS.[56]

Blackstone was no sooner published than he was reprinted (and
sold at $2 per volume) in Philadelphia in 1771–1772. Edmund Burke
remarked on the preoccupation of Americans with law and constitutional questions in his great *Conciliation* speech in the House of Commons on March 22, 1775:

> In no country, perhaps, in the world is the law so general a study.
> The profession itself is numerous and powerful, and in most
> provinces it takes the lead. The greater number of the deputies
> sent to the Congress were lawyers. But all who read, and most do
> read, endeavor to obtain some smattering in that science. I have
> been told by an eminent bookseller, that in no branch of his busi-
> ness, after tracts of popular devotion, were so many books as those
> of the law exported to the plantations. The colonists have now
> fallen into the way of printing them for their own use. I hear that
> they have sold nearly as many of Blackstone's *Commentaries* in
> America as in England. General Gage . . . states that all the people
> in his government are lawyers, or smatterers in law—and that in
> Boston they have been enabled, by successful chicane, wholly to
> evade many parts of one of your capital penal constitutions. . . .
> This study renders men acute, inquisitive, dexterous, prompt in
> attack, ready in defence, full of resources. In other countries, the
> people, more simple, and of a less mercurial cast, judge of an ill
> principle in government only by an actual grievance; here they
> anticipate the evil, and judge of the pressure of the grievance by
> the badness of the principle. They augur misgovernment at a dis-
> tance, and snuff the approach of tyranny in every tainted breeze.[57]

56. Kent, *Memoirs of Chancellor Kent,* 19.
57. Edmund Burke, *Selected Writings and Speeches,* ed. Peter J. Stanlis (Chicago:
Regnery Gateway Editions, 1963), 161.

Charles Warren concludes that the very meagerness of Americans' legal education in the period of the founding was in fact its strength. He finds truth in the reply of a great lawyer who, when asked how the lawyers who framed the United States Constitution had such a mastery of legal principles, replied—"Why they had so few books." Daniel Webster remarked that many other students read much more than he did, but that "so much as I read, I made my own." And Chancellor James Kent offers a similar explanation out of the fact that, studying during the Revolution, he had only one book—"Blackstone's *Commentaries,* but that one book he mastered." Warren concludes that this "sums up very concisely the cause of the greatness of many an early American jurist."[58]

§4. Conclusion

The centrality of education—broadly conceived as in antiquity as character formation—to the success of free government was a conviction of the founders, and some of the key sources have been mentioned. It is not much knowing but deep knowing harmonized by devotion to truth and justice that makes all the difference. We denizens of the information overload era are very far from understanding this critical point. Burke understood it and even conceded John Adams's hyperbolic claim of a decade earlier:

> A native of America [stated Adams] who cannot read and write is as rare an appearance as a Jacobite or a Roman Catholic, that is, as rare as a comet or an earthquake. It has been observed that we are all of us lawyers, divines, politicians, and philosophers.... [A]ll candid foreigners who have passed through this country, and conversed freely with all sorts of people here, will allow, that they have never seen so much knowledge and civility among the common people in any part of the world.... Be it remembered... that liberty must at all hazards be supported. We have a right to it, derived from our Maker. But if we had not, our fathers have earned and bought it for us, at the expense of their ease, their estates, their pleasure, and their blood. And liberty cannot be preserved without a general knowledge among the people, who

58. Warren, *History of the American Bar,* 187.

have a right, from the frame of their nature, to knowledge, as their great Creator, who does nothing in vain, has given them understanding, and a desire to know.[59]

Alexis de Tocqueville later spoke of "habits of the heart." And it is heart knowledge as well as head knowledge that Adams speaks of, what he and Jefferson termed "the principles of reason and pure Americanism."[60] The spirit of the founding displays significant kinship with the ancient and medieval principle that it is part of the purpose of political order to conduce to *habitual virtue,* to lay foundations for a life lived according to justice and truth, i.e., the inculcation of rudimentary righteousness through the imposed legal and institutional order of society. Only on such a foundation of habit can highest public and personal good be pursued and preserved—individual and social happiness as the prize of liberty. The political order is conceived as harmonizing with the "laws of nature and nature's God" in America as it comes from the hands of the founders, if we rightly remember it today.

Once again Tocqueville's keen eye saw something of this, and he expressed it in his encomium of the American jury system as "bound to have a great influence on national character." This is because juries

> instill some of the habits of the judicial mind into every citizen, and just those habits are the very best way of preparing people to be free. It spreads respect for the courts' decisions and for the idea of right. . . . Juries teach men equity in practice . . . teach each individual not to shirk responsibility for his own acts, and without that manly characteristic no political virtue is possible . . . invest each citizen with a sort of magisterial office. . . . Juries are wonderfully effective in shaping a nation's judgment and increasing its natural lights. . . . [The jury] should be regarded as a free school which is always open. . . . I think the main reason for the practical intelligence and the political good sense of the Americans is their long experience with juries in civil cases. . . . The jury is both the most effective way of establishing the people's rule and the most efficient way of teaching them how to rule.[61]

59. Charles Francis Adams, ed., *The Works of John Adams, Second President of the United States . . .* , 10 vols. (Boston: Little, Brown, 1850–56), 3:456.
60. Quoted from Sandoz, *GOL,* 35–36.
61. Tocqueville, *Democracy in America,* ed. Mayer, 274–76.

Such views seem to complement those of the founders precisely. Jefferson thought a Bill of Rights important, among other reasons, because it stated in the authoritative text of the fundamental law principles that would then become guides especially to judicial practice in support of liberty and justice in society. Such a text would, in effect, be a veritable *script* for acting and living well as free men in society at large. Herein lies the harmonizing of the educational and political vision of the founders—convinced as they are that America is not a fortuitous historical accident, but that it exemplifies through its authoritative documents and founding acts principles of timeless prudential truth. There is no warfare here between ancients and moderns, but an attempt to adapt and redefine abiding truth intrinsic to both in service of a newly articulated just regime. Hence the weight of Jefferson's words in his last year about the lack of novelty in the Declaration of Independence. "[I]t was intended," he wrote, "to be an expression of the American mind.... All of its authority rests then on the harmonizing sentiments of the day, whether expressed in conversation, in letters, printed essays, or in the elementary books of public right, as Aristotle, Cicero, Locke, Sidney, etc., & c."[62]

The Declaration and Constitution were conceived to be the groundwork of justice and happiness for the American community undertaking its historical pilgrimage. A basic *faith* in American institutions and the need for its inculcation through civic education is a consensus of the leading personalities of the period. Thus James Kent, inveighing against his imagined disparagement of republicanism and adulation of monarchy by John Adams, writes:

> I wish to make a firm stand against such pernicious tenets. They are as directly in the face of our institutions and manners as they are repugnant to our feelings and happiness. Besides, it is against moral fitness, no less than political duty, to be constantly instilling distrust and diffidence as to the Constitution of our country. An unshaken confidence, a reverential attachment to our established system, ought rather to be the lesson of the schools.[63]

62. Jefferson to Henry Lee, May 8, 1825, in *Life and Selected Writings of Thomas Jefferson*, ed. Koch and Peden, 719.
63. Kent, *Memoirs of Chancellor Kent*, 89.

His partisan spirit aside, the thrust of these convictions touches the central consideration and perennial necessity of civic education. In Kent's introductory lecture as professor at Columbia he stated the crux of the matter for aspiring law students, but not only for them:

> The importance of a knowledge of our Constitutional principles as a part of the education of an American lawyer arises from the uncommon efficacy of our courts of justice in being authorized to bring the validity of a law to the test of the Constitution.... I consider them, the course of justice, as the proper and intended guardians of our limited Constitution against the factions and encroachments of the legislative body.... A lawyer in a free country... should be a person of irreproachable virtue and goodness. He should be well read in the whole circle of the arts and sciences. He should be fit for the administration of public affairs and to govern the Commonwealth by his councils, establish it by his laws and correct it by his example.
>
> The people of this country are under singular obligations from the nature of their government to place the study of the law at least on a level with the pursuits of classical learning. The art of maintaining social order and promoting social prosperity is not with us a mystery for only those who may be distinguished by the adventurous advantages of birth and fortune.... A wide field is open to all—all may be summoned into public employment.... Extensive legal and political knowledge is requisite to render men competent to administer the government. A general initiation into the elementary learning of our law has a tendency to guard against mischief and at the same time to promote a keen sense of right and warm love of Freedom.[64]

A similar confidence in the principles and institutions of America is reflected in James Madison's attitude even at the end of his life, when the slavery question was becoming a nearly overwhelming concern. "The finest of Madison's characteristics... was his inexhaustible faith—faith that a well-founded commonwealth would be made immortal by the spirit of justice its principles instilled in the people."[65]

64. James Kent as quoted in Warren, *A History of the American Bar*, 352–53n.
65. Irving Brant, *James Madison: Commander-in-Chief, 1812–1836* (Indianapolis: Bobbs-Merrill, 1961), 504. This is given as the account by Harriet Martineau,

This is to suggest that the principles of our authoritative documents preeminently comprise—and were intended to comprise—a kind of syllabus for education in free government in America and, because of their universality and vision (with appropriate adaptations) for free government wherever it might have any chance of flourishing.

---

who visited the Madisons at Montpellier in 1834. Cf. Holmes, *The Religion of the Founding Fathers*, chap. 9; also Mark A. Noll, *America's God: From Jonathan Edwards to Abraham Lincoln* (New York: Oxford University Press, 2002), chap. 10.

4

Americanism

THE QUESTION OF COMMUNITY IN POLITICS

I write here in a synoptic way, summarizing themes addressed more fully in the previous three chapters for the purpose of concisely clarifying the meaning of *Americanism*. Let me open with the words on the subject from a representative expert, Theodore Roosevelt, who said the following just over a century ago:

> There is one quality which we must bring to the solution of every problem, — that is, an intense and fervid Americanism. We shall never be successful over the dangers that confront us; we shall never achieve true greatness, nor reach the lofty ideal which the founders and preservers of our mighty Federal Republic have set before us, unless we are Americans in heart and soul, in spirit and purpose, keenly alive to the responsibility implied in the very name of American, and proud beyond measure of the glorious privilege of bearing it. (1894)[1]

I shall suggest that it is, indeed, *Americanism* that best symbolizes who we are and shall understand that term as designating the "common sense" of the country's founding generation — its *homonoia* (like-mindedness) in Aristotle's usage, or *senso commune* in Vico's terminology. This is the way Thomas Jefferson and John Adams seem to have understood the term when they coined it at the end of the eighteenth

---

1. First published in *The Forum* (April 1894) and reprinted in *The Works of Theodore Roosevelt* (National Edition), 20 vols. (New York: Charles Scribner's Sons, 1926), 13:15. Citation kindly provided by Professor Gregory Russell.

century.[2] This understanding therefore appeals both to the old and new science of politics as denoting a complex matter of fundamental importance. Once the meaning has been clarified a bit, I shall try, by implication at least, to indicate how to meet some of the challenges we face in preserving and defending the convictions and the way of life historically built on Americanism. In this as in so much else Plato showed the way in the *Laws* when he characterized the process of preserving a just regime as *mache athanatos* (an undying struggle), a process our American forebears translated by the defiant phrase: *eternal vigilance is the price of liberty!* The universalism of Americanism was an element from the beginning and constitutes part of American exceptionalism. As one scholar explains matters:

> The self-interpretation of American society was correctly covered by the expression *Americanism*. It functions as the instrument of the self-understanding of a national universe; it also, however, takes the stage with a universal claim and constructs a cosmos that encompasses God, the world, man, society, and history in the American [mode]. The word *Americanism* originally referred to transatlantic neologisms but was used as early as the era of the Founding Fathers as a symbol for an American interpretation of order. . . . In this context Americanism means . . . awareness of a specific American mode of existence.[3]

The heart of the matter, and its most delicate aspect, is to connect Americanism with the biblical faith of Americans as the chief source of its strength and enduring resilience—and of its frequent arousal of anti-American sentiments from ideologues of every stripe, those self-anointed "elites" at home and abroad who readily enlighten and denigrate us at every waking moment on every conceivable subject. We remember that Burke identified the basis of the American consensus in the dissenting branch of Protestantism. Publius identified Providence's gift of "one united people" "speaking the same language, professing

2. For the usage of the term *Americanism* by Jefferson (in 1797) and Adams (in 1805) and its general meaning at the time of the founding, see the discussion in Sandoz, *GOL*, 35–40, esp. 38n30.

3. Jürgen Gebhardt, *Americanism: Revolutionary Order and Societal Self-Interpretation in the American Republic*, trans. Ruth Hein (Baton Rouge: Louisiana State University Press, 1993), 229–30.

the same religion, attached to the same principles of government" (*Federalist* No. 2). Tocqueville stressed one must never forget that religion gave birth to America and that American Christianity has kept a strong hold over the minds of the people, not merely as a philosophy examined and accepted, but as "an established and irresistible fact which no one seeks to attack or defend."[4] Not to be thought merely old-hat ideas, Samuel Huntington in 2004 challenged Americans to "recommit themselves to the Anglo-Protestant culture, traditions, and values that... have been the source of their liberty, unity, power, prosperity, and moral leadership as a force for good in the world." He forecast that, unlike the twentieth century, which was defined by contending ideologies, the twenty-first will be marked by the "revenge of God," who was prematurely certified dead, in fact murdered, by such nineteenth-century luminaries as Hegel and Nietzsche—i.e., by the resurgence of religions, with *culture* and *ethnicity* replacing *ideology* as the central terms of reference.[5] Anglo-America was a Bible-based culture for three hundred years, as Trevelyan observed, finding this stupendous religious movement unlike anything in the annals since Saint Augustine.

What are the consequences for Americanism? A great many, of which I mention only two here: first, a theory of human being as created *imago dei*, each person imperfect and sinful, yet graced with the defining unique capacity of communion with his Creator as this is experientially apperceived in the New Birth: an inward experience and assurance of election, a process of salvation that runs from conversion and justification, toward sanctification in imitation of Christ—a spiritual movement of maturation that runs from "ruin to recovery" of the divine image, as we have seen it powerfully argued in the soteriology of Isaac Watts and John Wesley during the eighteenth-century revival we call the Great Awakening. Second, there is a pervasive understanding of the course of human events as providentially guided, even as it is effected by human agents, i.e., by individuals exercising dominion through reason and volition over the creation as citizens no less than as pilgrims living in collaborative faith-grace partnership in immediacy to God. In both

4. Alexis de Tocqueville, *Democracy in America*, ed. J. P. Mayer, trans. George Lawrence, 2 vols. in 1 (Garden City, NY: Doubleday Anchor Books, 1969), 2:432.
5. Samuel P. Huntington, *Who Are We? The Challenges to America's National Identity* (New York: Simon & Schuster, 2004), xvii, 288.

respects the In-Between reality of time and history is consciously re-affirmed, vitally experienced as tensionally structured by the competing pulls of worldly immanent and transcendent divine reality.

So understood, Lincoln's "almost chosen people"[6] more often than not implies humility rather than hubris, as it has played out in American public affairs. Jingoism and imperialism are excesses, deformations— even tinging policy debates—of this "choseness," rather than optimal expressions of it. The sentiment of feeling *chosen*[7] is an expression of trembling assurance, but also one of a constant supplication for divine favor akin to that symbolized in the parable of the Prodigal Son who rejects, strays, and returns seeking mercy in a dynamic of faith experienced in rebellious apostasy, repentance, forgiveness, and renewed communion familiar in the prophetic writings of the Old Testament as well as in the Gospels (cf. Luke 15 with its echo of Psalm 51). The keen awareness of this dynamic in the consciousness of the American community at the time of the founding is reflected in many sources, but perhaps nowhere more poignantly than in the Continental Congress proclamations of national days of prayer, humiliation, repentance, and thanksgiving at various points during the Revolution—and intermittently proclaimed thereafter in our history as well. Such a day was proclaimed, it may be recalled, as the very first act of President George W. Bush's presidency in January 2001.[8]

6. Cf. the discussion in Walter Nicgorski and Ronald Weber, eds., *An Almost Chosen People: The Moral Aspirations of Americans* (Notre Dame: University of Notre Dame Press, 1976).

7. "Elect through the foreknowledge of God the Father, through sanctification of the Spirit, unto obedience and sprinkling of the blood of Jesus Christ" (1 Pet. 1:2). See the discussion in Sydney E. Ahlstrom, "The Religious Dimensions of American Aspirations," in *An Almost Chosen People,* ed. Nicgorski and Weber, 39–49, at 47.

8. The official text from the White House Web site reads as follows:

National Day of Prayer and Thanksgiving, 2001
By the President of the United States of America

A Proclamation

Nearly 200 years ago, on March 4, 1801, our young Nation celebrated an important milestone in its history, the first transfer of power between political parties, as Thomas Jefferson took the oath of office as President. On this bicentennial of that event, we pause to remember and give thanks to Almighty God for our unbroken heritage of democracy, the peaceful transition of power, and the perseverance of our Government through the challenges of war and peace, want and prosperity, discord and harmony.

>12

The Declaration of Independence[9] is a primary text for any understanding of Americanism and a concise, creedal statement of its meaning. But to be rightly understood it must be placed in the biblical context just limned. The evocation of transcendent divine Being in the Creator-creaturely relationship and the sense of providential governance of human affairs beyond any sectarian divisions are authoritatively communicated therein, as is also an anthropology hinting of man as *imago dei* and as, thereby, indelibly stamped with Liberty, expressed in the rhetorical mode of inalienable rights reflective of the Creator's salient attributes. The "Lockean" liberal political theory therein advanced thus ontologically foots on this anthropology as demanding consent for legitimacy of laws and of government itself, whose powers are thus inherently limited and whose cardinal purpose is *salus populi:* to serve its citizenry and not they it. The Declaration expressed the Whig consensus of Americans at the time, Jefferson later said.

President Jefferson also wrote, "The God who gave us life gave us liberty at the same time" and asked, "Can the liberties of a nation be secure when we have removed a conviction that these liberties are of God?" Indeed, it is appropriate to mark this occasion by remembering the words of President Jefferson and the examples of Americans of the past and today who in times of both joy and need turn to Almighty God in prayer. Times of plenty, like times of crisis, are tests of American character. Today, I seek God's guidance and His blessings on our land and all our people. Knowing that I cannot succeed in this task without the favor of God and the prayers of the people, I ask all Americans to join with me in prayer and thanksgiving.

NOW, THEREFORE, I, GEORGE W. BUSH, President of the United States of America, by the authority vested in me by the Constitution and laws of the United States, do hereby proclaim January 21, 2001, a National Day of Prayer and Thanksgiving and call upon the citizens of our Nation to gather together in homes and places of worship to pray alone and together and offer thanksgiving to God for all the blessings of this great and good land. On this day, I call upon Americans to recall all that unites us. Let us become a nation rich not only in material wealth but in ideals—rich in justice and compassion and family love and moral courage. I ask Americans to bow our heads in humility before our Heavenly Father, a God who calls us not to judge our neighbors, but to love them, to ask His guidance upon our Nation and its leaders in every level of government.

IN WITNESS WHEREOF, I have hereunto set my hand this twentieth day of January, in the year of our Lord two thousand one, and of the Independence of the United States of America the two hundred and twenty-fifth.

GEORGE W. BUSH

9. Cf. the discussion in Derek H. Davis, *Religion and the Continental Congress, 1774–1789: Contributions to Original Intent* (New York: Oxford University Press, 2000), chap. 6, "Religious Dimensions of the Declaration of Independence."

Jefferson and Adams meant all of this when they coined the term *Americanism* as early as 1797. But they also meant the *republicanism* nurtured in Western political philosophy by the most famous writings of our civilization, from the Israelite republic of seventy Elders (Numbers 11 and Deuteronomy 16, revived by James Harrington and Tom Paine), to Aristotle's "mixed" regime and rule of law, to Aquinas (whom Lord Acton thought the "first Whig"), to the Commonwealthmen of the English seventeenth century, especially John Milton and Algernon Sidney, whose language is soaked in biblical and classical understanding. From Richard Hooker by way of Locke their Americanism embraced the great principle that "laws they are not which public approbation hath not made so," an insistence upon *consent* that gave the American Revolution its motto, if it had one. The Constitution and laws of the land were intended, when time came, to inculcate republican virtues and customs into the minds and hearts of the citizenry and make them the habitual educational foundation of civic consciousness, thereby over time forming the uniquely American character. We may also mention that James Madison, as part of his own education, stayed on an extra term at the College of New Jersey to study Hebrew with John Witherspoon, so as to read the Old Testament in the original as he did the New Testament in *koine* Greek. This was the golden age of the classics in America, and the educated generation knew the Bible inside out and the Greek and Latin (especially "Tully") classics as second nature.

What emerges if we take the founding moment as paradigmatic for our purposes is a body of writing and thought in which faith in divine governance in human affairs (to remember Benjamin Franklin in the Philadelphia Convention) is buoyed by a sense of history that teeters uneasily and expectantly on the edge of possible eschatological fulfillment through the Parousia, a tenuous "enthusiasm" kept in check by the impenetrable obscurity of divine mysteries, one tempered by the rational watchful waiting that marks the human condition with uncertainty no less than expectancy, with the end to come like a thief in the night.[10] This scripturally grounded commonsense rationality Franklin's

10. Cf. Jesus' Olivet discourse (i.e., from the Mount of Olives, Matthew chaps. 24–25, etc.), esp. Matt. 24:31–46.

Poor Richard captured in the maxim "Work as if you were to live 100 years, pray as if you were to die tomorrow."[11]

The new epoch sensed to be possibly dawning was symbolized on the reverse of the Great Seal of the United States in the slogans "The year of our daring—1776" and "Novus ordo seclorum—The new Order of the Ages," with the Eye of Providence presiding over an unfinished pyramid. Not *my* will but *Thy will be done*, the prayer goes. No more than any other positive human achievement might any ecumenic kingdom ever be merely man's affair. But like every other great truth, this delicate matter too can be vulgarized and deformed by willful sophistry.

The fifth great strand of Americanism, along with the Bible, republicanism, so-called Lockean liberalism, and the classics, is common law constitutionalism. This tradition of law in practice, word, and experience mightily evoked the great Tree of Liberty, the ancient constitution, Magna Carta, the Petition of Right, Sir John Fortescue's Lancastrian constitution as revived two centuries later by Sir Edward Coke, whose crabbed *Institutes* became the reigning textbook for America's lawyers, as Jefferson attested. With it came a sturdy and intricate historical jurisprudence to augment the jurisprudence of divine and Stoic natural law that played such a key role in cogently justifying departure from the realm of England. When in old age Adams and Jefferson finally patched up their differences and wrote the great exchange of letters we have from them, Adams neatly identified the sources of *homonoia*, or unity of mind and spirit (Americanism), that carried the day for the Good Old Cause as Whig Liberty and Christianity. He fervently affirmed (in 1813) to his old comrade of battles now long past—his fellow "Argonaut," as he called Jefferson: "Now I will avow, that I then believed, and now believe, that those general Principles of Christianity, are as eternal and immutable, as the existence and attributes of God, and those Principles of Liberty are as unalterable as human Nature and our terrestrial, mundane System."[12]

11. From *Poor Richard Improved, 1757*, in *Benjamin Franklin: Writings*, ed. J. A. Leo Lemay, Library of America edition (New York: Viking Press, 1987), 1290.

12. John Adams to Thomas Jefferson, June 28, 1813, in *Adams-Jefferson Letters: The Complete Correspondence between Thomas Jefferson and Abigail and John Adams*, ed. Lester J. Cappon, 2 vols. in 1 (1959; repr., New York: Simon & Schuster/Clarion Books, 1971), 340.

Such Americanism—a highly differentiated complex of vital beliefs deeply held, forming the infrastructure of rational politics, adapting and augmenting as exigency demands—has sustained the nation into the present. Perhaps it still remains alive and well in the heartland despite all social amnesia, the educational depredations of ideologues and post-modernists, and the insidious deculturation wreaked by mendacity, neglect, and blissful ignorance. It has certainly structured resolve and from time to time been strengthened in moments of crisis and national peril, by decisions to fight for what the United States took to be right and in the national interest—most lately our just wars, both hot and cold, against the great tyrannies of the twentieth century, and the present war against terrorism. And it inspired by its potent universalism the French Revolution and both abolitionism and the civil rights revolution in this country.

Of course, especially by the steady affirmation as cardinal truth of man's tension toward the abiding divine Ground beyond nature and beyond all temporal reality, it has enraged the alienated and enlightened intellectuals who prefer their own trendy reductionist ideologies, favorite corrupting modern Gnostic variants of secularism. Such superior persons derisively sneer at the bucolic quaintness of those (including our founders, such notable patriots as Teddy Roosevelt, and most of the rest of us) who are unable to understand—as they well do—that all things are permitted, that might is right, and that the highest being for man is man himself. Throw in a dash of envy for material success, economic and political preeminence, and you have a recipe for being hated by voluble "elites" far and wide, at home and abroad—much to the bewilderment of ordinary folk and normal people.

"Anti-Americanism is at base a totalizing, if not a totalitarian, vision," one acute French observer explains, and he continues:

> The peculiar blindness of fanaticism can be recognized in the way it seizes on a certain behavior of the hated object and sweepingly condemns it, only to condemn with equal fervor the opposite behavior shortly after—or even simultaneously.... According to this vision ... Americans can do nothing but speak idiocies, make blunders, commit crimes; and they are answerable for all

the setbacks, all the injustices and all the sufferings of the rest of humanity.[13]

The fracturing of the sense of community fostered by Americanism proceeds apace at home, too. An insightful inventory of the various ingredients of anti-Americanism by a leading political scientist lays stress especially on the fashionable views of post-modernism, so dear to influential intellectual elites and widely disseminated in college classrooms, views eminently represented by the philosopher Martin Heidegger in his late phase. For Heidegger, America (for him then rivaled only by the Soviet Union in odiousness) embodies all that is despicable in modern progressive life. It is the existential enemy of Man and of civilization itself, he asserts in Nietzschean overtones. As James Caesar summarizes:

> Man needs an enemy to maintain his spirit. America is that enemy, and its threat is both external and internal. The internal threat is most insidious. America embodies all that is the worst in us, all that must be purified. America is the demonic, the thing inside us that is slowly stripping us of any spiritual quality. But though it is inside us, America does not fully possess us. We are not yet fully Americanized.[14]

This is the enemy to be fought against by "us"—Europeans or "we Germans of the Fatherland." World War Two unfortunately did not end the menace, it seems. The struggle continues in a multiplicity of ways. It is led by alienated self-loathing "homeless" *elites* unified from several ideological perspectives only by their own misery and by contemptuous disdain for the spiritual, material, and intellectual traditions of both the Enlightenment *and* of the Christian west still naively, crassly, and vigorously embraced by most normal Americans.

---

13. Jean-François Revel, *Anti-Americanism,* trans. Diarmid Cammell (San Francisco: Encounter Books, 2002), 143.

14. James W. Caesar, *Reconstructing America: The Symbol of America in Modern Thought* (New Haven: Yale University Press, 1997), 210. This instructive volume provides an excellent survey and analysis of the array of intellectual sources of animus against America that goes far beyond the hints given here.

5

Carrying Coals to Newcastle

VOEGELIN AND CHRISTIANITY

The question is about Eric Voegelin's relationship to Christianity. Was Voegelin a Christian? Is his philosophy a Christian philosophy? The personal and scholarly issues must be divided and subdivided for my few hints on these complicated subjects.

From the time I first heard him lecture, when I was a young undergraduate student in 1949, I never doubted that Voegelin was profoundly Christian, whatever the ambiguities of his formal church affiliation. It never dawned on me at the time to think otherwise, since the whole of his discourse was luminous with devotion to the truth of divine reality that plainly formed the horizon of his analytical expositions in class and of his scholarly writings as well, as I later found out. Voegelin made existential faith intellectually respectable, to put it bluntly—not something scientifically untenable and living off of obscurantism and polemical rearguard actions. That youthful judgment was valid then and, with appropriate qualification, remains so long years later.

His faith formed the bedrock of his personal *resistance* to National Socialism and strengthened his interpretation of philosophy as itself an act of resistance (from Socrates onward) against debilitating untruth. The signals are clear enough. Beginning each in a cold fury masked by matter-of-fact rhetorical understatement, in the 1933 race books Voegelin juxtaposed Max Scheler's personalistic philosophical anthropology, and then Thomas à Kempis's evocation of *imago dei* with Christ the exemplar of everyone's true humanity, to the Nazis' corrupt pseudo-scientific reductionist account. This he acidly derided as a "system of scientific superstition" that had brought the "knowledge of man to

114

grief." He ended *Political Religions* in 1938 (whose epigraph was Dante's incantation of hell: "Through me the way is to the City of Woe") with a grim, benedictory condemnation of fatuous *superbia* in words from the anonymous fourteenth-century mystic called the Frankfurter. Many years later, after returning to Europe, he assumed the mantle of charismatic authority in concluding his lecture on the Nazis and the German university with an electrifying evocation of Ezekiel's Watchman. The grounding of this early and persistent perspective in Augustinian mysticism is persuasively suggested by his previously unpublished meditations on Saint Augustine and on T. S. Eliot from the early 1930s and 1940s.[1] It vivified his early and persistent insight that the individual man is the intersection of time and eternity[2] and that human nature is a process-structure that is distinctively spiritual, as he stressed more than three decades later: "Through spirit man actualizes his potential to partake of the divine. He rises thereby to the *imago Dei* which it is his destiny to be."[3] The integrity of the individual human *person* thus conceived and affirmed, with its reflective consciousness, is the spring of resistance to evil and the responsive source of the love of truth—the very core of participatory (*metaxy* or In-Between) reality, never to be sacrificed to any collectivity of any kind whatever.[4] At the concrete level of political action, Voegelin's "identification of the Nazis as a satanic force for evil was sufficiently unambiguous even for the most dull-witted employee of the Gestapo to realize that the author [of *The Political Religions*] was not on [their] side."[5]

1. See Eric Voegelin, *CW* 2:8–10 (Max Scheler); *CW* 3:3–5 (Thomas à Kempis and Christ); *Political Religions,* in *CW* 5:71, 73; "The German University and the Order of German Society: A Reconsideration of the Nazi Era [1964]," in *CW* 12:1–35 *ad fin,* quoting Ezek. 33:7–9; "Notes on Augustine: Time and Memory," in *CW* 32: 483–501, dated ca. 1931–32 by the editors; "Notes on T. S. Eliot's *Four Quartets*," in *CW* 33:33–40, dated in the early 1940s by the editors. The Dante epigraph ("per me si va ne la citta dolente") is from the *Divine Comedy, Inferno,* Canto 3, line 1, printed in *CW* 5:20. For related discussion see below herein, chap. 8.
   2. Eric Voegelin, "Herrschaftslehre," MS chap. 1, p. 7 (ca. 1931); full citation in Sandoz, *VR,* 275n31; given below herein in chap. 8. The *Herrschaftslehre* is translated as chap. 4, "The Theory of Governance," in *CW* 32:224–372.
   3. Voegelin, "The German University," in *CW* 12:7.
   4. Eric Voegelin, "Reason: The Classic Experience," ibid., 265–91, at 290: "All 'philosophies of history' which hypostatize society or history as an absolute, eclipsing personal existence and its meaning, are excluded as false."
   5. Barry Cooper, *Eric Voegelin and the Foundations of Modern Political Science*

Voegelin was baptized and buried a Christian, the latter by process of long-deliberated choice of whose details our colleague Paul Caringella was intimately an eyewitness. Even the philosopher must face the ineluctable facts of the human condition and of his own mortality when dying and death loom as more than abstract metaphors. For his Lutheran form of interment service Voegelin asked that two passages from the New Testament be read: "Verily, verily, I say unto you, except a grain of wheat fall into the ground and die, it abides alone: but if it die, it brings forth much fruit. He that loves his life shall lose it; and he that hates his life in this world shall keep it unto life eternal" (Jn. 12:24–25); and "Love not the world, neither the things that are in the world. If any man love the world, the love of the Father is not in him. For all that is in the world, the lust of the flesh, and the lust of the eyes, and the pride of life, is not of the Father, but is of the world. And the world passes away, and the lust thereof: but he that does the will of God abides for ever" (1 Jn. 2:15–17). When Eric's wife, Lissy, asked him why he would want that second passage read, he is said to have replied, "for repentance."[6]

Does this then mean Voegelin was a Christian philosopher? While he took the fact and rich contents of *revelation* with utmost seriousness in all of his work, repeatedly dealing with it over the decades, the answer seems to be no. As is well-known he was no party man but sought to maintain the dispassionate, even fiercely independent stance of impartiality that he considered indispensable to the integrity of the scientific work to which he devoted his life.

> I have been called every conceivable name by partisans of this or that ideology. I have in my files documents labeling me a Communist, a Fascist, a National Socialist, an old Liberal, a new Liberal, a Jew, a Catholic, a Protestant, a Platonist, a neo-Augustinian, a Thomist, and of course a Hegelian—not to forget that I was supposedly strongly influenced by Huey Long.[7]

In a related vein Voegelin wrote professor (later U.S. Senator from North Carolina) John East as follows:

(Columbia: University of Missouri Press, 1999), 10. Cf. Voegelin, *The Political Religions,* in *CW* 5:19–73, at 24.

6. Personal communication from Paul Caringella by e-mail on Jan. 23, 2000.

7. Eric Voegelin, *AR,* 46.

The "pre-Reformation Christian" [label you mention] is a joke. I never have written any such thing. These *canards* arise because I frequently have to ward off people who want to "classify" me. When somebody wants me to be a Catholic or a Protestant, I tell him that I am a "pre-Reformation Christian." If he wants to nail me down as a Thomist or Augustinian, I tell him I am a "pre-Nicene Christian." And if he wants to nail me down earlier, I tell him that even Mary the Virgin was not a member of the Catholic Church. I have quite a number of such stock answers for people who pester me after a lecture; and then they get talked around as authentic information on my "position."[8]

Since there is no wrath like a dogmatist scorned, however, Voegelin was excoriated and calumniated by religious, ideological, and secularist zealots of all shades—and still is. But he accepted self-designation as a mystic-philosopher, perhaps to distinguish himself from the odd personalities sometimes inhabiting academic philosophy departments, and to identify his work as palpably like that (by his analysis) of the Hellenic philosophers of antiquity. As we read in *The World of the Polis:*

The [ancient] mystic-philosophers break with the myth because they have discovered a new source of truth in their souls. The "unseemly" gods of Homer and Hesiod must pale before the invisible harmony of the transcendental *realissimum;* and the magnificent Homeric epic that was enacted on the two planes of gods and men must sink to the level of "poetry" when the drama of the soul with its intangible, silent movements of love, hope, and faith toward the *sophon* is discovered [by Heraclitus].[9]

If the exploration of the human relationship to the transcendent divine Ground of being is the cardinal problem of philosophy, as Voegelin thought, and if he devoted his life to the task in its manifest diversity

---

8. Eric Voegelin to John P. East, July 18, 1977, in Hoover Institution Archives, Eric Voegelin Papers, microfilm reel 10.23. This letter was kindly called to my attention by Professor Timothy Hoye. Cf. William M. Thompson, "Eric Voegelin: A Pre-Nicene Christian?" *The Ecumenist* 38 (2001): 10–13; also see Ellis Sandoz, "Eric Voegelin a Conservative?" in *The Politics of Truth and Other Untimely Essays: The Crisis of Civic Consciousness* (Columbia: University of Missouri Press, 1999), chap. 9.
    9. Eric Voegelin, *OH* II, *The World of the Polis, CW* 15:311.

over time from prehistory into the present, the designation seems appropriate enough. As he explained to Alfred Schütz on one occasion:

> Philosophizing seems to me to be in essence the interpretation of experiences of transcendence.... There are degrees in the differentiation of experiences. I would take it as a principle of philosophizing that the philosopher must include in his interpretation the maximally differentiated experiences.... Now with Christianity a decisive differentiation has occurred.[10]

If in the course of his work of a lifetime he concluded that the open exploration of Man's tension toward transcendent divine being (while the universal attribute of mankind experienced-symbolized in many modes) is most optimally conducted in the light of the revelatory experiences of prophets and apostles, and the pneumatic-noetic exegesis by Greek philosophers of equivalent experiences, it is not too surprising that he should especially admire these. But more than this: In the confluence of these currents with medieval Christian mystic-philosophy, the *fides quaerens intellectum* of Anselm, Aquinas, and Eckhart, Voegelin saw a form of meditative technical philosophizing never surpassed, one that remains paradigmatic into the present. In that specific sense Voegelin may, after all, be a Christian philosopher: not by partisanship or creedal profession but by discerning and validating experientially a superiority perfecting the contemplative life, one implicit in it from distant antiquity that he sought to live by himself.[11] In this practice of meditative philosophy, he pushed well beyond conventional understanding to insist that *Reason* (*nous* in Plato and Aristotle) is itself a revelation (not merely "natural") and that the contemplative activity of rational inquiry emerges as a divine-human participation from questions that arise in the first place "because you have that divine *kinesis* in you that moves you to be interested." So-called " 'natural reason' is due to God's grace," and it lies at the very heart of philosophy itself.

> The movement in reality, which has become luminous to itself in noetic consciousness, has indeed unfolded its full meaning in the

10. Eric Voegelin to Alfred Schütz, Jan. 1, 1953, in *The Philosophy of Order: Essays on History, Consciousness, and Politics: For Eric Voegelin on His 80th Birthday, January 3, 1981*, ed. Peter J. Opitz and Gregor Sebba (Stuttgart: Klett-Cotta, 1981), 450.

11. Cf. Eric Voegelin, "Quod Deus Dicitur," in *CW* 12:376–94, and the analysis in Sandoz, *VR*, 258–63; see herein chap. 8.

Pauline vision [citing esp. Col. 2:9 and Rom. 8:22–23] and its exegesis through myth. The symbolism of the man who can achieve freedom from cosmic *Ananke,* who can enter into the freedom of God, redeemed by the loving grace of the God who is himself free of the cosmos, consistently differentiates the truth of existence that has become visible in the philosophers' experience of *athanatizein* [immortalizing], as in Aristotle, *Nicomachean Ethics* 1177b35.[12]

This settled analytical conclusion of the late Voegelin, with its far-reaching implications, gives cold comfort to radical secularists, naturalists, materialists, and sundry relativists for whom separation of "religion" from "philosophy" in experience and rational inquiry may be fervently axiomatic—if anything is!

Finally, the insistent exclusivity of putative "Christian" (doctrinal) truth Voegelin tempered with the mystic's tolerance as expressed by Jean Bodin, who wrote: "Do not allow conflicting opinions about religion to carry you away; only bear in mind this fact: genuine religion is nothing other than the sincere direction of a cleansed mind toward God."[13] And the universality of Christ Voegelin grandly understood in accord with Thomas Aquinas, who "asks 'whether Christ be the head of all men' (*ST* [*Summa theologiae*] III.8.2), and [who] answers unequivocally that he is the head of all men, indeed, and that consequently the Mystical Body of the Church consists of all men who have, and will have, existed from the beginning of the world to its end.... [Thus] the symbolism of *Incarnation* would express the experience, with a date in history, of God reaching into man and revealing Him as the Presence that is the *flow of Presence* from the beginning of the world to its end. History is Christ written large."[14] Elsewhere Voegelin writes:

12. *Conversations with Eric Voegelin,* ed. R. Eric O'Connor, Thomas More Institute Papers vol. 76 (Montreal: Thomas More Institute, 1980), 138–40; reprinted in *CW* 33:243–343. Cf. Eric Voegelin, "The Beginning and the Beyond: A Meditation on Truth," in *CW* 28:209–32. On *Nous* as revelatory, see "noetic pneumatic theophany" in Eric Voegelin, *OH* IV, *The Ecumenic Age, CW* 17:96–97, 305–308, 315–17, 324–25, 337, 375. Quoted extract from 316.

13. Jean Bodin's 1563 letter to Jean Bautru, as quoted in Sandoz, *VR,* 268, 276n37. See herein chap. 8 at n41.

14. Eric Voegelin "Immortality: Experience and Symbol," in *CW* 12:78. The symbolism of the divine experienced as "flowing presence" is fully developed in Eric Voegelin, "Eternal Being in Time," in *CW* 6:312–37, esp. 329–30. Cf. Paul Caringella,

> The Christ is the mystery of God in reality; in him are hidden all the treasures of wisdom and knowledge; for in him the divine reality, the *theotes*, is present in its whole fulness *(pan to pleroma);* and by responding to this maximal fulness through faith, all men will achieve the fulness of their own existence *(pepleromenoi).*[15]

Therefore, the real question may not be whether Voegelin was Christian, but whether Christianity is sufficiently Voegelinian to hold its place intellectually and spiritually in the unfolding reality experienced in modern human existence. Or is he, too, to be passed over and shunted aside like some of his great predecessors, beginning with Meister Eckhart?

"Voegelin: Philosopher of Divine Presence," in *Eric Voegelin's Significance for the Modern Mind,* ed. Ellis Sandoz (Baton Rouge: Louisiana State University Press, 1991), 174–205. Voegelin routinely referred to Jesus as "the Savior" and "the Messiah" in the first volume of *History of Political Ideas,* written in the early 1940s; e.g., Eric Voegelin, *History of Political Ideas,* vol. I, *Hellenism, Rome, and Early Christianity, CW* 19:108, 109, 119, 151f, 153, 162 f., 182 f. Among important late writings reflecting upon the meaning of Christ as revealed in scripture see esp. "The Gospel and Culture," in *CW* 12:172–212, with particular attention to the analysis of Col. 2:9 at 192 ff.; see also *Hitler and the Germans, CW* 31:204–209.

15. "The Beginning and the Beyond," in *CW* 28:173–232, at 183.

6

Medieval Rationalism or Mystic Philosophy?

THE STRAUSS-VOEGELIN DEBATE

The fascinating correspondence between Leo Strauss and Eric Voegelin raises more questions than it answers, if merely taken by itself.[1] There are, to be sure, a number of extremely valuable debates that arise between the two writers, especially in the letters of 1949 through 1951. Often, however, the exchange gives only straws in the wind and a sense of agreements and disagreements, but much that unites and much that separates them ultimately remains obscure. To account adequately for everything would require a review of the correspondence in the context of the entire corpus of the technical writing and teaching of both men. That large task cannot be undertaken on this occasion, although some tentative suggestions will be ventured by way of conclusion. Since this

---

1. For the letters see *Faith and Political Philosophy: The Correspondence between Leo Strauss and Eric Voegelin, 1934–1964*, trans. and ed. Peter Emberley and Barry Cooper (University Park, PA: Pennsylvania State University Press, 1993); rev. ed. omitting the interpretive essays ("Part Three: Commentaries") published under the same title and editorship by University of Missouri Press, 2004. The present chapter was included in the original edition, pp. 297–320. As Ernest L. Fortin commented: "What do we learn from the correspondence that we did not already know or could not know from other sources about Strauss's or Voegelin's thought? Not much, I suspect. Both authors have written extensively elsewhere on the subjects with which they deal here. There is nevertheless in the letters a certain bluntness or candor that would have been out of place in a piece written for publication.... Not surprisingly, neither one appears to have learned much from the other or to have budged in any way from his position" (Fortin, "Men of Letters: The Little-Known Correspondence between Leo Strauss and Eric Voegelin," *Crisis* [March 1991]: 33–36, at 36).

correspondence is an exchange between the two giants of political philosophy of our time, there should be no doubt of its importance and great intrinsic interest.

The tone of the exchange, stretching over the three decades from 1934 to 1964, is respectful and even warm to the extent of polite friendliness. It is a bit stiff, formal and civil, thawing eventually to "Mr. Strauss" and "Mr. Voegelin," never to Leo and Eric, but this does not inhibit a lively and frank discussion. Most of the efforts to define the intellectual relationship between the two men are made by Strauss, and these almost always point up differences. It is of some moment that only five of the fifty-one surviving letters published in the Peter Emberley and Barry Cooper edition were written after Voegelin published the first three volumes of *Order and History* (1956 and 1957), perhaps a significant fact. Moreover, Strauss makes little or no comment to Voegelin about what he has written on the basis of a profound study of the Bible—specifically of the Hebrew Old Testament—in *Israel and Revelation*,[2] his meticulous interpretation of the pre-Socratics that displays a philological and theoretical mastery of the some fifty-five Greek authors considered in *The World of the Polis*, nor the close textual analysis and interpretation given of the principal political writings of Plato and Aristotle as powerfully presented in the third of these volumes. Of course, there are gaps from missing letters, but this is mainly a problem for the correspondence during the years down to 1953 or so; and it seems extremely unlikely that a discussion of *Order and History* has disappeared.[3] There is the relocation (which could have played

2. There is mention by Voegelin in his letter of June 10, 1953, that he is "working on the Israelite chapter in [his] History" and "greatly regretted that we have no opportunity to speak occasionally." Strauss in his letter of June 23, 1953, responds that "the problem of history in the Old Testament" is "one of the most complex problems in intellectual history. I think perhaps the utopian plan would be to devote about ten years to the solution of this problem." He says not a word in subsequent correspondence about the long book on the subject published in 1956 as *Israel and Revelation*. Voegelin's lamentation about his command of Hebrew in the June 10 letter seems to have been partly modesty, since W. F. Albright in reviewing *Israel and Revelation* makes a point of noting that "his use of Hebrew is almost impeccable" (*Theological Studies* 22 [1961]: 275; see also the review by James B. Pritchard in *American Historical Review* 63 [1957–58]: 640–41).

3. I say this on the basis of Voegelin's careful habit of retaining carbon copies of his own letters and dutifully keeping a file of letters received. It is nearly inconceivable that an exchange with Strauss on *Order and History*, or any part of it, would have

a part in disrupting the correspondence) as the Voegelins moved from Baton Rouge to Munich in 1958. There he began a new phase of his career in Germany by establishing the Political Science Institute through his appointment to the chair in that discipline left vacant at the University of Munich since the death of Max Weber in 1928. The National Socialists were not keen on political science apparently.

But the silence is significant, no matter what allowances are made. And apart from rare occasions, such as the edition of this correspondence, when the matter is directly raised (or at the annual meetings of the Eric Voegelin Society when panels were devoted to the relationship in 1989 and 1990), the silence continues virtually into the present by latter-day Straussian scholars. Thus, a 1989 recall of critical exchanges with Strauss mentions Alexandre Kojève, C. B. Macpherson, Raymond Aron, Hans-Georg Gadamer, Karl Löwith, and Arnaldo Momigliana but passes over Voegelin—surely classified with Strauss as another "maverick" taking on the "authorities" and on much the same ground, i.e., an insistence on the indispensability of classical philosophy for a rational understanding of the human condition per se, not least of all of the contemporary world and its crisis.[4]

---

escaped this methodical practice. On the other hand, there appears to be no extant letter from Voegelin regarding Strauss's own Walgreen Lectures of 1949, *Natural Right and History* (Chicago: University of Chicago Press, 1953), after publication, despite a series of eager queries scattered through his earlier letters about when the book would appear. These materials now are organized in the Eric Voegelin Archive at Hoover Institution Library (Box 38.34; on microfilm reel 37.1), the source of forty of the fifty-one letters published in this collection. The two men continued to exchange publications, as can be seen from the very last letter (that of Sept. 7, 1964), in which Voegelin thanks Strauss for his apparently having had his publisher send him a copy of *The City and Man* (Chicago: Rand McNally, 1964).

  4. Thomas L. Pangle, ed., *The Rebirth of Classical Political Rationalism: An Introduction to the Thought of Leo Strauss; Essays and Lectures by Leo Strauss* (Chicago: University of Chicago Press, 1989), ix. Voegelin's name does not appear in the index to the volume. The only reference to Voegelin made by Strauss in print that I can think of is his comment that the former's 1949 review of the latter's study of Xenophon's *Hiero* was one of only two critiques from which "one could learn anything," the other being by Kojève. Voegelin then is identified as "one of the leading contemporary historians of political thought"—*not* as a *political philosopher,* a matter of consequence in the world of esoteric communication inhabited by such a careful writer as Strauss. Leo Strauss, "Restatement on Xenophon's *Hiero,*" in *What Is Political Philosophy? And Other Studies* (Glencoe, IL: Free Press, 1959), 96–103, on Voegelin at 96; cf. Voegelin to Strauss, January 14, 1949, letter 20; Strauss to Voegelin, April 15,

The silence may be the most important aspect for consideration. How is the silence to be interpreted? Perhaps these letters point toward an answer. A preliminary answer must be that Voegelin's publication of the initial volumes of *Order and History* finally put a period to the relationship that had been declining since his 1951 Walgreen Lectures at the University of Chicago, published as *The New Science of Politics.*[5] So, the further question to be wondered about is, exactly *why?* — to which the preliminary plausible answer must be that, from the perspectives of both men, persuasion had reached its limits, and there was little more to be said between them because of fundamental disagreement.

1949, letter 24; Strauss to Voegelin, August 8, 1950, letter 30; and Voegelin to Strauss, August 21, 1950, letter 31.

On exoteric and esoteric writing, see Leo Strauss, *Persecution and the Art of Writing* (Glencoe, IL: Free Press, 1952); see also Leo Strauss, "Exoteric Teaching," *Interpretation: A Journal of Political Philosophy* 14 (1986): 51–59, reprinted in *The Rebirth of Classical Political Rationalism,* ed. Pangle, 63–71. Receipt of *Persecution and the Art of Writing* is acknowledged by Voegelin in his letter of August 5, 1952, and the subject matter is referred to subsequently; the article from which the book grew, published in *Social Research* in 1941, was called to Voegelin's attention in Strauss's letter of February 13, 1943. There is no direct suggestion by Voegelin that Strauss himself engages in esoteric writing, but he shows interest in the subject and understands its ramifications, as hyperbolic remarks about John Locke intimate in his letter of April 15, 1953 (apparently never sent), and the letter of April 20, 1953, covering the same ground more circumspectly (see the editors' note to letter 42, dated April 15, 1953). Strauss responds by commending Voegelin for his acuity regarding types of esotericism (letter of April 29, 1953, penultimate paragraph).

An evenhanded discussion of Strauss's own employment of this technique in his writing is given in Bernard Susser, "Leo Strauss: The Ancient as Modern," *Political Studies* 36 (1988): 497–514, at 509; contrast the scathing denunciation of Strauss's "secret art of writing" (among other things) by Stephen Holmes, in "Truths for Philosophers Alone?" *Times Literary Supplement,* Dec. 1–7, 1989, 1319–20, 1322–24, ending in his declaration that Strauss "was no philosopher." Cf. the response by Thomas L. Pangle, *Times Literary Supplement,* Jan. 5–11, 1990, 11.

5. Eric Voegelin, *NSP;* Eric Voegelin, *OH,* vol. I, *Israel and Revelation* (Baton Rouge: Louisiana State University Press, 1956), vols. II and III, *The World of the Polis* and *Plato and Aristotle* (both Baton Rouge: Louisiana State University Press, 1957). For a bibliography of Voegelin's publications through 1981 see Sandoz, *VR,* 279–88; also Peter J. Optiz and Gregor Sebba, eds., *The Philosophy of Order: Essays on History, Consciousness, and Politics: For Eric Voegelin on His 80th Birthday, January 3, 1981* (Stuttgart: Klett-Cotta, 1980). "Agreement in Discord: Alfred Schütz and Eric Voegelin," the essay by Helmut R. Wagner in the latter volume (pp. 74–90), is particularly pertinent for understanding the Strauss-Voegelin relationship and the debt of both men to Husserl, as discussed in letters 6, 9, 10, and 11 in *Faith and Political Philosophy,* ed. Emberley and Cooper.

§1.

The air of mutual respect that pervades the correspondence is founded partly in common civility and Old World manners and partly in a recognition of the seriousness of each other's scholarship, with a sense that their exchanges constitute a conversation between *spoudaioi.* There is strong general agreement about the defectiveness of modern philosophy and the science of man from Machiavelli and Hobbes onward. Both see this as requiring a return to the Greeks, and Strauss remarks that radical doubt of all of the dogmas of the past three or four centuries is the beginning of wisdom. Voegelin more often than not is conciliatory, obliging, even deferential, seemingly intent on coaxing as much candor and insight as he can from his guarded correspondent. Clearly enough, sparring is going on, as each writer tests the other in various ways. There is eagerness for rapport, especially from Voegelin's side, but caution, wariness, and dubiousness, especially from Strauss's side. Now and then an issue becomes transparent for disagreement, the debate is joined, and sparks fly.

Thus, with enthusiasm Voegelin embraces Strauss's principle of understanding a thinker as he understood himself. And how is that? Voegelin, in characteristic fashion, elaborates the principle to mean that the conscientious interpreter has "to restore the experiences which have led to the creation of certain concepts and symbols; or: [since] symbols have become opaque . . . they must be made luminous again by penetrating to the experiences which they express." "We are in greater agreement than I first supposed," Voegelin concludes.[6] Still, Strauss remains silent on the key question of how and in what sense philosophy can be said to be experientially anchored.

That silence is broken in alarm and indignation, however, by an outburst provoked by Voegelin's use of the term *existential* in the *Gorgias* essay. Strauss writes:

> In his critique of Plato, Heidegger tries to find the way by rejecting philosophy and metaphysics as *such* . . . [But] insofar as I am serious and there are questions, I look for *the* "objective" truth. The sophist is a man to whom truth does not matter. . . . The passion

6. Voegelin to Strauss, March 12, 1949.

of *revelation* that moves the Platonic dialogue, this highest *mania*, cannot be understood within Kierkegaard's concept of "existence," and [the attempt to do so] must for the present be rejected as a radical illusion. . . . The question Plato *or* existentialism is today the ontological question—about "intellectuals" we (you and I) do not need to waste words, unless it were about how they finally have to be interpreted, namely within Platonic or existentialist philosophy.[7]

Clearly, Voegelin had struck a nerve. Strauss seems mollified by Voegelin's conciliatory explanation that existential*ism* (which he has no wish to defend) is not intended and that ontology is, indeed, centrally important. "I swear, I am not straying on existentialist paths; we are in agreement also on the question of ontology." However, Voegelin presses the point:

> The truth of ontology (including in particular philosophical anthropology) is not a datum, that can be recognized by anyone at any time. Ontological knowledge emerges in the process of history and biographically in the process of the individual person's life under certain conditions of education, the social context, personal inclination, a spiritual conditioning. *Episteme* is not just a function of understanding, it is also in the Aristotelian sense, a dianoetic arete. For this *non*-cognitive aspect of episteme I use the term "existential." * * * A history of political ideas in particular should investigate the process in which "truth" becomes socially effective or is hindered in such effectiveness. You see, it does not have to do with a negation or relativization of ontology, but rather with the correlation between perception in the cognitive and existential sense; this correlation is for me the theme of "history."[8]

To this Strauss responds with worries of why Voegelin puts "'truth' in quotation marks? Is truth only so-called truth, the illusion of a respective period?" The closest classical equivalent to existential, he believes, is *practical*, understood as the contradiction of *theoretical*. "If I am not

---

7. Strauss to Voegelin, December 17, 1949. The essay in question is Voegelin's "The Philosophy of Existence," *Review of Politics* 11 (1949): 477–98; it is included in revised form in *OH* III, chap. 2.

8. Voegelin to Strauss, January 2, 1950.

totally mistaken," Strauss goes on, "the root of all modern darkness from the seventeenth century on is the obscuring of the difference between theory and praxis." An intervening letter from Voegelin is lost, but it apparently allayed Strauss's worst fears. He writes:

> The question is whether there is a pure grasp of truth as essential human possibility, quite regardless of what the conditions and actualization of this possibility are, or whether there is *not* such a grasp as essential possibility. When you say "only at such and such a time did that order of the soul emerge," you leave open, if this order of the soul is the natural telos of Man or a "coincidence," that it *could* also not have emerged, does it not deprive it of the status of a telos? However that may be, it seems to me nonetheless, that we are in more fundamental agreement than I believed.[9]

Strauss's questions go unanswered in this context. At an earlier place, Strauss writes of "the science established by Plato and Aristotle: the postulate of an exact ethics and politics in Plato; Aristotle's adhering to the ideal of exactness despite the abandonment of its application to the human things; the necessarily higher ranking of physics over ethics and politics for at least Aristotle and his successors."[10] Whether the exactness of the theoretical sciences, in contrast to the practical ones, equates with the pure grasp of truth as possibility for Strauss remains unclear, and he seems to leave it "open." At a later place, he speaks of his Walgreen Lectures, published as *Natural Right and History,* as presenting the "*problem* of natural right as an unsolved problem," thus holding out the conception of philosophy itself as "an uncompletable ascent." Philosophy on the classical model is disclosed as an unsuspected third way to the conventional alternatives of choosing between "positivism-relativism-pragmatism and neo-Thomism," whereby it is shown that the consequence of one's ignorance is "that one must strive after knowledge."[11]

A not dissimilar third way is disclosed by Voegelin from his study of the same sources. The paradigm of true philosophy is provided by Plato and Aristotle; but underlying classical philosophy itself, by

9. Strauss to Voegelin, April 10, 1950.
10. Strauss to Voegelin, November 24, 1942.
11. Strauss to Voegelin, December 10, 1950.

Voegelin's reading, is *faith* in the divine cosmos as the primal experience articulated in myth and differentiated through noesis in philosophy. It may be true that classical philosophy is "ahistorical" in that it is a loving search of the heights and depths of reality to discern the process and structure of being by the spiritually sensitive man who seeks abiding truth. But the modern derailment of philosophy from Descartes to Hegel (which Voegelin considers as a unit) deforms this questing dimension of philosophizing by transforming the uncompletable ascent described as the *love of wisdom* in Plato into the possession of exact truth as the *system of science*.[12] "I would permit myself a correction to your formulation," therefore, Voegelin writes,

> that "*all* earlier philosophy" was unhistorical. Philosophy [deformed into] the system, from Descartes to Hegel, seems to me to form a unity insofar as the idea of a philosophical, closed, "system" dominates. The idea of "system" though, the possible exhaustive penetration of the mystery of the cosmos and its existence by the intellect, is itself a gnostic phenomenon, a drawing in of eternity into the time of the individual thinker. I would therefore restrict your comment on philosophy [to] the Platonic-Aristotelian sense....
>
> With regard to the "second thesis" of your letter, that philosophy is radically independent of faith, ... I do not see how you get around the historical fact of the beginning of philosophy in the attitude of faith of Xenophanes, Heraclitus, and Parmenides.[13]

§2.

We come now to the crux of the disagreement between the two writers. Strauss, in the earlier letter, had written that this second thesis was "the root of *our* disagreement" (86), and in this he was not wrong. In

---

12. The contrast between love of wisdom as the form of classical philosophy and the system of science with particular attention to Hegel as a deformation of modern philosophy commanded Voegelin's attention repeatedly throughout the rest of his life, one may note. See Voegelin, *OH* II:16–19; Eric Voegelin, "Hegel: A Study in Sorcery [1971]," in *CW* 12:213–55; cf. *CW* 12:89–91, 300; and Eric Voegelin, *OH*, vol. V, *In Search of Order,* intro. by Ellis Sandoz (Baton Rouge: Louisiana State University Press, 1989), 48–70 and *passim.*
13. Voegelin to Strauss, December 4, 1950.

response to Voegelin's asserted "historical fact" Strauss flatly denies it and adds: "whatever *noein* might mean, it is certainly not *pistis* in some sense. On this point Heidegger... is simply right."[14] This becomes the "one point where our paths separate," Strauss states, although Voegelin reads *Philosophy and Law* (1935; English translation, 1987) and finds that Strauss had in that earlier book held a view much like his own. But this, too, Strauss denies. The "classics are the Greeks and not the Bible," he argues. "The classics demonstrated that truly human life is a life dedicated to science, knowledge, and the search for it." "I believe still today," writes Strauss, "that the *theioi nomoi* is the common ground of the Bible and philosophy—humanly speaking. But I would specify that short of that, it is the problem of the multitude of *theioi nomoi,* that leads to the diametrically opposed solutions of the Bible on the one hand, of philosophy on the other."[15]

The sharp contrast between a Middle Ages based on revelation and a classical antiquity not so grounded, according to Strauss, leads him to this further statement:

> There is a double interest not to disguise this essential difference in any way. First, the interest in revelation, which is by no means merely natural knowledge. Secondly, human knowledge, *episteme.* You yourself have said of yourself that science matters very much to you. For me, it matters a great deal to understand it as such. . . . The classics demonstrated that truly human life is a life dedicated to science, knowledge, and the search for it. . . . Every synthesis is actually an option either for Jerusalem or for Athens.
>
> Well, you speak of the religious foundation of classical philosophy. I would not do so.[16]

Of course, "religious foundation" was not part of Voegelin's speech, either, but words put in his mouth by Strauss.[17] He passes over the matter, however, and his responsive analysis qualifies the sharp distinction

14. Strauss to Voegelin, December 10, 1950.
15. Strauss to Voegelin, February 25, 1951.
16. Ibid.
17. On the point, see the instructive discussion of the transformation of the "living order of Israel" into "the 'religion of the book'" in Voegelin, *OH* I:376–79, also 120, 288, 381; cf. ibid., II:218–19. On *nous* and *pistis* in Plato's *Republic,* see ibid., III:113–14.

between "human knowledge and revealed knowledge," by noticing that the latter *is* human insofar as it is the knowledge of concrete persons who experience it as stemming from a divine source and (while pointedly rejecting psychologizing explanations, i.e., Feuerbach's and Marx's), he arrives at the following important formulations.

> Revelation, then, is humanly debatable because it, like all knowledge, is human knowledge. . . . It distinguishes itself from "mere" human knowledge in that its contents are experienced as "being addressed" by God. And through this experience of "being addressed" the essential contents of revealed knowledge are given: (1) a man who understands himself in his "mere" humanness in contrast to a transcendental being; (2) a world-transcendent Being, who is experienced as the highest reality in contrast to all worldly being; (3) a being who "addresses," and therefore, is a person, namely, God; (4) a man who can be addressed by this Being, who thereby stands in a relation of openness to Him. In this sense I would venture the formulation: the fact of revelation is its content.[18]

This sense of revelation as the *experience of divine presence*[19] is shown to require the development of self-reflective consciousness whereby the man separates himself clearly from the divine, the movement from compactness toward differentiation, a "process in which man de-divinized himself and realized the humanity of his spiritual life."[20] This achievement of Greek philosophy is absorbed by Christianity in the early centuries. The erotic orientation toward divine Being of man in Plato meets with no response, however, in contrast with the *amicitia* of Thomas—a contrast familiar from the *New Science of Politics* but qualified by Voegelin in later work so as to take account of his subsequent understanding of both reason and revelation in Hellenic philosophy, as suggested below.[21]

18. Voegelin to Strauss, April 22, 1951.
19. See the analysis of this defining theme by Paul Caringella, "Voegelin: Philosopher of Divine Presence," in *Eric Voegelin's Significance for the Modern Mind,* ed. Ellis Sandoz (Baton Rouge: Louisiana State University Press, 1991), 174–206.
20. Voegelin to Strauss, April 22, 1951.
21. Cf. Voegelin, *NSP,* 76–80. For the later work, especially pertinent are the essays reprinted in *CW* 12, including "Immortality: Experience and Symbol" (52–94), "Equivalences of Experience and Symbolization in History" (115–33), "Reason: The Classic Experience" (265–91), "Wisdom and the Magic of the Extreme: A Meditation"

Strauss's response is to appeal to Christian *dogma* rather than enter into a discussion that appeals to experiential analysis, which Voegelin is steadily stressing. The former suggests that there may yet be a common ground between himself and Voegelin, if only the latter accepts dogma in the Catholic sense, "because [he writes] my distinction between revelation and human knowledge to which you object is in harmony with the Catholic teaching. But I do not believe that you accept the Catholic teaching."[22] By this is meant the clear doctrinal distinctions reflected by the dichotomies natural human knowledge and supernatural revelation, reason and faith, science and religion, in particular— and again Strauss is right. Because, just as Voegelin has here discerned the human element in revelation and the presence of revelatory experience (faith) as undergirding Greek philosophy from its pre-Socratic beginnings through its climax in Plato and Aristotle, so also is he moving in the direction that takes him, in the decades ahead, to an analysis of reason (*Nous* and *noesis*) in classical philosophy that greatly widens our understanding of it and attributes the notion of merely "natural reason" to a misunderstanding fostered by the medieval Christian philosophers.[23] The human reality of philosophy no less than of Judaic and Christian revelation is the *metaxy* or participatory reality of the In-Between of divine-human encounter, to hint at the later formulations.

(315–75), and "Quod Deus Dicitur," (376–94). Of decisive importance for the matters at hand is Eric Voegelin, "The Beginning and the Beyond: A Meditation on Truth," in *CW* 28:173–232.

22. Strauss to Voegelin, June 4, 1951.

23. See the works cited in n21, especially Voegelin, "The Beginning and the Beyond," in *CW* 28:210–11, for the present point. The relationship of *noesis* and *pistis* is analyzed in *CW* 12:273–74. That, and in what respects, Voegelin's position leaves him vulnerable on multiple grounds to being charged with the so-called "modernist" heresy condemned by Roman Catholicism is observed and discussed by Fortin, "Men of Letters," *Crisis,* 34–35. Voegelin long ago clearly understood this problem himself, as is explicit in his letter to Alfred Schütz, January 1, 1953: "All that I have said about the problem of 'essential Christianity' is ... untenable from the Catholic standpoint and would have to be classified as a variant of that Modernism which has been condemned as a heresy" (letter in *The Philosophy of Order,* ed. Opitz and Sebba, 449–57, at 57). On the meaning and extent of the heresy *modernism,* see Richard P. McBrien, *Catholicism: Study Edition* (Minneapolis: Winston Press, 1981), 55–56, 218–23, 644–55. On his concern for Christian orthodoxy, on the other hand, see Voegelin, "Response to Professor Altizer's 'A New History and a New but Ancient God?'" in *CW* 12:292–302, at 292–95; also "Quod Deus Dicitur," in *CW* 12:376–83.

How closely faith and reason verge can instructively be seen from a passage from Voegelin's Candler Lectures of 1967, entitled "The Drama of Humanity," where he was able to enumerate ten meanings of Reason in Plato and Aristotle, as follows.[24]

Reason is:

1. the consciousness of existing from a Ground, an awareness filled with content and not empty. Reason is thereby the instrument for handling world-immanent reality. Rebellion against reason since the eighteenth century creates a void in this dimension that must then be filled by substitutes.
2. the transcendence of human existence, thereby establishing the poles of consciousness: immanent-transcendent.
3. the creative Ground of existence which attracts man to itself.
4. the sensorium whereby man understands himself to exist from a Ground.
5. the articulation of this understanding through universal ideas.
6. the perseverance through lifetime of concern about one's relation to the ground, generative of existential virtue: *phronesis* (wisdom, prudence), *philia* (friendship), and *athanatizein* (to immortalize human existence).
7. the effort to order existence by the insight gained through understanding the self to be existentially linked to the Ground and attuned to it: the major intellectual operation of so translating consequences of this insight as to form daily habits in accordance with it.
8. the persuasive effort to induce conscious participation of the self, and other men's conscious participation, in transcendent reason (Plato's *peitho*). The problem of communicating and propagating the truth of being.
9. the constituent of man through his participation in (the reason of) the Ground; or, the constituent force in man *qua* human through participation in the divine *Nous* which is his specific essence.

---

24. Quoted from Ellis Sandoz, "The Philosophical Science of Politics Beyond Behavioralism," in *The Post Behavioral Era,* ed. George J. Graham and George W. Carey (New York: McKay, 1972), 301–302, taken from Voegelin's Candler Lectures of 1967, titled "The Drama of Humanity," now available in *CW* 33, chap. 10; the meanings of *reason* are given and elaborated in *CW* 33:214–16. The listing also is given and discussed in "Anxiety and Reason," *CW* 28, chap. 2, p. 88.

10. the constituent of society as the *homonoia* or "like-mindedness" of Everyman in a community formed through recognition of the reason common to all men. In Aristotle, if love within the community is not based upon regard for the divinity of reason in the other man, then the political friendship *(philia politike)* on which a well-ordered community depends cannot exist. The source of the Christian notion of "human dignity" is the common divinity in all men. Nietzsche perceived that if that is surrendered then there is no reason to love anybody, one consequence of which is the loss of the sense and force of obligation in society and, hence, of its cohesiveness.

If any of the enumerated components of reason is lost, imbalanced constructions result which eventuate in psychological and social breakdowns and disintegrations. As is suggested by this listing of the meanings of reason in Plato and Aristotle, noetic reason is philosophic or scientific reason, an activity of the consciousness articulated out of experience in a variety of interrelated symbolisms and symbolic forms.

In his Aquinas Lecture of 1975, entitled "The Beginning and the Beyond," Voegelin characterizes the relationships between philosophy and revelation in this way:

The dichotomies of Faith and Reason, Religion and Philosophy, Theology and Metaphysics can no longer be used as ultimate terms of reference when we have to deal with experiences of divine reality with their rich diversification in the ethnic cultures of antiquity, with their interpretation in the cultures of the ecumenic empires, with the transition of consciousness from the truth of the intra-cosmic gods to the truth of the divine Beyond, with the contemporary expansion of the horizon to the global ecumene. We can no longer ignore that the symbols of "Faith" express the responsive quest of man just as much as the revelatory appeal, and that the symbols of "Philosophy" express the revelatory appeal just as much as the responsive quest. We must further acknowledge that the medieval tension between Faith and Reason derives from the origins of these symbols in the two different ethnic cultures of Israel and Hellas, that in the consciousness of Israelite prophets and Hellenic philosophers the differentiating experience of the divine Beyond was respectively focused on the revelatory appeal and the human quest, and that the two types of consciousness had to face new problems when the political events of the Ecumenic Age cut them loose from their moorings in the ethnic cultures and forced their confrontation under the multicivilizational conditions of an ecumenic empire.[25]

Had Leo Strauss lived to read these words, it seems likely that his reaction might have been much as it was in his ironic letter of June 4, 1951: "Said in one sentence—I believe that philosophy in the Platonic sense is possible and necessary—and you believe that philosophy understood in this sense was made obsolete by revelation. God knows who is right."

§3.

One has the familiar sense of ships passing in the night, after this review of some of the salient passages in the correspondence. Is there more to it than that? What conclusions can be drawn, however tentatively?

The restraining sentiment to be remembered as a kind of maxim of civility for whatever we conclude about the debate under consideration may be taken from a remark Strauss made to Voegelin: "[T]he agreement in our intentions . . . , so long as we have to combat the presently reigning idiocy, is of greater significance than the differences [between us], which I also would not wish to deny."[26]

That said, some of the differences can be noted, on the assumption that the agreements have become clear enough by now. What lies behind the basic disagreement is expressed already in 1942 by Strauss and is accurate for the entire subsequent relationship with Voegelin: "The impossibility of grounding science on religious faith. . . . Now you will say. . . that the Platonic-Aristotelian concept of science was put to rest through Christianity and the discovery of history. I am not quite persuaded of that."[27]

25. Voegelin, *CW* 28:210–11. For references to "Ecumenic Age" and related matters, see Voegelin, *OH,* vol. IV, *The Ecumenic Age* (1974; available, Columbia: University of Missouri Press, 2000), esp. 114–70.

26. Strauss to Voegelin, April 17, 1949.

27. Strauss to Voegelin, November 24, 1942.

Behind these formulations stand two philosophers both victimized and appalled by the deculturation and banality of modernity who devoted their lives to the recovery of true philosophy, Strauss on the basis of the medieval Arabic and Jewish philosophy of Averroës, Alfarabi, and Maimonides, Voegelin by a far-reaching critical revision of the medieval Christian philosophy of Augustine, Anselm, Aquinas, and Eckhart. This is not to question that, from their divergent perspectives, both men took classical philosophy and the science of man and being it achieved with utmost seriousness nor that each deeply, even fervently, believed his interpretation to be both true to the texts and in accord with the "real" self-understanding Socrates, Plato, and Aristotle had of the philosopher's calling. It is entirely understandable that a "nonbeliever," as Strauss termed himself, and a mystic philosopher in the Christian tradition would not see eye to eye about ultimate things.

How, indeed, could it be otherwise? And both Strauss and Voegelin believed that they avoided religious dogma out of devotion to the quest for the truth of being, one in the name of ancient rationalism, the other in the name of the fundamental experiences and their noetic and pneumatic articulation through several modes of symbolization. Thus, to Voegelin the core problem of all philosophy was the problem of transcendence—meaning not the immanent transcendence of Husserl and of the nature-based philosophy of Strauss, but the transcendence of divine Being. His definition is given at the beginning of *Order and History* in the following words and are taken as true to philosophy as Plato perfected it:

> Philosophy is the love of being through love of divine Being as the source of its order. The Logos of being is the object proper of philosophical inquiry; and the search for truth concerning the order of being cannot be conducted without diagnosing the modes of existence in untruth. The truth of order has to be gained and regained in the perpetual struggle against the fall from it; and the movement toward truth starts from a man's awareness of his existence in untruth. The diagnostic and therapeutic functions are inseparable in philosophy as a form of existence. And ever since Plato, in the disorder of his time, discovered the connection, philosophical inquiry has been one of the means of establishing islands of order in the disorder of the age. *Order and History* is a philosophical inquiry concerning the order of human existence in

society and history. Perhaps it will have its remedial effect—in the modest measure that, in the passionate course of events, is allowed to Philosophy.[28]

As one commentator remarked after surveying the Voegelinian corpus, "Voegelin adumbrates a philosophy of spiritual ascent, of which there are famous examples, such as Plotinus, Plato, St. Bonaventura, and Meister Eckhart."[29] If the understanding of Reason is so expanded as to reassert the participatory and intuitive dimensions of classical philosophy's Nous, the understanding of faith and revelation also is reevaluated—and it emphatically is *not* creedal, doctrinal, or dogmatic faith that is at issue in Voegelin's work. In reflectively groping toward his later (1975) formulation of the matter quoted at the end of the preceding section, he finds in Strauss's *Philosophy and Law* (1930) substantial agreement with his own understanding of the fundamental experience of the divine Cosmos as the background of all experiences of order. "I have the impression that you have retreated from an understanding of the prophetic (religious) foundation of philosophizing (with which I would heartily agree) to a theory of *episteme* and that you refuse to see

28. Voegelin, *Israel and Revelation*, xiv. The understanding of philosophy given here is closely akin to that of Jonathan Edwards: "True virtue most essentially consists in benevolence to Being in general. Or to speak more accurately, it is the consent, propensity and union of heart to Being in general, that is immediately exercised in a general good will." "True virtue consists in love to Being in general." "When I speak of an intelligent being's having a heart united and benevolently disposed to Being in general, I thereby mean *intelligent* Being in general. Not inanimate things or beings." "From what has been said, 'tis evident that true virtue must chiefly consist in love to God; the Being of beings, infinitely the greatest and best of beings." Edwards quoted from *Dissertation II. The Nature of True Virtue*, in *The Works of Jonathan Edwards*, vol. 8, *The Ethical Writings*, ed. Paul Ramsey (New Haven: Yale University Press, 1989), 540, 541, 542, 550, respectively. See the discussion herein, chap. 1, §5, and nn63, 64, 78, 79, and related text.

For the express statement that *transcendence* is the "decisive problem of philosophy," see Eric Voegelin, *Anamnesis: Zur Theorie der Geschichte und Politik* (Munich: Piper Verlag, 1966), 36, 46–48; the first page refers to a line in Voegelin's letter to Alfred Schütz of September 17–20, 1943, which Voegelin invites Strauss to get from Schütz and read if he is interested, and Strauss, then, reads and reacts to; for this important exchange see *Faith and Political Philosophy*, ed. Emberley and Cooper, 18–36. Note: pagination is identical in the original and reprint editions.

29. Paul G. Kuntz, "Voegelin's Experiences of Disorder out of Order and Vision of Order out of Disorder...," in *Eric Voegelin's Significance for the Modern Mind*, ed. Sandoz, 138.

the problem of *episteme* in connection with experience, out of which it emerges." Almost sorrowfully, Voegelin continues: "Why you do this, I do not know. And how this position can work, when it comes to the treatment of a concrete problem (for example, to an interpretation of a Platonic myth), I cannot predict—for that I would first have to see from you a concrete implementation."[30]

As noticed earlier, Strauss acknowledges that "the Law has primacy" and that "I basically stand on the same ground" as he did fifteen years before, but with deeper understanding. "I believe still today that the *theioi nomoi* is the common ground of the Bible and philosophy—humanly speaking." But the multitude of divine laws so confuse things as to lead to solutions diametrically opposed to one another in the Bible and in philosophy. He rejects any blending of the two, to repeat, contending that every "synthesis is actually an option either for Jerusalem or for Athens."[31] For Voegelin, the theoretization of this problem by Augustine is essentially valid for an understanding of the relationship of science (especially metaphysics) and revelation.

> Revealed knowledge is, in the building of human knowledge, that knowledge of the pregivens of perception (*sapientia,* closely related to the Aristotelian *nous* as distinguished from *episteme*). To these pregivens belongs the experience of man of himself as *esse, nosse, velle,* the inseparable primal experience: I am as knowing and willing being; I know myself as being and willing; I will myself as a being and a knowing human. (For Augustine in the world sphere, the symbol of the trinity: the Father—Being; the Son—the recognizable order; the Spirit—the process of being in history). To these pregivens belongs further the being of God beyond time (in the just characterized dimensions of creation, order, and dynamic) and the human knowledge of this being through "revelation." Within this knowledge pregiven by *sapientia* stirs the philosophic *episteme*.[32]

---

30. Voegelin to Strauss, February 21, 1951, letter 36. Thus, already in 1957 Voegelin wrote of the meaning of *Nous:* "even in Aristotle it still has an amplitude of meaning from intellection to faith" (*OH* II:208).

31. Strauss to Voegelin, February 25, 1951, letter 37. The primacy of law in Strauss's thought and its medieval roots are carefully explored in Hillel Fradkin, "Philosophy and Law: Leo Strauss as a Student of Medieval Jewish Thought," *Review of Politics* 53 (Winter 1991): 40–52, esp. 49–52.

32. Voegelin to Strauss, April 22, 1951, letter 38.

Strauss remains adamant, however, in seeing this as a problem traditionally comprehensible in terms of faith and knowledge, and not of universal faith but as a particularly Christian, and by extension, a Jewish, problem. Hence, the problem is not a universal-human one but "presupposes a *specific* faith, which philosophy as philosophy does not and cannot do. Here and here alone it seems to me lies the divergence between us—also in the mere historical."[33] The richness and subtlety of the debate does not lend itself to adequate summary. The prefiguration of the outcome is Strauss's early reaction: "What you wrote about Plato and Aristotle, naturally interests me quite directly. . . . I do not hold this interpretation to be correct. But it is toweringly superior to nearly all that one gets to read about Plato and Aristotle."[34]

The gentleness and civility of Strauss himself, it must be said, is not always emulated by all who identify with his cause, and the silence we have noticed as descending on our correspondents after publication of the initial volumes of *Order and History* was briefly if stridently shattered by a long essay in the *Review of Metaphysics* in which Voegelin's whole interpretation of Hellenic philosophy was resoundingly rejected as (among other reasons) existentialist, theologico-historicist, Christian, faith and not science, empiricist, mystical, Toynbeean, Thomistic, too concerned with experience and too little concerned with reason, theological, neglectful of the political, egalitarian, liberal, reductionist in seeing Plato's myths as revelation, oblivious to the tension between theory and practice, inverting the classic philosophic theory of the relationship between being and history (historicism, again), blocking instead of fostering access to Greek philosophy because of Christian assumptions in quasi-Hegelian dress. "Voegelin is forced by his commitments both to reject Hellenism and at the same time to preserve it in unrecognizable form." "He excludes the possibility of a non-empiricist and non-mystical philosophy." "It is not easy," the author patronizingly sighs, "to make such a judgment of what may well be a devout man's life work."[35] After this blast, there was little more that could usefully be said. Silence reigned.

33. Strauss to Voegelin, June 4, 1951, letter 39. For "mere historical," see letter 35.
34. Strauss to Voegelin, December 12, 1942, letter 5.
35. Stanley Rosen, "*Order and History*," *Review of Metaphysics* 12 (December 1958): 257–76, at 258, 268, 276, and *passim*. The reader is helpfully directed (at

§4.

In modern philosophy the hard line drawn between religion and philosophy is exemplified in Benedict de Spinoza's attitude as expressed in the *Tractatus theologico-politicus* (1670), where the principle is laid down as follows:

> Between faith or theology, and philosophy, there is no connection, nor affinity. I think no one will dispute the fact who has knowledge of the aim and foundations of the two subjects, for they are as wide apart as the poles.
>
> Philosophy has no end in view save truth; faith . . . looks for nothing but obedience and piety. Again, philosophy is based on axioms which must be sought from nature alone.[36]

"The core of Strauss's thought is the famous 'theological-political problem,' a problem which he would say 'remained *the* theme of my studies' from a very early time."[37] Strauss's gloss on the quoted Spinoza passage suggests that the philosopher who knows truth must refrain from expressing it out of both convenience and, more so, duty. If *truth* requires one not to accommodate opinions to the Bible, *piety* requires the opposite, "i.e., that one should give one's own opinions a Biblical appearance. If true religion or faith, which according to him requires not so much true dogmas as pious ones, were endangered by his Biblical criticism, Spinoza would have decided to be absolutely silent about this subject." But, of course, to thicken this tangle, the rule of speaking "*ad captum*

267n) to "a definitive discussion [of the relation between religion and philosophy], with full references," namely, Strauss's *Persecution and the Art of Writing*.

36. Benedict de Spinoza, *Writings on Political Philosophy*, ed. A. G. A. Balz, trans. R. H. M. Elwes (New York: Appleton-Century-Crofts, 1937), 16.

37. Steven B. Smith, "Leo Strauss: Between Athens and Jerusalem," *Review of Politics* 53 (Winter 1991): 75–99, at 78. The early book by Strauss was the study of Spinoza's *Tractatus* written in 1925–1928 and published as *Die Religionskritik Spinozas als Grundlage seiner Bibelwissenschaft; Untersuchungen zu Spinozas Theologisch-Politischem Traktat* (Berlin: Akadamie Verlag, 1930; English translation, 1965). As he remarks to Voegelin, "Hula was telling me that you are interested in Arabic political philosophy. That was once my speciality" (February 20, 1943, letter 7). Strauss recurs to a comparison by Voegelin of Averroës with Husserl's treatment of Aristotle's *De Anima* Bk. 3, and to his medieval studies, including Maimonides and his "Essay on the Law of the *Kuzari*" on October 11, 1943, letter 11.

vulgi" means so as to satisfy the dominant opinion of the multitude, which in Spinoza's situation was that of a secularist Jew speaking to a Protestant Christian community.[38] It was Spinoza's intention to emancipate philosophy from its position as mere handmaid of scripture. "In his effort to emancipate philosophy from its ancillary position, he goes to the very root of the problem—the belief in revelation. By denying revelation, he reduces Scripture to the status of the works of the Greek poets, and as a result of this he revives the classical conception of Greek philosophers as to the relation between popular beliefs and philosophic thought."[39]

Behind both Spinoza and Strauss stand the great Spanish Islamic philosophers of the medieval period who insisted upon philosophy as a purely "rational" enterprise based on Aristotle and steering a middle way, one infected neither by dogmatic religion nor by traditional mysticism— to take the case of Averroës, the great twelfth-century *falasifa* Ibn Rushd. It may be useful to recall that Thomas Aquinas's *Summa Contra Gentiles* is the Western Christian "comprehensive systematic work against the Arabic-Aristotelian philosophy. In 1270, thirteen Averroistic propositions were condemned by Étienne Tempier, the bishop of Paris, and the year 1277 brought the sweeping condemnation of 219 propositions, including besides the Averroistic proper, several of Thomas Aquinas which seemed equally dangerous."[40] By the Averroist tradition, philosophy is considered to be "the systematic application of demonstrative reasoning to the world." Such philosophy starts from indubitable first principles and cannot be empirical, since philosophy is conceived as a demonstrative science and there can be no indubitable premises about any part of the world as experienced, much less about the whole cosmos.[41] Philosophers are capable of arriving at truth

---

38. Strauss, *Persecution and the Art of Writing*, 142–201, at 168, 178.

39. Harry Austryn Wolfson, *Philo: Foundations of Religious Philosophy in Judaism, Christianity, and Islam*, 2 vols. (Cambridge, MA: Harvard University Press, 1947), 1: 163. For Spinoza's "grand assault on traditional philosophy," see ibid., 2:160–64. Cf. Strauss, *Persecution and the Art of Writing*, 188–91.

40. Eric Voegelin, "Siger de Brabant," *Philosophy and Phenomenological Research* 4 (June 1944): 507–25, at 511. This essay is reprinted in *CW* 20, *History of Political Ideas*, vol. II, chap. 11.

41. George F. Hourani, *Averroës: On the Harmony of Religion and Philosophy* [a translation of Ibn Rushd's *Decisive Treatise*], (London: Luzac, 1961), 20–21. A recent critical bilingual edition is *Averroës: The Book of the Decisive Treatise Determining the*

directly and, thus, at the highest level, have no need of scripture or revelation—a teaching that necessitates discretion in communication. As a thoroughly rationalistic enterprise, not mysticism but only philosophy allows union with the divine, since that requires knowledge of the theoretical sciences.[42] There are levels of human nature and levels of discourse and truth to match.

> For the natures of men are on different levels with respect to [their paths to] assent. One of them comes to assent through demonstration; another comes to assent through dialectical arguments, just as firmly as the demonstrative man through demonstration, since his nature does not contain any greater capacity; while another comes to assent through rhetorical arguments, again just as firmly as the demonstrative man through demonstrative arguments.[43]

Ibn Rushd identifies the elite (philosophers) as those who are taught by demonstrative argument, the theologians (a mere subclass of the masses) as those suitable for dialectic, and the masses themselves as those who can understand only through imaginative and persuasive language. Farabi names only two classes, the elite and the masses.[44] This view, of course, requires secret or artful teaching and caution by philosophers. Thus, Farabi endorses Plato's techniques of concealment and Aristotle's methods. They "used different methods but had the same purpose of concealment; there is much abbreviation and omission in Aristotle's scientific works, and this is deliberate. . . . Different expressions of truth suit different levels of understanding. . . . Zeno said: 'My teacher Aristotle reported a saying of his teacher Plato: "The summit of knowledge is too lofty for every bird to fly to."' "[45] Finally, there is the

---

Connection between the Law and Wisdom and Epistle Dedicatory, trans. with an intro. and notes by Charles E. Butterworth (Provo, UT: Brigham Young University Press, 2001).

42. Hourani, *Averroës,* 27–28.

43. Ibid., 49 (*The Decisive Treatise,* 6.17–21), cf. p. 92. In this work the judge and philosopher Averroës defends philosophy on the basis of *Law*—which is to say, politically. Thus, "If teleological study of the world is philosophy, and if the Law commands such a study, then the Law commands philosophy," a sentence that stands as the summary of chapter 1 (ibid., 44; cf. 83n7).

44. Ibid., 92.

45. Hourani, *Averroës,* 106.

agreement of the greatest Jewish philosopher, Maimonides, who writes of Genesis 1:1 ("In the beginning God created heaven and earth."): "It has been treated in metaphors in order that the uneducated may comprehend it according to the measure of their faculties and the feebleness of their apprehension, while educated persons may take it in a different sense."[46] Strauss's convinced adherence to this paradigm of philosophy and philosophizing is stated and hinted in many ways, such as the following from his 1962 preface to the English translation of *Spinoza's Critique of Religion:* "I began . . . to wonder whether the self-destruction of reason was not the inevitable outcome of modern rationalism as distinguished from pre-modern rationalism, especially Jewish-medieval rationalism and its classical (Aristotelian and Platonic) foundation."[47]

Voegelin's attitude toward this model of philosophizing—and hence toward the Straussian approach to philosophy in the degree to which it is indebted to this model, a matter to be more fully ascertained than I can more fully attempt here—is suggested by his study of Siger de Brabant, a Latin Averroist. The notions of the grades of human nature and levels of communication just noticed, Voegelin finds, show "the inclination to treat the non-philosophical man as an inferior brand and even to compare him to animals, an attitude which seems to crop up as soon as the Christian insight into the equal spiritual dignity of all men is abandoned." Along with the elitist idea, which may be confined to "the intellectual sphere of the *vita philosophi* . . . [comes also] the liberal idea of the educated man as a social type superior to the uneducated common man, the *vilis homo.* . . . The bourgeois implications are obvious, for the ideal of intellectual life is coupled with the idea that the man of substance is morally superior to the poor man."[48]

More generally, then, Voegelin remarks of the *falasifa* that "philosophy had become in the Arab environment, more so than it was with Aristotle, a form of life for an intellectual elite."[49]

46. Moses Maimonides, *The Guide for the Perplexed,* trans. M. Friedlaender, 2nd ed. (London: G. Routledge and Sons, 1904), 4.

47. Leo Strauss, *Spinoza's Critique of Religion,* trans. E. M. Sinclair (New York: Schocken Books, 1965), 31; also reprinted in Leo Strauss, *Liberalism Ancient and Modern* (New York: Basic Books, 1968), 257.

48. Voegelin, "Siger de Brabant," 520.

49. Ibid., 512.

Philosophy did not mean for them a branch of science, but signified an integral attitude towards the world based on a "book," much as the integral attitude of the orthodox Muslim would be based on the Koran. The sectarian implication is beyond doubt; the *falasifa* represent a religious movement, differing in its social structure and content of doctrine from other Islamic sects, but substantially of the same type. . . . The great Arabic philosophical discussions did not center in the *Organon* or *Physics* of Aristotle, but were concerned with the twelfth book of *Metaphysics* and the third book of *De Anima* as transmitted by the Commentary of Alexander of Aphrodisias. . . . The keystone of the canon was the so-called *Theology of Aristotle,* an abridged paraphrase of the last three books of the *Enneads* of Plotinus. The Neo-Platonic mysticism and the Commentary of Alexander of Aphrodisias to *De Anima* were the dynamic center of Arabic philosophy, furnishing the principles of interpretation for the comments on Aristotelian works proper. They made possible the evolution of the idea of the Active Intellect as an emanation from God arousing to activity the passive intellect of man. The aim of human life is in this system the achievement of the complete union, the *ittisal,* of the human intellect with the Active Intellect. Behind the dry technical formula of the oneness of the Active Intellect in all human beings, lie a mystical experience and a well-developed religious attitude giving their meaning to the theoretical issues. The clash between Faith and Reason in the thirteenth century is at bottom a clash between two religions, between Christianity and the intellectual mysticism of the *falasifa.*

. . . . It was this mythical Aristotle who dominated the *falasifa* and through their mediation became known to the West. It was not primarily the content of his work that created the disturbance; the Aristotelian results could be assimilated, as Albertus Magnus and Thomas Aquinas have demonstrated. The danger was the mythical Aristotle as a new spiritual authority of equal rank with the Christian revelation and tradition. The Aristotle who was a *regula in natura et exemplar* could be a model requiring the conformance of man in the same sense in which the Christ of St. Francis could be the standard of conformance for the Christian.[50]

50. Ibid., 514–16.

The gulf that separates Eric Voegelin and Leo Strauss and some of the possible reasons for it will by now have become more evident, even if the heart of their rival modes of philosophy remains to be explored. That is a task readers must undertake for themselves, if they are drawn to pursue the quest for Truth in the loving search of the Ground called Philosophy.

7

Gnosticism and Modernity

"The temptation to fall from uncertain truth into certain untruth"

Since its first appearance in German in 1959, Voegelin's *Science, Politics, and Gnosticism.* has become a classic of modern political theory.[1] It demonstrates the power of Voegelin's thought, its lucidity of expression, and provides an analysis of the demonic in modern existence of unique insight and cogency. It also displays the grounds of the new science of politics with its debt to classical and Christian philosophy and to the vocation of diagnosing the maladies of contemporary political existence and supplying their therapies—within the modest limits of reason and science. I want briefly to reflect on the character of Voegelin's analysis and its commonsense as well as philosophical foundations. In addition, I wish to clarify the meaning and place of the by now-celebrated thesis that key aspects of radical modernity are "Gnostic," and how that thesis relates to other facets of Voegelin's philosophy of human affairs.

It should first be said that *Science, Politics, and Gnosticism* extends, deepens, and to some extent qualifies the argument first made in *The New Science of Politics* (1952) that the "essence of modernity is Gnosticism." It also continues to display the "new science" with its anchoring

---

1. This essay is an adaptation of the author's introduction to the English-language edition of Eric Voegelin, *Science, Politics, and Gnosticism*, trans. William J. Fitzpatrick (1968, Henry Regnery Publishers; repr., Wilmington, DE: ISI Books, 2004). Citations herein will be to this edition and abbreviated as *SPG*.

in ordinary experience and utilization of the Aristotelian method. The latter is the great strength of Voegelin's philosophizing, since he begins with commonsense understanding as a given and ascends analytically to a clarification of the key experiences of reality in which everyman shares and through which he becomes—if philosophically inclined and drawn by reason's persuasiveness—at least potentially a partner in the inquiry of truth. Particularly the first section of the volume, delivered as the inaugural lecture of the new professor of political science at the University of Munich on November 26, 1958, is calculated to deal in a direct way with the subject matter of the modern crisis of human existence in a fashion intelligible and brilliantly informative to a general audience. The talk of "Gnosticism" will be less immediately accessible, of course, until some of the particulars come into view. But this is no more than a momentary obstacle to understanding.

The context of Voegelin's discourse is a philosopher's search for truth and his own personal resistance to untruth in its manifold forms, especially as it affects the political situation from which his philosophizing took rise.[2] This is to say nothing pretentious; for Voegelin believed that the vocation of the philosopher shared much with the vocation of all other human beings, and he directly and powerfully evoked this perspective (grounded in personal experience with National Socialism) in an early passage of his *Antrittsvorlesung*.[3] As his principal philosophical mentor, Plato, contended, the philosopher is no more than an exemplary human being—not a species apart. Thus, in addressing his new colleagues and the assembled studentry of the University of Munich on a solemn occasion of high ceremony, the subject matter and truth status of his discourse were clarified in the following blunt words as applicable to each and every one present—and to any eventual readers as well:

> We shall now try to present the phenomenon of the prohibition of questions through an analysis of representative opinions. Thus,

2. The publication of three intimately related texts in one volume fosters the sense of Voegelin's advancing analysis of the place of religious experiences in modern politics from 1938 to 1958. Cf. *CW* 5, *Modernity without Restraint; Political Religions; Science, Politics, and Gnosticism; and New Science of Politics.*

3. Cf. Klaus Vondung, "National Socialism as a Political Religion: Potentials and Limits of an Analytical Concept," *Totalitarian Movements and Political Religions* 6 (June 2005): 87–95.

this effort will present not only the phenomenon, but the exercise of analysis as well. It should show that the spiritual disorder of our time, the civilizational crisis of which everyone so readily speaks, does not by any means have to be borne as an inevitable fate; ... on the contrary, everyone possesses the means of overcoming it in his own life. And our effort [here] should not only indicate the means, but also show how to employ them. No one is obliged to take part in the spiritual crisis of a society; on the contrary, everyone is obliged to avoid this folly and live his life in order. Our presentation of the phenomenon, therefore, will at the same time furnish the remedy for it through therapeutic analysis.[4]

The philosopher as physician of the soul is evoked. A commentator reflecting on the overall character of Voegelin's philosophizing offers these helpful remarks:

To understand Voegelin's philosophy of order-disorder, it is necessary to recognize that his philosophy is the protest of good against evil. ... Behind Voegelin the historian is Voegelin the prophet crying, "Woe unto them that call evil good and good evil" (Isa. 5:20). The judgments upon the kinds of philosophy available involve sorting out the evil from the good. The powerful forms politically have been fascist (including the worst variety of the Nazis) and the communist; and the degenerate or "derailed" modern philosophy has only feeble protests against collectivist tyrannies of Right and Left. The bad forms are very bad, and Voegelin has no nice academic party manners that inhibit him from calling Karl Marx a "swindler" and his master, Hegel, a charlatan who played "con games". ... By "true" philosophy Voegelin means basically good philosophy. It is classical and Christian, the heritage of Plato, Aristotle, St. Augustine, out of whom came St. Thomas Aquinas and scholasticism. ... The conception Voegelin has of good and true philosophy is so noble that any practicing philosopher would tremble to try to do more than suggest what it is. Philosophy, which has the role of saving us from evil, is "the love of being through love of divine Being as the source of its order" (*OH* I, xiv). I call Voegelin an "Augustinian" because philosophy must develop "pairs of concepts which cast light on both good and evil" (*OH* III, 68–69). Voegelin presents a City of God

4. Voegelin, *SPG*, 17.

against and above the City of Man. The social function of true philosophy is to resist disorder and form the community that "lives through the ages."[5]

Protecting philosophy against perversion is vital to the larger task of protecting human existence itself against perversion and tyranny. The issues are matters of life and death urgency (*OH* I:xiii). Hence the startling juxtaposition in Voegelin's analysis of famous philosophers like Marx, Comte, and Hegel prohibiting questions that might undermine their systems' credibility and the refusal to ask questions by the commandant of the extermination camp at Auschwitz, Rudolf Höss, with indubitable life-and-death consequences. No SS leader would even think of questioning his orders: "Something like that was just completely impossible," said Höss in a newspaper interview a few weeks before Voegelin lectured. "This is very close to the wording of Marx's declaration," Voegelin wrote, "that for 'socialist man' such a question 'becomes a practical impossibility.' Thus, we see delineated three major types for whom a human inquiry has become a practical impossibility: socialist man (in the Marxian sense), positivist man (in the Comtean sense), and national-socialist man."[6]

The line drawn in the material before us is mainly between philosophy and anti-philosophy in the form of Gnosticism. What are the differences between them? Voegelin states the two principles as follows: "Philosophy springs from the love of being; it is man's loving endeavor to perceive the order of being and attune himself to it. Gnosis desires dominion over being; in order to seize control of being the gnostic constructs his system. The building of systems is a gnostic form of reasoning, not a philosophical one."[7] First, last, and forever, philosophy is the love of wisdom, not its definitive possession, *contra* Hegel's system and claim to *actual knowledge (wirkliches Wissen)* in the *Phenomenology.* The closure against divine reality—variously effected through the philo-

---

5. Paul G. Kuntz, "Voegelin's Experiences of Disorder out of Order and Vision of Order out of Disorder . . . ," in *Eric Voegelin's Significance for the Modern Mind*, ed. Ellis Sandoz (Baton Rouge: Louisiana State University Press, 1991), 115, 117. (The internal citations of *OH* reference various volumes of Voegelin's *Order and History* in the original Louisiana State University Press edition.) Cf. Sandoz, *VR*, 141–42.
6. Voegelin, *SPG*, 20.
7. Ibid., 32.

sophically costumed *libido dominandi* disguised by systems, the prohibition of pertinent questions, and the murder of God—is the leading
rhetorical attribute of modern eristic that, thereby, allows evocation of
the pretended superman *(Übermensch)* as autonomous Man. Such intentional falsifications of reality through linguistic debauchery and
perversions of philosophy Voegelin analyzes in terms of Gnosticism in
its various forms.

The entire text under consideration explains in detail just why this
is so. To ask some of the key questions: Does Voegelin really contend
that modern mass ideological movements and dominant "philosophical"
schools in the modern world are vitiated by being in some sense con-
tinuations of the various anti-Christian sects denominated and discredited as heretical because "Gnostic" in antiquity—for instance, the
Manichaeans and Valentinians? Yes, he does. He argues both a historical
continuity and an experiential *equivalence* between the ancient movements and such fashionable modern phenomena as positivism, Marxism, Freudianism, existentialism, progressivism, utopianism, revolutionary activism, fascism, communism, national socialism, and the rest
of the "*isms.*" Aside from the tracing of historical transmission by a
substantial body of scholarship whose work taken all together tends to
demonstrate the validity of the imputation of Gnosticism to much of
modern thought, there is the experiential analysis. The latter hinges on
the two related experiences of *alienation* from the world as a hostile
place and *rebellion* against the divine Ground of being.

In consequence, arising from the lust for power, the leading attributes
of modern Gnosticism are: (1) immanentist programs for the transformation of the world; and (2) atheism and the deification of Man as
the superman, autonomous master of nature and maker of history in
the wake of the death of God. Modern Gnosticism is, however, especially distinguished from ancient Gnosticism by its renunciation of
"vertical" or otherworldly transcendence and proclamation of a "hori-
zontal" transcendence or futuristic parousia of Being (Martin Heidegger) or intramundane salvific doctrines as ultimate truth. It thus takes
the form of speculations on the meaning of history construed as a
closed process manipulated by the revolutionary elite who understand
the path, process, and goal of history in its movement from stage to
stage toward some sort of final perfect realm (Hegel, Marx, Comte,
National Socialism). This characteristic of radical immanentization or

secularization of reality means that the "reality" question underlies all of the lesser issues. This, in turn, gives rise to Voegelin's utilization of the symbol *Second Reality* for the dream-world constructs of the Gnostic ideologues whose closure against divine Being, or reductionist exclusion of troublesome aspects of reality by forbidding questions, mutilates and falsifies the consciousness of reality given through common experience. The flavor and depth of Voegelin's presentation powerfully emerges in the following passage from his second essay in the book, "The Murder of God":

> The aim of parousiastic gnosticism [as in Marx, Nietzsche, and Heidegger] is to destroy the order of being, which is experienced as defective and unjust, and through man's creative power to replace it with a perfect and just order. Now, however the order of being may be understood—as a world dominated by cosmic-divine powers in the civilizations of the Near East, or as the creation of a world-transcendent God in Judaeo-Christian symbolism, or as an essential order of being in philosophical contemplation—it remains something that is given, that is not under man's control. In order, therefore, that the attempt to create a new world may seem to make sense, the givenness of the order of being must be obliterated; the order of being must be interpreted, rather, as essentially under man's control. And taking control of being further requires that the transcendent origin of being be obliterated: it requires the decapitation of being—the murder of God.[8]

The Crucifixion of Christ as the murder of God in Hegel, for instance, is not an event but the feat of a dialectician. The "substance of the order of being—which, for the [true] philosopher, is something given—is systematically construed as a succession of phases of consciousness which proceed in dialectical development. . . . God has died because he was no more than a phase of consciousness that is now outmoded. . . . [T]he spirit as system requires the murder of God; and, conversely, in order to commit the murder of God the system is fashioned."[9]

The elements of reductionism, transformation of the world, and systems construction in Thomas More, Thomas Hobbes, and Hegel

8. Ibid., 38–40.
9. Ibid., 51–53.

figure prominently in the diagnosis of "pneumopathology" given in the concluding essay, entitled "*Ersatz* Religion: The Gnostic Mass Movements of Our Time."[10] This piece was not part of the original 1959 German edition but first appeared in *Wort und Wahrheit* about a year later. It largely summarizes and elaborates the argument of *The New Science of Politics'* fourth chapter. In identifying the leading characteristics of the Gnostic attitude, Voegelin stresses that "Knowledge— *gnosis*—of the method of altering being is the central concern of the gnostic."[11]

This focus on changing the world as an exercise in futility with disastrous consequences for mankind is repeatedly countered by Voegelin's insistence on the stability and givenness of reality. The point must be underscored: The only reality we have is reality experienced.[12] Thus, the utopia of More is possible only by leaving sin (*superbia,* pride of life) out of his account of human nature—which More knew was an impossibility, hence utopian, even if subsequent utopians have not. Hobbes sustains his system in *Leviathan* by occluding reality and denying any *summum bonum,* relying instead upon the *summum malum* of fear of violent death as his first principle. Hegel's system is contrived only by the game of dialectic, the unfolding of consciousness to an end of history in the identity of the human logos and divine Logos in the person of Hegel himself—thereby obscuring the mystery of history that is unknowable as extending into an opaque and indefinite future.[13]

10. Ibid., 76.

11. Ibid., 65.

12. This stance of Voegelin's is directly challenged by the Marquette University theologian Robert M. Doran in "Theology's Situation: Questions to Eric Voegelin," in *The Beginning and the Beyond,* Papers from the Gadamer and Voegelin Conferences, supplementary issue of *Lonergan Workshop,* vol. 4, ed. Fred Lawrence (Chico, CA: Scholars Press, 1984), 82–83. Important issues are here at stake that cannot be explored further in the present context or apart from a consideration of Voegelin's later writings.

13. Voegelin's wrestle with Hegel runs through much of his later work up to and including the final volume of *Order and History,* vol. V, *In Search of Order* (1987; available, Columbia: University of Missouri Press, 2000; also as *CW* 18). Noteworthy is "On Hegel: A Study in Sorcery" [1971] in *CW* 12:213–55. His general relationship to German Idealism is insightfully discussed by Jürgen Gebhardt, "Toward the Process of Universal Mankind," in *Eric Voegelin's Thought: A Critical Appraisal,* ed. Ellis Sandoz (Durham, NC: Duke University Press, 1982), 67–86. No attempt is made herein systematically to cite the relevant work by and about Voegelin on the wide-ranging

What alternatives to these ingenious but demonstrably—and intentionally, to the point of swindling and "demonic mendacity"—false "solutions" to the problems of existence in an admittedly imperfect world does our philosopher proffer?[14] Philosophy and faith considered experientially, in Voegelin's account, yield alternatives lacking in the dogmatic certitude provided by the Gnostic doctrines. He summarizes—after an analysis of the meaning of Christian faith and preparatory to a consideration of the experiences of transcendence in Judaism, philosophy, and Islam—as follows:

> The temptation to fall from uncertain truth into certain untruth is stronger in the clarity of Christian faith than in other spiritual structures. But the absence of a secure hold on reality and the demanding spiritual strain are generally characteristic of border experiences in which man's knowledge of transcendent being, and thereby the origin and meaning of mundane being, is constituted.[15]

Against the imaginative manipulators of Second Realities of all persuasions, Voegelin stands firm on ground prepared by Plato, Aristotle, and Augustine. "The nature of a thing cannot be changed; whoever tries to 'alter' its nature destroys the thing. Man cannot transform himself into a superman; the attempt to create a superman is an attempt to murder man."[16] The Christian solution to the imperfection of the world remains open: "[T]he world throughout history will remain as it is and . . . man's salvational fulfillment is brought about through grace in death."[17] "The world . . . remains as it is given to us, and it is not within man's power to change its structure." Thus, More "in his revolt against the world as it has been created by God, arbitrarily omits an element of reality in order to create the fantasy of a new world."[18] "Hegel identifies his human logos with the Logos that is Christ, in order to make the meaningful process of history fully comprehensible.

---

matters at issue in *SPG*. A comprehensive bibliography and guide to this literature is available, however, in Geoffrey L. Price, *Eric Voegelin: A Classified Bibliography, Bulletin of the John Ryland's University Library of Manchester* 76 (Summer 1994): 1–180.

14. Voegelin, *SPG*, 26.
15. Ibid., 83.
16. Ibid., 47–48.
17. Ibid., 64–65.
18. Ibid., 75–76.

In the three cases of More, Hobbes, and Hegel, . . . the thinker suppresses an essential element of reality in order to be able to construct an image of man, or society, or history to suit his desires. . . . The constitution of being[, however,] remains what it is—beyond the reach of the thinker's lust for power. . . . The result, therefore, is not dominion over being, but a fantasy satisfaction."[19]

The materials discussed here primarily date from around 1960. Voegelin, of course, meditated these and related issues for another quarter-century before his life ended in 1985. The introduction to the 1974 volume of *Order and History,* volume IV, *The Ecumenic Age,* pursued the experiential analysis of Gnosticism in a meditation on the "Beginning and the Beyond" which augmented and further solidified the theory as presented in earlier work. But it also qualified his original analysis by giving weight to other factors of importance in structuring "modernity." He developed, in addition, the important notion of "Egophanic revolt" that supplemented the theory of rebellion and deformation presented in the earlier contexts. The posthumously published *Order and History,* volume V, *In Search of Order* (1987), alludes at several points to the problems of Gnosticism in a matter-of-fact way. As is evident from the earlier work itself as well as the later publications, Voegelin was constantly revising and refining his insights. Unsurprisingly there were important revisions to the earlier analyses in light of new evidence. As he commented in the *Autobiographical Reflections,* whose original text dates from 1973:

> Since my first applications of Gnosticism to modern phenomena . . . , I have had to revise my position. The application of the category of Gnosticism to modern ideologies, of course, stands. In a more complete analysis, however, there are other factors to be considered in addition. One of these factors is the metastatic apocalypse deriving directly from the Israelite prophets, via Paul, and forming a permanent strand in Christian sectarian movements right up to the Renaissance. . . . I found, furthermore, that neither the apocalyptic nor the gnostic strand completely accounts for the process of immanentization. This factor has independent origins in the revival of neo-Platonism in Florence in the late fifteenth century.[20]

19. Ibid., 73.
20. Eric Voegelin, *AR,* 66–67. The passage continues in relevant comment. A more fully annotated version is *CW* 34, *Autobiographical Reflections, Glossary of Terms,*

A valuable subsequent statement came in a reported conversation in 1976 where Voegelin replied to a question, in part as follows:

> I paid perhaps undue attention to gnosticism in the first book I published in English, *The New Science of Politics*. . . . I happened to run into the problem of gnosticism in my reading of [Hans Urs] von Balthasar. But in the meanwhile we have found that the apocalyptic tradition is of equal importance, and the Neoplatonic tradition, and hermeticism, and magic, and so on. [Still] . . . you will find that the gnostic mysticism of Ficino is a constant ever since the end of the fifteenth century, going on to the ideologies of the nineteenth century. So there are five or six such items—not only gnosticism—with which we have to deal. If all new types have to be brought in, the simple doctrine is no longer very useful. And something new may be found out tomorrow.[21]

The power of Voegelin's analysis makes *Science, Politics, and Gnosticism* both a pleasure to read and an illumination of superior order. It remains for us to remember that his theory of Gnosticism is merely (as we have just seen Voegelin acknowledge) a powerful if limited facet of a great thinker's philosophy of history and human affairs.

---

and Cumulative Index, ed. with intro. by Ellis Sandoz (Columbia: University of Missouri Press, 2006).

21. *Conversations with Eric Voegelin*, ed. R. Eric O'Connor, Thomas More Institute Papers vol. 76 (Montreal: Thomas More Institute, 1980); reprinted in and quoted from *CW* 33:338. For a good survey and analysis of the other pertinent factors, see David Walsh, *After Ideology: Recovering the Spiritual Foundations of Freedom* (1990; repr., Washington, DC: Catholic University of America Press, 1995), 99–135, and the literature cited therein. For Voegelin's "revisions," see Klaus Vondung, "Rereading Eric Voegelin's *Order and History*," *International Journal of Classical Studies* 11 (Summer 2004): 80–94, esp. at 90–92. The influence of the Gnosticism thesis is far greater than is commonly assumed. It can be seen without direct mention of Voegelin, for instance, in such disparate works as political scientist Zbigniew Brzezinski's *Out of Control: Global Turmoil on the Eve of the Twenty-First Century* (New York: Scribner, 1993); the bestseller by Harold Bloom, *Omens of Millennium: The Gnosis of Angels, Dreams, and Resurrection* (New York: Riverhead Books, 1996); and the technical study by N. Deutsch, *The Gnostic Imagination: Gnosticism, Mandaeism, and Merkabah Mysticism* (Leiden: Brill, 1995). Also Stefan Rossbach's important *Gnostic Wars: The Cold War in the Context of a History of Western Spirituality* (Edinburgh: Edinburgh University Press, 2000).

8

The Spirit of Voegelin's Late Work

The principal work by Voegelin written in the final years of his life and published posthumously includes the final volume of *Order and History*, entitled *In Search of Order*, his deathbed meditation dictated to Paul Caringella, "Quod Deus Dicitur," and the unfinished Aquinas Lecture titled "The Beginning and the Beyond: A Meditation on Truth."[1] While a great deal need not be made of the patently incomplete character of each of these documents, construing the silence of omissions has led to various interpretive debates in the secondary literature about the possibly "changed" views of the "late" Voegelin on crucial matters. The principal issues raised deserve brief mention and clarification from my perspective at the outset of this discussion.

§1.

In particular, there have been questions raised about the triumph of his "scientific" side over his "spiritual" side in the final writings—a false dichotomy, in my view. There was a hinted emergence of two "schools" of interpretation pitting a German against an alleged American interpretation of the master's thought. Such an odd outbreak of nationalism aside, the emergence of an interpretive divergence of some sort seems undeniable. But its depth and justifiability when measured against Voegelin's texts themselves are questions that are more opaque and probably must remain so as largely accounted for by the predispositions

---

1. *OH*, vol. V, *In Search of Order* (*CW* 18); "Quod Deus Dicitur," chap. 14 in *CW* 12:376–94; and "The Beginning and the Beyond: A Meditation on Truth," chap. 5 in *CW* 28:173–232.

of the interpreters and not merely or even primarily by complexities in the work being interpreted.[2] To put matters simply: Was Eric Voegelin a scientist to the marrow of his bones? Yes. Was he a mystic-philosopher in all of his work from the 1920s until the very end of his life? Yes—by express self-declaration so from the 1960s. Can one be both mystic-philosopher and political scientist in the philosophical sense established in classical antiquity by Plato and Aristotle? Yes—and that was Voegelin's position as I read it, as I think he himself intended it, and as I have tried to portray it in my own studies of him. I do not see a change of heart in the late Voegelin on these basic issues. The silences in his late writings on the specific subject of Christianity cannot be construed as evidence of a change of heart. To argue otherwise involves something akin to reading tea leaves. The subject matter of Christianity lay ahead in *In Search of Order,* as he plainly indicates, and time ran out before he ever got to it. Shall we then fault Voegelin for an untimely death? He did all he could. Moreover, the experience of transcendent divine Reality is obviously and profoundly the subject of "Quod Deus Dicitur," evidently the latest of all the late writings. There is a different tone in the last volume of *Order and History* to which we must be attentive, to be sure. In "Quod Deus Dicitur," however, the tone is familiar, and one hears a mystic-philosopher speaking until he can speak no more—and quoting in the process from a document that contains (so far as I know) one of the most direct statements of his abiding devotion to Christianity ever reduced to the printed page,[3] as well as from the final part of *In Search of Order.*

2. The gist of the debate among conscientious students of Voegelin's work can best be gauged from a representative published exchange: Jürgen Gebhardt, "The Vocation of the Scholar," and its answer by Frederick G. Lawrence, "The Problem of Eric Voegelin, Mystic Philosopher and Scientist," in *International and Interdisciplinary Perspectives on Eric Voegelin,* ed. Stephen A. McKnight and Geoffrey L. Price (Columbia: University of Missouri Press, 1997), 10–58. Lawrence relies in part upon Paul Caringella's unpublished paper "Voegelin's *Order and History,*" quoted *in extenso* by Lawrence ibid., 36–42; more fully see Paul Caringella, "Eric Voegelin: Philosopher of Divine Presence," in *Eric Voegelin's Significance for the Modern Mind,* ed. Ellis Sandoz (Baton Rouge: Louisiana State University Press, 1991), 174–205. I do not mean to suggest that this is the only debate over the meaning of Voegelin's work, of course.

3. Of Voegelin's last days Paul Caringella, who sat by his bedside, gives this account:

Eric Voegelin began dictating "Quod Deus Dicitur" on January 2, 1985, the day before his eighty-fourth birthday. He revised the last pages on January 16;

I take the "two-Voegelin" characterization to be at best misleading: There is one Voegelin whose complex and profound thought deserves to be understood on its own terms. But there may be real issues here nonetheless. Some evidently center, in part, on uneasiness with a perceived "religious" Voegelin and, in part, on the question of an academically "useable" Voegelin in a period of rampant scientism where religion is passé or worse. This evident climate of opinion seems bleakly dominant for the foreseeable future, and it is plainly dominant at the expense of the life of the soul—as it always has been. Thus, it may be arguably true that the power and stature of Eric Voegelin's scholarly achievement can never gain any real attention in the "mainstream" intellectual life of our time, if it is portrayed as fundamentally grounded in spiritual experiences and is, thus, in some sense "religious" and to be dismissed out of hand as such. There is more than a little to this argument, I must agree, and it poses something of a dilemma. To speak as I do in following the sources of a "philosophical science" rooted in the work of a "mystic-philosopher" who affirms the cardinal importance of human participation in the divine Ground of being, of the reality of the life of the spirit as the basis of noetic science, may seem to invite a strategic catastrophe for the intellectual and academic cause of Eric Voegelin. This is not because of what Voegelin did in fact achieve. Rather it is because of the company he may seem to be keeping (i.e.,

---

further revisions were made on January 17 and in the afternoon of January 18, his last full day before his death on Saturday the nineteenth at about eight in the morning.

When the dictation reached Anselm's prayer, Voegelin provisionally inserted pertinent pages from an earlier manuscript, with minor adjustments. He similarly adapted at the beginning of Sec. 5 a paragraph from his "Response to Professor Altizer" (...1975...). His discussion of Hesiod's *Theogony* and Plato's *Timaeus* in the last pages and in the planned conclusion is based on the full analytical treatment in the last thirty-odd pages of the unfinished fifth and last volume of his *Order and History.*

Quoted from *CW* 12:376–77n. The response to Thomas J. J. Altizer mentioned (the "document" I referred to in the text) is reprinted in ibid., 292–303. One must also consider in this connection other late work, of course: "Wisdom and the Magic of the Extreme," ibid., 315–75, esp. the paragraph beginning "But who is this person of the Christ really?" (369). Voegelin's incomplete Aquinas Lecture at Marquette University, "The Beginning and the Beyond: A Meditation on Truth," in *CW* 28:173–232, contains a portion that is incorporated into "Quod Deus Dicitur" (*CW* 12: 193–203). See also Ellis Sandoz, "*In Memoriam* Eric Voegelin," *Southern Review* 21 (1985):372–75.

obscurantists, crackpots, fanatics, and other deluded enthusiasts as the religious are regularly caricatured by Hollywood, the public media, and sneering intellectuals, for instance) when his work of a lifetime is so characterized and pigeonholed. He himself had mild misgivings on this score, fearful of possibly being identified as one more California guru. It is at least possible that the austere style of presentation of *In Search of Order* was partly intended as a prophylaxis against any such absurd confusion. Perhaps there is a perception and packaging problem, in short. Protecting the core of the work of an erudite and absolutely solid analytical philosopher certainly assumes importance on this consideration.

Well, what shall we do about that, one wonders? Let him become a phenomenologist or a hermeneuticist or, perhaps, a quasi-Catholic philosopher so that the learned academy in its devotion to these respected strands of scholarship will at least be able to breathe a collective sigh of relief and relate him to their own respectable professional endeavors? Voegelin's debts and suggested similarities to Husserl, Heidegger, Gadamer, and Scheler could be stressed.[4] The connective tissue is truly there, the contexts and affinities legitimately cited, and the philosophical company suitably distinguished. Much good could come of it, to be sure. But can the decisive *differences* unique to Voegelin survive such processes of comparison and assimilation, I wonder? Some such move does serve to underscore the steady and sustained interest of Voegelin early and late in devising the groundwork for a more adequate political science, one that thereby could be rendered more palatable to secular-minded contemporary academics and to their students. There is something to be said in favor of this approach, considered as a stratagem. Better half a loaf than no bread at all, to think along with these advocates and to think politically. The real Voegelin is a scandal, we might whisper softly to ourselves in dark of night. We crave respectability and seek to make an impact, to be successful—not simply to disappear

4. Valuable on Voegelin's Augustinianism and relationship to Max Scheler's writings is William Petropulos, "The Person as *Imago Dei*: Augustine and Max Scheler in Eric Voegelin's *Herrschaftslehre* and *The Political Religions*," in *The Politics of the Soul: Eric Voegelin on Religious Experience*, ed. Glenn Hughes (Lanham, MD: Rowman & Littlefield, 1999), 87–114; also William Petropulos, "Eric Voegelin and German Sociology," in *Manchester Sociology Occasional Papers No. 50*, ed. Peter Halfpenney, Department of Sociology, University of Manchester (February 1998).

into the abyss of forgotten labors, unread books, and lost opportunities purged from memory, lemmings into the sea. Prudence itself dictates such a course, goes the siren song. Moreover, conscientious scholars with the best of good intentions will disagree over the meaning of the complicated material they are studying and do so in good faith. Honest disagreements are simply inevitable.

Under these circumstances, I can only say that, tempting as it may be, the prudential calculation—if that becomes the driving consideration—is inadmissible as distorting the material on principle, if and when it is carried out to the neglect of the overall content of Voegelin's work. To look for the context of Voegelin's science, to relate it to its origins in the history of German *Geisteswissenschaft*, and to see it as developing that scholarly mode as a dimension of contemporary philosophy and science may be entirely legitimate, providing the account does not become reductionist in the process.[5] To discover ways in which Voegelin's work fits into the broad spectrum of movements of contemporary theory is valuable and important—if one does not ideologize his thought in the process by (say) supposedly rescuing him from the conservative-reactionary camp by assimilating him to a left-liberal position more compatible with the interpreter's own political commitments. It has to be stressed (as I have done elsewhere on more than one occasion) that Eric Voegelin was, indeed, above all a philosopher and a scientist, not a party hack or politically correct ideologue of any stripe. Nobody is entitled through any device whatever with impunity to turn him into one posthumously.[6] Details regarding the complex debate

5. The fecund ambiguity of the German word *Geist* (translated in the more explicit English language as either *mind* or *spirit* or *ghost*) is a stumbling block that lies at the basis of much debate; and it certainly makes a significant difference in understanding, depending on which meaning is imputed to the term in various contexts. The substantive matters at issue are pursued with vigor and seriousness especially by Jürgen Gebhardt. Cf. Gebhardt, epilogue to *In Search of Order*, *CW* 18:125–34, esp. *ad fin;* Gebhardt, his portion of the editors' introduction to *On the Form of the American Mind [Geist]*, *CW* 1:ix–xxv; Gebhardt, editor's introduction to *History of Political Ideas*, *CW* 25:1–35, esp. 21 ff.; Peter von Sivers, editor's introduction to *History of Political Ideas*, *CW* 20:1–18, esp. 14–18, where interesting parallels with quantum theory are drawn.

6. See Ellis Sandoz, "Eric Voegelin a Conservative?" and "Voegelin's Philosophy of History and Human Affairs," in *The Politics of Truth and Other Untimely Essays: The Crisis of Civic Consciousness* (Columbia: University of Missouri Press, 1999), 139–44 and esp. 163–69.

over the scope of meditation and meaning of *science* in Voegelin's late work must be left to other occasions.[7] However, it is important to remind ourselves of the rudiments of Voegelin's noetic science as he has stated matters himself. Such a concise statement is given in *Science, Politics, and Gnosticism* §1, where the *episteme politike* is discussed, and its reliance on Aristotle's *Analytica Posteriora*, with a caveat and elaboration—as follows:

> When we speak of scientific analysis, we wish to emphasize the contrast with formal analysis. An analysis by means of formal logic can lead to no more than a demonstration that an opinion suffers from an inherent contradiction, or that different opinions contradict one another, or that conclusions have been invalidly drawn. A scientific analysis, on the other hand, makes it possible to judge of the truth of the premises implied by an opinion. It can do this, however, only on the assumption that truth about the order of being—to which, of course, opinions also refer—is objectively ascertainable. And Platonic-Aristotelian analysis does in fact operate on the assumption that there is an order of being accessible to a science beyond opinion. Its aim is knowledge of the order of being, of the levels of the hierarchy of being and their interrelationships, of the essential structure of the realms of being, and especially of human nature and its place in the totality of being. Analysis, therefore, is scientific and leads to a science of order through the fact that, and insofar as, it is ontologically oriented. . . . The decisive event in the establishment of *politike episteme* was the specifically philosophical [i.e., noetic] realization that the levels of being discernible within the world are surmounted by a transcendent source of being and its order. And this insight was itself rooted in the real movements of the human spiritual soul toward divine Being experienced as transcendent. In the experiences of love for the world-transcendent origin of being, in *philia* toward the *sophon* (the wise), in *eros* toward the *agathon* (the good) and the *kalon* (the beautiful), man became philosopher. From these

---

7. Cf. Sandoz, *VR*, chap. 7, "*Principia Noetica:* The Voegelinian Revolution," 188–216. The method of Voegelin's meditative inquiry is clarified in a number of places, among the most important being the following: his use of the "Aristotelian procedure" explained in *The New Science of Politics*, 31, 52, 80, in light of the critique of positivism given in the introduction to that book; *OH* III, *Plato and Aristotle*, esp. chaps. 3, 6–9.

experiences arose the image of the order of being. At the opening of the soul—that is the metaphor Bergson uses to describe the event—the order of being becomes visible even to its Ground and origin in the Beyond, the Platonic *epekeina,* in which the soul participates as it suffers and achieves its opening.

Only when the order of being as a whole, unto its origin in transcendent Being, comes into view, can the analysis be undertaken with any hope of success; for only then can current opinions about right order be examined as to their agreement with the order of being. When the strong and successful are highly rated, they can then be contrasted with those who possess the virtue of *phronesis,* who live *sub specie mortis* and act with the Last Judgment in mind.[8]

For those ready to object that this was formulated in 1958 and things changed afterward (and of course some things did change, but not the foundations of Voegelin noetic science), there is a pertinent reply by Voegelin to the question of a shift from the 1966 version of the theory of consciousness and the elaboration set forth in his final book, an answer he gave in March 1983.

> Questioner: "... could you comment on any developments in your notion of intentionality from *Anamnesis* to the first chapter of [*In Search of Order*]?"
> Voegelin: "Well, I don't know if it's a development. It's just a more accurate description of the complexes; of the problem of complex itself; of the concept of tension (it's better developed); all of these tensions and systems of complexes."

---

8. The entire section should be consulted. Quoted from Voegelin, *Science, Politics, and Gnosticism: Two Essays,* intro. by Ellis Sandoz (1968; repr., Wilmington, DE: ISI Books, 2004), 12–14; cf. *Modernity without Restraint, CW* 5:258–59. See also "Anxiety and Reason," in *What Is History?, CW* 28:52–110, esp. beginning with the question "What is Reason?" (88 ff.) and the listing of ten primary meanings followed by an analysis; listing given herein, 132–33. An extensive discussion of some pertinent issues is provided in Barry Cooper, *Eric Voegelin and the Foundations of Modern Political Science* (Columbia: University of Missouri Press, 1999). Some of my discussion herein overlaps that given in "Voegelin's Philosophy of History and Human Affairs," in *Politics of Truth,* by Sandoz, 144–70; also Sandoz, "Our Western Predicament— A Voegelinian Perspective on Modernity," in *Politik und Politeia: Formen und Probleme politischer Ordnung, Festgabe für Jürgen Gebhardt zum 65. Geburtstag,* ed. Wolfgang Leidhold (Würzburg: Koenigshausen & Neumann Verlag, 1999), 521–33.

Questioner: "But you wouldn't deny anything you said in *Anamnesis?*"

Voegelin: "No. I rarely have something to deny because I always stick close to the empirical materials and do not generalize beyond them. . . . I would only hesitate to go beyond the formulation of the tensions and the complexes, because I see no real experiences of anything going beyond that formulation."[9]

§2.

Our brief reflections on the two principal writings open with "Quod Deus Dicitur," and then turn to *In Search of Order.* Voegelin does in some degree move beyond earlier formulations even as he reiterates some of them in exploring the tension toward the divine *Realissimum* in his final meditation. In the process he gives hints on the Christian experiential horizon—a subject definitely on his mind. I say that advisedly, given the title of the meditation and on the grounds that, not only do we have here his very last utterances dictated during the last sixteen days of his life, but also because of Lissy Voegelin's report of their conversations to this effect, with Voegelin telling her: "At last I understand Christianity!" And she responding: "Yes, Eric, but you're going to take it with you!"[10] So he did. We have only a fragment, much of it drawn from previous writings. Does this confirm these earlier views? I think it does, and it thereby argues the continuity of Voegelin's thought. What is the tenor of the meditation?

"A dry soul is wisest and best," wrote Heraclitus, and Voegelin agreed.[11] On occasion of his discussion of Heraclitus, he concluded with the following:

The transcendental irruption which makes the generation of the mystic-philosophers an epoch in the history of mankind has pro-

---

9. *The Beginning and the Beyond,* Papers from the Gadamer and Voegelin Conferences, supplementary issue of *Lonergan Workshop,* vol. 4, ed. Fred Lawrence (Chico, CA: Scholars Press, 1984), 126–27.

10. Oral communication to the author by Lissy Voegelin after Eric Voegelin's death.

11. Heraclitus, Fragment B 118, quoted from the *Anthology* of John Stobaeus in Jonathan Barnes, *Early Greek Philosophy* (Harmondsworth: Penguin Books, 1987), 109; quoted by Voegelin in *OH* II, *The World of the Polis,* 238.

foundly affected the problem of social order up to the present because the old collective order on the less differentiated level of consciousness is under permanent judgment *(krisis)* by the new authority, while the new order of the spirit is socially an aristocratic achievement of charismatic individuals, of the "dry souls" who can say: "I have come to throw fire on the earth. . . . Do you believe I have come to bring peace to the earth? No, I tell you, rather division" (Luke 12:49, 51).[12]

The spirit of his "Quod Deus Dicitur" is in this same vein of affective austerity and invocation of the authority of the dry souls for their insight. He wishes to know "what is said to be God?"—what is called *"It,"* as the comprehending Divinity of the Beyond of the gods of myth and doctrine is symbolized in the language of *In Search of Order.* He explores this question during his final days and hours in sustained converse, as was his anamnestic method, with the great philosophical meditatives of history. Beginning from the formulation in the title as given by Thomas Aquinas (*Summa theologiae* 1.2.3), he analytically moves in succession to Anselm of Canterbury and Hegel, to Plato, to Psalm 13 (in the Vulgate, 14 in KJV), nods to Jeremiah and Isaiah, moves back to Plato's resistance to the sophists and especially to Gorgias and the distinction between *apodeixis* and *epideixis* for properly understanding the so-called "proofs" of God's existence, to the meaning of *theology* in the *Republic* and *Laws,* to the ambivalent responsiveness of Aristophanes, to the recollection of the "One" in Parmenides's differentiation of the Beyond of the many gods of Hesiod, to the meaning of the differentiation in Plato's one "God" in the *Timaeus,* to end with thoughts remembered from *In Search of Order:*

> For Hesiod, Zeus is no god unless there is a divine reality Beyond the gods. In these Hesiodian symbolizations we recognize the first intimations of the comprehending *(periechon)* Beyond that ultimately becomes the *epekeina* of Plato.[13]

The material intended for further reflection but unable to be directly attended to, noted by Caringella, consisted of the following: the

12. Ibid., 240.
13. Voegelin, "Quod Deus Dicitur," in *CW* 12:376–92, sentence quoted from 392; cf. *In Search of Order, CW* 18:87–89.

all-enfolding divine of Anaximander and Aristotle's commentary on it; the prayer of Plotinus (*Enneads* 5.1.6); the prayer of the *Timaeus* (48d–53c); Goethe's "mental prayer"; the equivalent Christian experiences-symbolizations in Colossians 2:9: "For in [Christ] dwells all of the fulness [*pleroma*] of the Godhead bodily"; and in Aquinas's *tetragrammaton* (*ST* 1.13.11.1).[14]

Voegelin's meditative path is an exploration of the consciousness of God experienced, not as an objectified *thing*, but rather as "the partner in a questing search that moves within a reality formed by participatory language." Moreover, the "noetic search for the structure of a reality that includes divinity is itself an event within the reality we are questioning. . . . [A]t every point . . . we are faced with the problem of an inquiry into something experienced as real before the inquiry into the structure of its reality has begun."[15] This is a primary event: *Our reason in search of our faith is at the same time our faith in search of our reason!* The quest is an event and a historical process, seen against the background of two major civilizational contexts: (1) the emergence of "God" from the polytheistic background of Hellas and (2) the emergence of "God" from "the tension between doctrinal and mystical theology in the Christian societies since antiquity."[16] These experiences-symbolizations produce an array of language dominating discourse on the subject but "stabilized" at a comparatively compact level of intentionalistic topics ranging from philosophy and religion through natural theology and supernatural theology, without ever "penetrating to the fundamentally paradoxic structure of thought that is peculiar to the participatory relation between the process of thought and the reality in which it proceeds."[17] The *paradox* (a prominent issue in the analysis of *In Search of Order*) principally lies in the relationship between (a) the divine-human encounter experienced in the search and (b) the reflective symbols arising in particular cultural and linguistic contexts that must be utilized in giving it noetic expression. In the instance of Thomas, the scriptural faith of I AM THAT I AM (Ex. 3:14; *ego sum qui sum*, in the Vulgate) is presupposed in the question concerning what is called

14. Voegelin, "Quod Deus Dicitur," in *CW* 12:392–94.
15. Ibid., 376–77.
16. Ibid., 377.
17. Ibid., 378.

God, at the core of which is the tension experienced-symbolized between necessary Being and contingent being. "There is no divinity other than the necessity in tension with the contingency experienced in the noetic question."[18] The nub of the paradox lies in the intentional, parochial, finite *means* of symbolization inevitably employed by philosophers (and other meditatives) to articulate the *experiential event* of their participatory encounter with the trans-finite divine Beyond. The breaking out of the doctrinal impasse that compactly obscures the problem of paradox composes significant parts of the history of Western philosophy (both differentiating and deforming)—sometimes, for instance, in terms of the so-called proofs of the existence of God from Plato to Aquinas through Descartes and Leibniz to Kant's rejection of such supposed efforts as untenable. But what, in fact, really is occurring in these places, Voegelin argues, is not syllogistic proofs but noetic analysis of the paradox of reality just circumscribed. So discerned by Hegel as being, not proofs, but descriptive analyses of the process of the Spirit *(Geist)* itself, he wrote: "The rising of thought beyond the sensual, the thought transcending the finite into the infinite, the leap that is made by breaking from the series of the sensual into the supersensual, all this is thought itself, the transition is *only thought itself.*"[19] Clarifying though this is, Hegel's subsequent error is to deform his insight into the paradoxic structure by construing it as the definitive solution of the problem of divinity in the process of thought and by then incorporating it into his finished conceptual system—thereby obscuring through "hypostatization" that "the noetic movement itself, the divine-human encounter, is still an active process in tension toward the symbols of faith."[20] Philosophy, Voegelin steadily insists, is ever the questing love of divine wisdom in the spiritual man responsive to the appeal of *It-reality;* philosophy can, therefore, never become the perfected real science or knowledge *(wirkliches Wissen)* imagined by the libidinous systematizer and his epigones.[21]

Despite the deformation, however, Voegelin finds Hegel close to the optimal expression of the problem as experienced by Anselm of

18. Ibid., 379.
19. Ibid., 381, quoting Hegel, *Encyklopaedie,* 1830, §50, italics in original as translated and quoted by Voegelin.
20. Voegelin, "Quod Deus Dicitur," 381.
21. Cf. Voegelin, "On Hegel: A Study in Sorcery," in *CW* 12:213–55, at 223.

Canterbury; but he oversteps the bounds stated by Anselm in *Proslogion* XV: "'Oh Lord, you are not only that than which a greater cannot be conceived, but you are also greater than what can be conceived.' This is the limit of noetic conceptual analysis disregarded by Hegel." Voegelin then continues with this telling passage:

> The noetic quest of Anselm ... assumes the form of a prayer for an understanding of the symbols of faith through the intellect. Behind the quest, and behind the *fides* the quest is supposed to understand, there now becomes visible the true source of the Anselmian effort in the living desire of the soul to move toward the divine light. The divine reality lets the light of its perfection fall into the soul; the illumination of the soul arouses the awareness of man's existence as a state of imperfection; and this awareness provokes the human movement in response to the divine appeal. The illumination, as St. Augustine names this experience, has for Anselm indeed the character of an appeal, and even of a counsel and promise. For in order to express the experience of illumination he quotes John 16:24: "Ask, and you will receive, that your joy may be full." The Johannine words of the Christ, and the Spirit that counsels in his name, words meant to be understood in their context, express the divine movement to which Anselm responds with the joyful countermovement of his quest (XXVI). Hence, the latter part of the *Proslogion* consistently praises the divine light in the analogical language of perfection. Anselm's prayer is a *meditatio de ratione fidei* as he formulates the nature of the quest in the first title of the *Monologion*. The praying quest responds to the appeal of reason in the *fides;* the *Proslogion* is the *fides* in action, in pursuit of its own reason. St. Anselm, we must therefore conclude, clearly understood the cognitive structure as internal to the *metaxy,* the In-Between of the soul in the Platonic sense.[22]

Voegelin's reliance on Saint Augustine must be stressed in connection with any assessment of the argument of *In Search of Order.* Thus, as he indicated in a letter to Leo Strauss:

> With respect to the relationship of science (and especially metaphysics) and revelation, Augustine seems to me in principle to

---

22. Voegelin, "Quod Deus Dicitur," 383–84. A printer's error in the original cites John 6:24, here corrected; cf. n3, above.

have shown the way. Revealed knowledge is, in the building of human knowledge, that knowledge of the pregivens of perception (*sapientia,* closely related to the Aristotelian *nous* as distinguished from *episteme*). To these pregivens belongs the experience of man of himself as *esse, nosse, velle,* the inseparable primal experience: I am as knowing and willing being; I know myself as being and willing; I will myself as a being and a knowing human. (For Augustine in the worldly sphere, the symbol of the trinity: the Father—Being; the Son—the recognizable order; the Spirit—the process of being in history). To these important pregivens belongs further the being of God beyond time (in the just characterized dimensions of creation, order, and dynamic) and the human knowledge of this being through "revelation." Within this knowledge pregiven by *sapientia* stirs the philosophic *episteme.* I must confess that these pregivens appear to me quite acceptable.[23]

The source of Voegelin's use of *It* to symbolize the encompassing divine Reality is vaguely given as the common expression "It rains"[24] and ascribed elsewhere to Nietzsche and to Karl Kraus, but it evidently also partakes of the neo-Platonic "light mysticism" of Saint Augustine and contemplatives influenced by his (and their) writings, including Anselm. Thus, Augustine writes:

By the Platonic books [i.e., Plotinus, *Enneads* 5.1.1, etc.] I was admonished to return into myself. With you [Lord] as my guide I entered into my innermost citadel, and was given power to do so because you had become my helper (Ps. 29:11). I entered and with my soul's eye, such as it was, saw above that same eye of my soul the immutable light higher than my mind—not the light of every day, obvious to anyone, nor a larger version of the same kind which would, as it were, have given out a much brighter light

23. Eric Voegelin to Leo Strauss, April 22, 1951, in *Faith and Political Philosophy: The Correspondence between Leo Strauss and Eric Voegelin, 1934–1964,* trans. and ed. by Peter Emberley and Barry Cooper (1993; repr., Columbia: University of Missouri Press, 2004), 82–83; also "Notes on Augustine: Time and Memory," chap. 8 in *CW* 32:483–501. In the letter to Strauss quoted in the text, Voegelin is remembering the Trinitarian anthropology given in Saint Augustine's *Confessions* 13.11.12, where the theme of *On the Trinity* is announced; cf. Augustine, *Confessions,* trans. with an intro. and notes by Henry Chadwick (Oxford: Oxford University Press, 1991), 279–80.

24. *In Search of Order, CW* 18:30. Cf. the discussion in "The Beyond and Its Parousia," a lecture given in 1982, in *CW* 33:396–414, at 398.

and filled everything with its magnitude. It was not that light, but a different thing, utterly different from all our kinds of light. It transcended my mind, not in the way that oil floats on water, nor as heaven is above earth. It was superior because it made me, and I was inferior because I was made by it. The person who knows the truth knows it, and he who knows it knows eternity. Love knows it. Eternal truth and true love and beloved eternity: you are my God. To you I sigh "day and night" (Ps. 42:2). When I first came to know you, you raised me up to make me see that what I saw is Being, and that I who saw am not yet Being. And you gave a shock to the weakness of my sight by the strong radiance of your rays, and I trembled with love and awe.[25]

In Julian of Norwich one finds the following meditation on I AM as more fully revealed in the Trinity:

> *I it am.* That is to say, *I it am, the Might and the Goodness of the Fatherhood; I it am, the Wisdom of the Motherhood; I it am, the Light and Grace that is all blessed Love; I it am, the Trinity, I it am, the Unity: I am the sovereign Goodness of all manner of things. I am that maketh thee to love: I am that maketh thee to long: I it am, the endless fulfilling of all true desires.*[26]

§3.

The balance achieved by Anselm is never surpassed (as Voegelin's loving recollection of it implies), and the important implications can best be

25. Augustine, *Confessions* 7.10.16, ed. Chadwick, p. 123; cf. ibid., 10.24.52: "This light itself is one, and all those are one who see it and love it" (p. 209).

26. Cited from Julian of Norwich, *Revelations of Divine Love*, chap. 59 (italics and punctuation *sic*), as given in Evelyn Underhill, *Mysticism: A Study in the Nature and Development of Man's Spiritual Consciousness*, 12th ed. (1910; repr., New York: Meridian Books/Noonday Press, 1955), 113; cf. the discussion of *It* as the divine Darkness of the soul, when immersed in "the Cloud of Unknowing" in ascent into the "unknown of the intellect" that transcends "sight and knowledge." "This acknowledgment of our intellectual ignorance, this humble surrender, is the entrance into the 'Cloud of Unknowing'" (ibid., 348–49). This limit also marks the ultimate boundary of noesis, as Voegelin attests in many places, esp. *Anamnesis*, pt. 3, §4, "Tensions in the Knowledge of Reality [*Wissensrealität*]" (Munich: Piper Verlag, 1966), 323–40; trans. and ed. Gerhart Niemeyer (1978; Columbia: University of Missouri Press, 1990), 183–99, which discusses philosophy's limits and concludes with attention to Thomas Aquinas and Pseudo-Dionysius.

studied by the reader in the original. The stance of Voegelin at the end of his days is of a man living in responsive openness to the divine appeal. He finds that what is at stake is not God but the truth of human existence with the persuasive role of the philosopher unchanged since antiquity, the persistent partisan for reality—experienced in the propagation of existential truth: This is the scholar's true vocation. If there is an "answer" given to the question of his unfinished meditation, it may be glimpsed in an affirmation of the comprehending Oneness of divinity Beyond the plurality of gods and things. At the end of Voegelin's long struggle to understand, Reality experienced-symbolized is a mysterious ordered (and disordered) tensional oneness moving toward the perfection of its Beyond—not a system.[27]

It is right, I think, to approach *In Search of Order* from the perspective gained through the foregoing consideration of "Quod Deus Dicitur." While the analysis there is directed toward the paradoxic structure of linguistic articulation of meditation as carried out by a philosopher, i.e., responsively by Voegelin himself, the substance of the study is that sketched already. Therefore, only the barest hints of the book need be attempted here.[28] This is because the dense intricacy of the analysis does not lend itself to cogent abridgment. But it is also because Voegelin himself is emphatic that no discursive teaching whatever can be derived from the class of decisive experiences such as the one just traced in Anselm. This is one further paradox to be considered, of course. Although he was writing explicitly about Plato's "*fides* of the Cosmos" in the *Timaeus* that "becomes transparent for the drama of the Beyond enacted, through the tensional process of the Cosmos, from demiurgic Beginning to a salvational End," Voegelin's strictures apply more generally, *viz.*:

> No "Principles," or "absolutes," or "doctrines" can be extracted from this tensional complex; the quest for truth, as an event of participation in the process, can do no more than explore the structures in the divine mystery of the complex reality and, through the analysis of the experienced responses to the tensional

27. Voegelin, "Quod Deus Dicitur," 291–92; *In Search of Order*, 109; Voegelin, *OH* IV, *The Ecumenic Age*, 233–35.

28. The reader may also wish to consult the original and more recent introductions I prepared for the book's 1987 and 1999 republication as part of the *Collected Works* (*CW* 18).

pulls, arrive at some clarity about its own function in the drama
in which it participates.[29]

This is not a new insight on Voegelin's part, as one commentator summarizes his early perspective on the subject of participatory experience: "[A]nalysis of noetic acts and the person as the center of noetic
acts revealed spirit to be incapable of reification. Spiritual and intellectual acts can only be understood by persons committing the same acts."
With reference to the writings of Othmar Spann and Max Scheler,
but also of the young Voegelin,

> the "primacy of the spirit" in the human community is found in
> the primal community of man and God. In meditation as the
> ground form of philosophizing the conditions of noetic under-
> standing are attained. Because the divine Ground of being resists
> reification, so too do the noetic acts of the person. The meditative
> movement of human consciousness, the *via negationis* which
> breaks every reification which interrupts communication between
> spirit and spirit *(Gezweiung)*, is therefore the quintessential act
> of the human person. In the highest form of community, the
> *unio mystica*, the human discovers his true being *in deo* and
> through this his brother-and-sisterhood in humankind. This
> experience also gives the person the criteria for judging the un-

---

29. *In Search of Order*, 123. William James pertinently observed over a century
ago:

> This incommunicableness of the [mystic's experience] is the keynote of all mys-
> ticism. Mystical truth exists for the individual who has the [experience], but for
> no one else. In this . . . it resembles the knowledge given to us in sensations more
> than that given by conceptual thought. Thought, with its remoteness and abstract-
> ness, has often enough in the history of philosophy been contrasted unfavorably
> with sensation. It is a commonplace of metaphysics that God's knowledge cannot
> be discursive but must be intuitive. . . . [W]e have seen . . . that mystics may em-
> phatically deny that the senses play any part in the very highest type of knowl-
> edge which their [experiences] yield.

James, *The Varieties of Religious Experience: A Study of Human Nature*, Being the Gif-
ford Lectures on Natural Religion Delivered at Edinburgh in 1901–1902 (New York:
Modern Library, n.d.), 396. I have substituted "[experiences]" in James's text for his
transport(s), since Voegelin never reported having had any of the latter. *Vision* and the
whole range of meditative experience is analyzed by Voegelin in "Wisdom and the
Magic of the Extreme," in *CW* 12, esp. 345–71; see the discussion in Sandoz, *VR*,
218–25.

truthfulness of speculation which reduces humankind to mere worldly existence.[30]

What then is *In Search of Order* about? Is there a guiding thread through the maze that gives meaning to the enterprise to the degree that it lies before us, an unfinished meditation? Perhaps the rule of reading is given in Voegelin's reiterated statement that the ineffable becomes effable in divine-human experience. In other words: The mystery of transcendent divine Being is not directly experientiable but only its effects (to use the "old" language of tradition and of his own earlier writings) as explored in the participatory quest of truth. The book is about Voegelin's quest of truth and the terms of that quest as the form of philosophizing dictated by his examination of the structure of his own reflective consciousness. We may grandly speak of his "theory of consciousness," of course. But the discipline of *In Search of Order* and its teaching for all who enter the quest for the truth of divine Reality is to avoid every intentionalist construction and every abstraction so as to stick to the concrete terminology of radically empirical analysis. Thus, the old objectification of the dichotomous pairs immanent and transcendent and even of experience and symbolization all but disappears from the pages of this last book. That is not because Voegelin is safely back in the fold of naturalistic science in the mode of quantum theory or of hermeneutics. Rather it is because the rigor of analysis in the In-Between as participatory is more directly—i.e., economically and succinctly—articulated experientially by Plato's *epekeina* (Beyond) than it is when the more easily hypostatized language of entities and things creeps in as the mode of expressing the *tension* toward the divine Ground whose exploration is noesis proper. The disciplined vocabulary attempts to obviate intentionality in favor of the participatory perspective of the noetic quest, and thereby to make deformative lapses into doctrinalization, dogma, and hypostatization of the experiential tension's structure-process less likely in thought and discourse. These considerations should not, of course, be so construed as to obscure Voegelin's insistence upon the paradoxical Parousia of It-reality also in experiences of thing-reality, as intimated (for instance, within the biblical

---

30. Petropulos, "Eric Voegelin and German Sociology," 5, 21.

horizon) in Ephesians 4:6: "One God and Father of all, who [is] over all, and through all, and in all you." As one commentator summarizes: "Consciousness as *metaxy* or 'In-Between,' then, always participates intentionalistically in 'thing-reality' and luminously in 'It-reality' at the same time."[31]

Thus "God," so far from being abolished—to venture illustrations not given by Voegelin himself, to help clarify a cardinal point—is apperceived as the divine presence encountered in every waking hour. Reason *(Nous)* itself is not "natural" but partakes of the divine-human encounter and collaboration to understand. *Parousia* is so expanded as to include the experienced presence of the divine It-reality celebrated by meditatives as widely different as William Blake and the Psalmist, who experience the creation as transparent for the Creator behind it, and for the undisclosed (ineffable) divine depth Beyond, intimated through it—in harmony with the principle of *analogia entis.* While it may not be set to music, *In Search of Order* is Handel's "Hallelujah Chorus" in the chaste discourse of classical philosophy, the noetic effusion of a dry soul. It may not be poetry, but it is nonetheless filled with glimmerings of a mind ready

> To see the world in a grain of sand,
> And a heaven in a wild flower;
> Hold infinity in the palm of your hand,
> And eternity in an hour.[32]

It breathes the vision of the Psalmist that

> The heavens declare the glory of God; and the firmament showeth his handiwork. Day unto day uttereth speech, and night unto night showeth knowledge. *There is* no speech nor language, *where* their voice is not heard. Their line is gone out through all the earth, and their words to the end of the world. In them hath he set a tabernacle for the sun. Which *is* as a bridegroom coming out of his chamber, *and* rejoiceth as a strong man to run a race.[33]

31. Robert McMahon, "Eric Voegelin's Paradoxes of Consciousness and Participation," *Review of Politics* 61 (1999): 117–39, at 124. Cf. Thomas W. Heilke, *Eric Voegelin: In Quest of Reality* (Lanham, MD: Rowman & Littlefield, 1999), esp. chap. 1.
32. William Blake, from *Auguries of Innocence,* in *The Pocket Book of Verse,* ed. with an intro. by M. E. Speare (New York: Washington Square Press, 1940), 86.
33. Ps. 19:1–5 (KJV).

Already in his doctoral dissertation of 1922 on "Wechselwirkung und Gezweiung" (Interaction and Spiritual Community), following Max Scheler and Othmar Spann, and in the *Herrschaftslehre* (Theory of Governance), Voegelin understands the individual human person to be potentially *imago dei,* "the intersection of divine eternity and human temporality," and he never relinquished that fundamental insight into man and reality. As he later wrote, he regarded the experience of the Divine ground of being as the central problem of all philosophizing— whatever terminology he found from time to time to be most felicitous in exploring and articulating the experience.[34] A decade *after* Voegelin wrote the *Herrschaftslehre* T. S. Eliot wrote:

34. For the doctoral dissertation, "Wechselwirkung und Gezweiung" (1922), and the "'primacy of the spirit' [as the] crux of Voegelin's argument" therein, see the analysis of Petropulos, "Eric Voegelin and German Sociology," 5; the dissertation itself is published in translation as "Interaction and Spiritual Community: A Methodological Investigation," in *CW* 32:19–140. The quotation from Voegelin, "Herrschaftslehre" (ca. 1931), is given as follows in the original, at MS chap. 1, p. 7, in Eric Voegelin Papers, Hoover Institution Archives, Stanford University, Box 53.5: "Die Person, sagten wir, sei der Schnittpunk von göttlicher Ewigkeit und menschlicher Zeitlichkeit; in ihr offenbart sich die Endlichkeit also das Wesen der Welt. Person ist die Erfahrung der Grenze, und der ein Diesseitig-Endliches sich gegen ein Jenseitig-Unendliches absetz." This document is published in translation as "The Theory of Governance," in *CW* 32:224–372, and the passage quoted comes at the end of the section on Augustine and is rendered: "The person is . . . the point of intersection between divine eternity and human temporality; in the person finitude is revealed as the essence of the world. The person is the experience of the limits demarcating world-immanent finiteness from the transcendent infinite" (236). In 1953 Voegelin wrote: "Philosophizing seems to me to be in essence the interpretation of experiences of transcendence; these experiences have, as an historical fact, existed independently of Christianity, and there is no question that today too it is equally possible to philosophize without Christianity." "Essentially my concern with Christianity has no religious grounds at all." Quotations from Eric Voegelin to Alfred Schütz, January 1, 1953, in *The Philosophy of Order: Essays on History, Consciousness, and Politics: For Eric Voegelin on His 80th Birthday, January 3, 1981,* ed. Peter J. Opitz and Gregor Sebba (Stuttgart: Klett-Cotta, 1981), 450, 449, respectively. By "religious" grounds Voegelin means no doctrinal or dogmatic grounds: His interest is empirical or experiential— and pneumatic or revelatory (religious) experiences interested him greatly, as is evident. For later (1965) expression of the human person as *imago dei,* cf. Voegelin, "The German University and the Order of German Society: A Reconsideration of the Nazi Era," in *CW* 12:1–35, at 17: In the context of a discussion of Thomas Mann, for instance, Voegelin there writes that "suffering . . . belongs to the essence of man, for though it is man's destiny to be *imago Dei,* the possibility is also present not to live up to it—to fall away from it and to close oneself off." Cf. the discussion in chap. 5, herein.

> But to apprehend
> The point of intersection of the timeless
> With time, is an occupation for the saint—
> ....
> For most of us, there is only the unattended
> Moment, the moment in and out of time,
> The distraction fit, lost in a shaft of sunlight,
> The wild thyme unseen, or the winter lightning
> Or the waterfall, or music heard so deeply
> That it is not heard at all, but you are the music
> While the music lasts. These are only hints and guesses,
> Hints followed by guesses; and the rest
> Is prayer, observance, discipline, thought and action.
> The hint half guessed, the gift half understood, is
> Incarnation.
> Here the impossible union. . . .[35]

There is a thread to follow, indeed, and the continuity from Voegelin's young manhood onward is striking. Thus in his first book (published in 1928) he devotes a remarkable chapter to Jonathan Edwards's spirituality and writes: "In the first half of the eighteenth century, in the person of Jonathan Edwards, the separation of dogma from mysticism begins in [America]." As we observed in chapter 5, in *The History of the Race Idea* (1933) Voegelin opened his critique of the Nazi reductionist biological anthropology by resolutely juxtaposing classical and Christian understanding of human existence that it pretended finally to replace, as presented by Max Scheler and by Thomas à Kempis in *Imitation of Christ:* " 'Every day is to be lived as if it were the last, and the soul should always be anxious for the world beyond the senses. Perfect calm of the soul can be found only in the eternal gaze upon God—. . . but this is not possible while I am in this mortal

---

35. T. S. Eliot, from part V of "The Dry Salvages" (1941), in *Four Quartets,* quoted from Eliot, *The Complete Poems and Plays, 1909–1950* (New York: Harcourt, Brace & World, Inc., 1952), 136. Copyright © 1971 by Esme Valerie Eliot. Quoted by permission. I am grateful to Professor Todd Breyfogle for this citation. See Voegelin's study from the early 1940s of T. S. Eliot's *Four Quartets,* published in *CW* 33:33–40: "Voegelin's interpretation is governed by the fact that the work is the spiritual autobiography of a Christian poet" (p.4).

state.'"³⁶ As previously noticed, *The Political Religions* (1938) concluded with Voegelin's contemptuous rejection of Nazi pretensions by invoking the Frankfurter: "The inner-worldly religiosity experienced by the collective body—be it humanity, the people, the class, the race, or the state—as the *realissimum* is abandonment of God. . . . According to the *German Theology* the belief that man is the source of good . . . is anti-Christian renunciation."³⁷ The epistemological issues were reflected in *The New Science of Politics* (1952) where Voegelin restricted existential faith to the arena of consciousness (glossing Hebrews 11:1) and revelation to the experiential *fact* of God's presence in reflective consciousness:

> The experience of mutuality in the relation with God, of the *amicitia* in the Thomistic sense, of the grace that imposes a supernatural form on the nature of man, is the specific difference of Christian truth. The revelation of this grace in history, through the incarnation of the Logos in Christ, intelligibly fulfilled the adventitious movement of the spirit in the mystic philosophers [of antiquity]. The critical authority over the older truth of society that the soul had gained through its opening and its orientation toward the unseen measure [in Plato] was now confirmed through the revelation of the measure itself. In this sense, then, it may be said that the fact of revelation is its content.³⁸

Four years later in *Israel and Revelation* (1956) Voegelin formulated the matter at issue in these words: "Philosophy can touch no more than the being of the substance whose order flows through the world."³⁹ The apparent meagerness of the contemplative's result is stressed by Voegelin on a number of occasions, partly a paradoxical outgrowth of

---

36. Voegelin, *On the Form of the American Mind* [*Geist*], 131. Thomas à Kempis as quoted in Voegelin, *The History of the Race Idea from Ray to Carus, CW* 3:4–5. Cf. his discussion in the companion volume from 1933, Voegelin, *Race and State, CW* 2: 19–36, 102–13, and *passim;* see also chap. 5 herein.
37. Voegelin, *Modernity without Restraint, CW* 5:71.
38. Ibid., 150–51. On *faith,* see ibid., 187n24. For the underlying analysis of these matters supplemental to the discussion in *The New Science of Politics,* cf. my section of "The General Introduction to the Series," *History of Political Ideas,* vol. I, *CW* 19:30–37, and citations therein.
39. Voegelin, *OH* I, *Israel and Revelation,* 411. Cf. the discussion in Sandoz, *Politics of Truth,* 156–69 and notes.

what he took to be one of the most important insights of Jean Bodin in the midst of the sixteenth-century religious civil wars in France, an insight framed in Bodin's letter of 1563 to his friend Jean Bautru: "I had written to you in prior letters to this effect: do not allow conflicting opinions about religion to carry you away; only bear in mind this fact: genuine religion is nothing other than the sincere direction of a cleansed mind toward God."[40] Near the end of his life Voegelin stressed the signal importance of the sentiment and its prudential consequences for our pluralistic world: "Understanding the problem of mysticism as the simple doctrinal understanding of *phronesis* would be desirable as a task for educators today: reading Bodin's *Lettre a Jean Bautru*... as a fundamental text in every university of the future, which every student must learn."[41]

§4.

In Search of Order can thereby be seen as Voegelin's valedictory analysis of a set of interrelated problems that he struggled with for more than sixty years. He did so from a remarkably consistent and resolute perspective

---

40. Translated in Paul Lawrence Rose, ed., *Jean Bodin: Selected Writings on Philosophy, Religion, and Politics* (Geneva: Droz, 1980), 81. This theme and the religious toleration consequential to mystical insight is the subject of Bodin, *Colloquium of the Seven about the Secrets of the Sublime; Colloquium Heptaplomeres de Rerum Sublimium Arcanis Abditis,* trans. with intro, annotations, and critical readings by Marion Leathers Daniels Kuntz (Princeton: Princeton University Press, 1975). The matter is thematic in David Walsh, *The Third Millennium: Reflections on Faith and Reason* (Washington, DC: Georgetown University Press, 1999). For Voegelin's study of Jean Bodin, see Voegelin, *History of Political Ideas,* vol. V, *CW* 23:180–251, with the *Letter to Jean Bautru* discussed at 188–90: "This definition of true religion remains a constant in the work of Bodin" (188n10).

41. *The Beginning and the Beyond,* ed. Lawrence, 106; on the same page Voegelin remarks: "I got into these problems of mysticism as a teenager, not because of religious education in school (I went to a Protestant Sunday School), but because Hindus came to give lectures. But one must get it from somewhere." Quoted from *CW* 33:426. Elsewhere he remarked relatedly: "I can quite definitely see that I got the practice of meditation by reading *Upanishads,* by reading the *Symposium* of Plato, by reading the *Confessions* of Saint Augustine. These are the classics of meditation to which one has to return—not Madame Guyon." Quoted from *Conversations with Eric Voegelin,* in *CW* 33:304. Cf. *AR,* chap. 25, "Consciousness, Divine Presence, and the Mystic Philosopher," 112–14.

of affirmation of man's participation in divine Being as the *sine qua non* of his very humanity. If anything is surprising about the book, it lies, I have tried to suggest, primarily in the subtle shift of vocabulary away from objectivation, in the tautness of the prose, in the emphasis upon the mysterious impersonal depth of *It-reality* beyond the doctrinal *God* of ready invocation—all in the interest of so refining the participatory mode of discourse as more tellingly to express the philosopher's meditative process as the truly cooperative divine-human event of In-Between reality Voegelin experienced it as being. Voegelin rigorously adapts the radical empiricism of Plato and James to express the process of noetic meditation in quest of truth—the Anselmian *fides quaerens intellectum* that emerges as the standard of true philosophizing. Moreover, as William Petropulos convincingly shows, this is not new in principle: *Meditation* as the essence of philosophizing is characteristic of Voegelin's published work from age twenty-one onward. Chief among Voegelin's purposes in making these stylistic adjustments is a desire to safeguard insights through analytical precision against attack by those pests of every age, the dogmatists, sophists, and *nabala:* "The fool [*nabal*] hath said in his heart, *There is* no God"—i.e., the spiritually obtuse among us of unlimited abundance. The type is analyzed in detail in "Quod Deus Dicitur." There Voegelin concludes that it is primarily for such pneumopathological personalities that "proofs" of the existence of God must have been devised; and he draws the distinction between apodictic and epideictic proofs, a distinction lost on fools.[42] The status of such "proofs" is clarified, for instance, in relation to Bonaventure's *Itinerarium,* or *Journey of the Mind to God:*

> The reasons taken from the exterior world, although not denied by Saint Bonaventure, are not of primary importance; they are stimuli inducing us to think and to become aware of the immediacy of our cognition of God. The being perceived in any created being cannot be perceived in its ultimate meaning without the knowledge of the Being which is God. Neither can any absolute and final and evident truth be known with certitude without the

---

42. Cf. Petropulos, "Eric Voegelin and German Sociology"; also Petropulos, "The Person as *Imago Dei:* Augustine and Max Scheler in Eric Voegelin," in *The Politics of the Soul,* ed. Hughes. Quotation from Ps. 14:1 (KJV); Voegelin, "Quod Deus Dicitur," 384–90.

divine light shining through the objects and ideas. This light is always there; we have but to pay full attention to it. When we bring to full awareness the content of our first idea, it is impossible for us to think that God does not exist.[43]

Finally, the drift of my suggestions of what Voegelin is about in his last book, whose very title conveys the author's attitude of an open quest of reality, is borne out in many places but powerfully so in two passages that give the philosopher's perspective on the search for truth and its *ontic* status:

> In the analysis of Saint Thomas . . . there appears the personal God who bears the proper name "God," but behind the God who speaks his Word and hears the word of prayer, there looms the nameless, the impersonal, the tetragrammatic God [YHWH or JHVH]. The God who is experienced as concretely present remains the God beyond his presence. The language of the gods, thus, is fraught with the problem of symbolizing the experience of a not-experientiable divine reality. . . . [I]f the consciousness of experience and symbolization remains alive . . . the succession of the gods becomes a series of events to be remembered as the history of the Parousia of the living, divine Beyond. Not the Beyond but its Parousia in the bodily located consciousness of questioning man, the experience of the not-experientiable divine reality, has history: the history of truth emerging from the quest for truth. Under this aspect, the serious effort of the quest for truth acquires the character of a divine comedy.[44]

In a later passage he says:

> [T]he quest for truth is ultimately penultimate. In the quest, reality is experienced as the mysterious movement of an It-reality through thing-reality toward a Beyond of things. Neither the

43. Bonaventure, *The Journey of the Mind to God,* trans. Philotheus Boehner, ed. with intro. and notes by Stephen F. Brown (Indianapolis: Hackett, 1993), 67–68n151.
44. Voegelin, *In Search of Order,* 83–84. Cf. William James's discussion of "ineffability" and "noetic quality" as two leading marks of mystical experience, in James, *Varieties of Religious Experience,* 371; Evelyn Underhill critically expands James's analysis in *Mysticism,* 81, 380. For a wide-ranging comparative study, see R. C. Zaehner, *Mysticism Sacred and Profane* (1957; repr., London: Oxford University Press, 1961).

things nor the non-things involved in this process are objects external to it; they are structures in the process, discerned through the quest for truth. Moreover, as the things and non-things are not external to the quest, the quest and its language are not external to them; in reflective distance, the quest itself is discerned as a "placed" event in the mysterious movement. For the questioner has to tell the story of his struggle for the unflawed order from his position in the flawed order of thingly existence; and he can tell it, therefore, only in the flawed language that speaks of non-things [God, the soul, consciousness, etc.] in the mode of things.

This flawed language includes the language of the "gods." Hence, the story of the quest does not put an End to the mystery but can only deepen the insight into its paradoxic penultimacy.... When the paradoxic experience of not-experientiable reality becomes conscious in reflective distance, the questioner's language reveals itself as the paradoxic event of the ineffable becoming effable. This tension of effable-ineffable is the paradox in the structure of meditative language that cannot be dissolved by a speculative meta-language of the kind by which Hegel wanted to dissolve the paradoxic "identity of identity and non-identity." In reflective distance, the questioner rather experiences his speech as the divine silence breaking creatively forth in the imaginative word that will illuminate the quest as the questioner's movement of return to the ineffable silence. The quest, thus, has no external "object" but is reality itself becoming luminous for its movement from the ineffable, through the Cosmos, to the ineffable.[45]

Setting aside the intentionalism of its formulation thirty years earlier, considered as "the analysis of existential consciousness," Voegelin wrote, "[t]he present analysis thus confirms the statement by which this study on *Order and History* opened, the statement: 'The order of history emerges from the history of order.'"[46]

On more than one occasion in his writings Voegelin asserts the authority of the philosopher as truth-sayer amid the crisis of an age of mendacity and rebellion. He chides the Oxford political philosophers for abdicating duty and invokes from Marcus Aurelius the image of

45. Voegelin, *In Search of Order,* 119–20.
46. Ibid., 47.

"the philosopher—the priest and servant of the gods."[47] He reminds his auditors in Munich of the solemn words of the Watchman of Ezekiel (33:7): "So, you, son of man, I have made a watchman for the house of Israel; whenever you hear a word from my mouth, you shall give them warning from me."[48] Jürgen Gebhardt rightly recurs to this element of Voegelin's work in noting that for him, when the church has abandoned its duty of spiritual leadership (as it had, for instance, during the Hitler period), "it is the philosopher-scholar who is called upon to accept the office of *magisterium* and defend it against intellectual usurpers."[49] The theme is humbly sounded in *In Search of Order* when the old philosopher finally writes for the last time of Parmenides and philosophy:

> The Being he has differentiated is the structure of the It-reality in consciousness....The thinker has become the speaker of the It-reality with such self-assertive assurance that the balance of consciousness is disturbed. That he also is the speaker of a bodily located consciousness, of a human being known as Parmenides, becomes problematic.... The excitement that carried the "knowing man" from assertive to self-assertive symbolization provoked the balancing resistance of the "philosopher," of Socrates-Plato who knows that he does not know and, even more important, who knows why he does not know.[50]

47. Voegelin, "The Oxford Political Philosophers," *Philosophical Quarterly* 3 (April 1953): 97–114 *ad fin;* cf. *The Communings with Himself of Marcus Aurelius Emperor of Rome, Together with His Speeches and Sayings,* ed. with revised text and trans. by C. R. Haines (London: William Heinemann, 1924), 3.4.3 (p. 51).

48. Quoted in Voegelin, "The German University," in *CW* 12:35.

49. Gebhardt, "The Vocation of the Scholar," 18. Voegelin's condemnation of the churches' dereliction and abdication of their responsibilities of spiritual leadership was bare-knuckled and scathing, as in the original foreword to *The Political Religions,* only recently published: "A consideration of National Socialism from the standpoint of religion must begin with the assumption that there is evil in the world; and not just as a deficient mode of being, as a *negativum,* but as a genuine substance and force that must be combated. But here we approach Manichean problems, and in general, a representative of the organized church will prefer to let his church and the entire world be destroyed by evil than to scorch his finger on a problem of dogma.... These circles react with somewhat more life only... when they fear a loss of revenue" (*CW* 33:22). Cf. more fully *Hitler and the Germans, CW* 31, esp. chaps. 4 and 5, which caused a sensation in Munich when delivered as a course of lectures at the university entitled "Introduction to Political Science" during spring semester 1964.

50. Voegelin, *In Search of Order,* 103–104.

A profound serenity descends upon Voegelin's meditative quest, his faith in search of understanding, and the mood is synoptically captured in a sentence near the end of *The Ecumenic Age:* "Things do not happen in the astrophysical universe; the universe, together with all things founded in it, happens in God."[51]

51. Voegelin, *The Ecumenic Age, CW* 17:408 (334 in the original LSU Press edition).

9

Truth and the Experience of Epoch in History

It is uneasily suspected that we may be living through some sort of grand transition or even epoch in the history of mankind. Since an *epoch*, like Nessy, is much rumored, seldom seen, difficult to discern in the impenetrable fog of futurity, and—if this really is one—will be the first one directly experienced by the living generations of mankind, what is it and what, if anything, does one *do* about it? What are its traits, pitfalls, and promises? At the outset a caveat is in order: The word *epoch* can mean either a brief moment or an extended period of time, longer than an age. Thus, there is inherent ambiguity, which may be just as well. But what might it mean in the present instance?

§1.

In the period between 1989 and 1991 the Soviet communist empire collapsed, and the Cold War ended. The events of fifteen years ago were even confused with the end of history itself, so palpable was the existential dislocation that had befallen the world.[1] A rebirth of freedom, perhaps an American renaissance, was sensed and proclaimed

1. The best-known example is Francis Fukuyama, *The End of History and the Last Man* (New York: Free Press, 1992), which has been widely discussed. For a critique see esp. Barry Cooper, *The End of History: An Essay on Modern Hegelianism* (Toronto: University of Toronto Press, 1984) as directly supplemented by Barry Cooper, "The End of History: Déjà-vu All Over Again," *History of European Ideas* 19, nos. 1–3 (1994): 377–83.

with the flickering hope of creation of just government the unlikely fruit of the travail that had beset the world for the previous half-century. The most resolute of the old idolatries now collapsed or undone in the pinnacles of power, neither putative leaders nor their peoples knew just how to fill the void left in the spewing wake of flotsam that obscured the anomie of the new existence and whose rubble made the shattered dream of universal power's most fitting monument. The perplexing moment between eras was our precise historic location, then: a horrific past behind us, a daunting array of possible futures lie unknowably before us. This kaleidoscope we call the pluralistic field of human existence, of history in the making. Anyone lulled into believing history was over at the time has since been jolted by the resurgence of radical Islamist jihadism and instructed by the Afghani and Iraqi populations' electorate founding, amid civil strife, sectarian violence, against all the odds and historical precedents, a constitutionally representative government as the unlikely aftermath of theocratic and secular despotism.

Together with the sense of epoch (however defined), there also came a sense of great opportunity if we didn't bungle it. It was a moment of pivotal opportunity curiously akin to the watershed discerned by American founders in 1787 and expressed by Publius on the first page of *The Federalist Papers:*

> [I]t seems to have been reserved to the people of this country, by their conduct and example, to decide the important question, whether societies of men are really capable or not, of establishing good government from reflection and choice, or whether they are forever destined to depend, for their political constitutions, on accident and force. If there be any truth in the remark, the crisis, at which we are arrived, may with propriety be regarded as the era in which that decision is to be made; and a wrong election of the part we shall act, may... deserve to be considered as the general misfortune of mankind.

It is instructive to recall that the direct objective of this plea, to persuade the American people (the New York electorate specifically) to ratify the Constitution of the United States, was achieved—but barely so, by the narrowest of voting margins in the key states of Virginia and New York. Yet that document now continues as the world's oldest existing written constitution still the basis of a national government.

This is just cause for hope and celebration. Yet for reason and justice to prevail in human governance, as invited and exemplified by the American founding, it should not be forgotten that both had to be compromised in order to accommodate diversity of viewpoint and the passions, interests, and convictions that divided the relatively homogenous American community. Thus, as is well known and to take the principal example, slavery remained under the Constitution as the *sine qua non* of ratification and union at the time. Only bitter civil war fought seventy-five years later could end it, and by that drastic means only at the sacrifice of the generous understanding of the "federal system" that was one of the glories of the original constitutional achievement. Moreover, it must be noted, the legacies of slavery endure to this very day when race and ethnicity remain cardinal traits of the conflicted domestic politics of the United States.

Both the success of the American founding and its shortcomings are instructive for immediate concerns. As marvelous as freedom's moment is, whenever and however it occurs, the constraints of reality soon impose themselves in various ways. For it seems that there is a *reality* to be accounted for that steadily curbs human dealings, and that freedom is never absolute. In other words, for example, whatever else it may mean a felicitous moment does not and cannot alter the human condition itself, i.e., the abiding terms of human existence in the world as experienced over millennia, a matter to which we must recur. Thus, while operating within a highly developed *civic culture*, the uncommonly gifted American founders were fortunately able to rely upon a widely held differentiated consciousness of reality and a commonsense understanding of politics in a general populace that sufficiently agreed upon basic conditions of free association so as to form a coherent national community, one evoked as "We the People of the United States."[2]

---

2. Exactly who the *People* were in 1787 is a matter of cardinal importance here left aside. But it was heavily debated subsequently in America as the slavery question heated up and abolitionism gained momentum in disputing the meaning of political equality and its ramifications. Most memorably the issues can be followed at the climactic stage in the papers of Abraham Lincoln from the time of his speech in Springfield, Illinois, of June 26, 1857, on the Dred Scott Decision onward, and it is the theme of the Lincoln-Douglas debates during the following year. See Abraham Lincoln, *Speeches and Writings, 1832–1865*, ed. Don E. Fehrenbacher, 2 vols. (New York: Library of America, 1989), 1:390–402, 426–433, 495–821, *passim*. A thoughtful and generally pertinent discussion of the meaning of the political community

Even within such a uniquely favorable context, as observed, the Americans succeeded by the skin of their teeth. The achievement itself, however truly glowing it was by all historical comparisons (such as the contemporaneous French Revolution, its course and aftermath), was so flawed that it hardly sufficed as the foundation of peace and justice in the country. Political order finally broke down in 1860. It could only be reconstituted through a war that lasted four years, the bloodiest in American history, one that was followed by a period of coercive rule over the vanquished states of the South ("Reconstruction") that persisted for more than a decade after open warfare concluded.

The leading lights of the period 1765–1791 in pursuing the American experiment knew from the outset that they were embarked on a chancy venture. They were cognizant at the time of the deficiencies of their own handiwork and spelled out the grounds of the overall enterprise in language that reflected its problematic character. *Experience must be our only guide. Reason may mislead us,* John Dickinson of Pennsylvania sagely reminded his colleagues in the Federal Convention, to reiterate. "We must follow the example of Solon," Pierce Butler of South Carolina said, "who gave the Athenians not the best Government he could devise; but the best they would receive."[3] "What is government itself but the greatest of all reflections on human nature?" James Madison inquired. "If men were angels, no government would be necessary. If angels were to govern men, neither external nor internal controls on government would be necessary. In framing a government which is to be administered by men over men, the great difficulty lies in this: You must first enable the government to control the governed; and in the next place, oblige it to control itself." Easier said than done, all admitted then and might admit now.[4]

These reminders imply something about *reality.* Briefly stated, it is the basis of the argument here that human nature, nature itself, history, and the spiritual realm identified philosophically from Plato onward as

---

from the perspective of seventeenth-century England and the birth of liberalism is provided by Peter Laslett, *The World We Have Lost: England before the Industrial Age,* 2nd ed. (New York: Charles Scribner's Sons, 1971), 188–92.

3. Quoted from Max Farrand, ed., *Records of the Federal Convention of 1787,* rev. ed., 4 vols. (1911; repr., New Haven: Yale University Press, 1966), 1:125.

4. Quotation from *Federalist* No. 51. See chaps. 1 and 2 herein for further discussion.

metaphorically lying "beyond" *(epekeina)*[5] the cosmos and, thus, transcendent and divine—the Ground of all being—are abidingly present as the structure-process of the Whole within which all events occur and solely within whose order (so far as it is known) they become intelligible and meaningful. An epoch in history, considered in this perspective, may mark substantial changes in man's political and social life, but it cannot alter man himself or the basic fabric of reality of the world. The opportunities opened by an epochal moment continue to inhere within the stable context of reality as experienced over the millennia as attested through all modes of apprehension, natural scientific, philosophic, and revelatory. Men have not become angelic nor the world heavenly, to accent the negative side. On the contrary, from the Garden of Eden to present-day Iraq and Afghanistan the evidence is overwhelming. *Human beings are virtually ungovernable*—an inference that we are obliged to accept as an axiom of politics, past, present, and future.

§2.

Human affairs are constantly being ambushed by new experiences. Thus, a (perhaps *the*) cardinal mark of the putative epoch we are considering is the tentative emergence of a significant fraction of living mankind from a dreamworld deformation of reality, one propagated by ideological empires for nearly a century as the common denominator of modern tyranny. Whole nations are emerging into the true light of day with the hope and distinct possibility of recovering as the new climate of opinion a balanced sense of reality in daily existence and a decent political order in society. For if anything distinguishes the era of ideology and Gnostic totalitarianism, it is the pattern of perverse distortions of the human, historical, and ontological dimensions of reality that defines it beyond the evil banalities of brutality, torment, and terror. Yet novel forms of these very dreamworld experiences emerge in real life to shatter the serenity of the newly liberated world.

These *Second Reality* experiences, as they are called, form one of the principal focal points of Eric Voegelin's analysis of modernity. Thus, it is

5. Plato *Republic* 509B. For analysis see Eric Voegelin, *Order and History,* 5 vols. (1956–1987; available, Columbia: University of Missouri Press, 2000), 3:112–17.

clear that the gist of Voegelin's effort, the grit around which he created his pearl, arose because of his own personal, intellectual, and spiritual resistance to the Nazi horror experienced as a profound affront to his humanity, that of his fellow citizens, ultimately one endangering mankind itself, and identified more broadly as *evil* fomenting the crisis of modernity. As he already wrote in a moment of passionate clarity after his desperate escape from Vienna and the Gestapo in 1938:

> Today, no major thinker in the Western world is unaware, nor has failed to express the fact, that the world is undergoing a severe crisis, a process of withering, which has its origin in the secularization of the spirit and the ensuing severance of a consequently purely secular spirit from its religious roots. No major thinker is ignorant of the fact that recovery can only be brought about by religious renewal, whether within the framework of the Christian churches or outside it. A significant renewal can proceed only from great religious personalities, but it is possible for everyone to prepare himself and to do what he can to prepare the ground in which resistance to evil may grow.[6]

The quest for order and truth is biographically as well as philosophically grounded in the *resistance to untruth* and spiritual disorder massively encountered experientially directly in the rise of Hitler's National Socialism and all that accompanied it.

The element is abidingly central, not merely to Voegelin's attitude and philosophical effort, but to our own circumstances. Indeed, we must concede that the *crisis* experienced in 1938 (as just delineated) palpably continues into the present, thereby casting its shadow across the *epoch* we seek to discern. The evidence mounts as statesmen and pundits strive adequately to come to grips with the exigencies of the post-9/11 world and war against terrorism here and globally. Suddenly, the arguments from *The Political Religions* find new applicability as global terror masks its atrocities in political Islamism and *Jihad*.[7] In the liberated nations of Central Europe, meanwhile, the members of

---

6. Voegelin, "Foreword to the Second Edition of *The Political Religions* (1939)," in *CW* 33:22–23.

7. Cf. Barry Cooper, *New Political Religions, or An Analysis of Modern Terrorism*, Eric Voegelin Institute Series in Political Philosophy (Columbia: University of Missouri Press, 2004).

the intellectual elite could choose either to lead or to disdain direct involvement in the political well-being of their societies in the midst of
transition or crisis. After a decade-and-a-half the report is mixed at
best. Old habits die hard if they die at all, as Aristotle first observed.
But freedom and democracy have been powerfully affirmed as the anti-
dotes in the attempts everywhere to resist the new tyranny of Islamism
now clearly perceived as the new religiously grounded *totalitarianism*.
For the individual the temptation is great, often sanctioned by traditions
lacking in civic culture and so nearly inescapable, to leave politics to
the politicians and to go virtuously about one's business while the void
at the top is left to be filled by rabble unconcerned with either truth or
justice or by alienated opportunists obsessed exclusively with a consum-
ing desire for power. The process is infinitely more complicated in the
traditional societies of the Middle East where apolitical tribal politics
against a theocratic background has been the only alternative to outright
tyranny for millennia and the differentiation of the free political individual person, as in Christian societies, never occurred and is therefore
largely unknown except in the deformation manifested in possessive
individualism.

Thus, Voegelin's energetic message on occasion of his inaugural lecture at Munich in 1958 was aimed at apolitical German intellectuals
in the wake of World War Two, including primarily the university faculty members gathered for the occasion, at least some of whom had
prospered during Hitler's tyranny through complicity or merely by
minding their own academic business. But his words have wider application and underscore his insistence on the individual person's *duty of
resistance to corruption as the badge of citizenship*—corruption, in the
lecture's context, taking the form of the Gnostic ideologue's trick of
forbidding pertinent questions about reality, its genesis and order.
Voegelin's energetic statement, to repeat, aimed at the conscience of
each individual: "No one [Niemand] is obliged to take part in the
spiritual crisis of a society; on the contrary, everyone [jedermann] is
obliged to avoid this folly and to live his life in order."[8]

A comparable point, as it happens, was stressed by President Václav
Havel of Czechoslovakia in his remarkable address to the United States

8. Voegelin, *SPG,* 17, *WPG,* 33.

Congress in February 1990, when he spoke of putting "morality ahead of politics" and accepting "the burden of political responsibility." He said:

> We are still incapable of understanding that the only genuine back-bone for all our actions—if they are to be moral—is responsibility. Responsibility to something higher than my family, my country, my company, my success. Responsibility to the order of Being, where all our actions are indelibly recorded and where, and only where, they will be properly judged. The interpreter or mediator between us and this higher authority is what is traditionally referred to as human conscience. If I subordinate my political behavior to this imperative mediated to me by my conscience, I can't go far wrong.

He then went on to state:

> If the hope of the world lies in human consciousness, then it is obvious that intellectuals cannot go on forever avoiding their share of responsibility for the world and hiding their distaste for politics under an alleged need to be independent. It is easy to have independence in your program and then leave others to carry that program out. If everyone thought that way, pretty soon no one would be independent.[9]

There is obvious congruence between Voegelin's attitude and that voiced by Václav Havel, the moral as well as political leader of free Czechoslovakia during the first weeks of his presidency after the Velvet Revolution. In practice it means that it is not satisfactory for there to be one government in Washington, Warsaw, or Prague, and another in the realm of thought and spirit referenced here as *conscience* and *the order of Being*. Rather, concord must be sought within the limits of the possible within the political community and between it and higher truth. Every person, whether an intellectual or merely a citizen, is obliged to pursue this harmony of the political order with the higher order of Being, and only so can liberty and justice prevail. Every person's duty under free government was similarly stated in the famous Burkean maxim: *All that is needed for evil to triumph is for good men to do nothing.*

9. Quoted from the *Congressional Record–House*, Feb. 21, 1990, p. H 395.

Because deformed consciousness of reality is a pervasive malady of radical modernity (centering in the expectation of the magical transfiguration of man and the world as we know them into some perfect third realm of freedom populated with new men, transformations effected through revolutionary activism, as in Marxism or national socialism, or through the indefinite progress of natural science), certain cautions may be mentioned. Civic obligation is not a counsel of perfection, nor one conceived in the spirit of utopian expectation; nor does it collapse the spiritual into the political sphere. Rather it is to observe their tensional relationship as the In-Between *(metaxy)*, the preeminent sphere of human existence and of purposeful action in creating and preserving decent government. It is to state a constantly noticed obligation to be pursued under terms of life in the world that, with due regard for human frailty, must obtain in all moderate politics. It represents the core principle of civic culture underlying just rule, and free government grounded in consent, wherever and in whatever form it exists. Such politics is exemplified in such previously noticed commonsense reminders of the facts of the human condition as Madison's observation that government is itself the greatest of all reflections on human nature—while, paradoxically insisting that political rule demands our aspiration to, and conformity with, higher truth. It remains forever true, he wrote, that "[j]ustice is the end of government. It is the end of civil society. It ever has been, and ever will be pursued, until it be obtained, or until liberty be lost in the pursuit."[10] Upon this rock the American political experiment was founded and upon it continues to this day, a foundation quite consciously incorporating truth uncovered in classical Hellenic and Stoic philosophy and in Judaeo-Christian revelation.

§3.

We rightly recall American matters in sketching a Voegelinian philosophical perspective on present events for several reasons. While he was born in Germany and driven out of the University of Vienna and

10. *Federalist* No. 51, in *The Federalist,* ed. Jacob E. Cooke (Middletown, CT: Wesleyan University Press, 1961), 349, 352.

Austria by Hitler, Eric Voegelin became an American citizen in 1944 and regarded his own experience of the *(then)* comparatively ideology-free civic culture in America as a basic influence on his philosophy after he first imbibed it as a young man in his late twenties, as is attested in his first book, *Über die Form des amerikanischen Geistes* (1928).[11] During his initial twenty-year stint in America (1938–1958), Voegelin continued his study of all aspects of Americana, and he regularly taught courses each semester on American government during sixteen years at Louisiana State University.[12] The American experience was, thus, a matter of scientific or philosophic as well as practical political consequence, since both science and politics originate in commonsense experience and rationality. Common sense thus concretely grounded (philosophically represented by Thomas Reid and the eighteenth-century Scottish school of that name) runs through all of Voegelin's mature work and distinguishes his empiricism.[13] It served him at every turn to put into focus the facts of human existence, even when he was conducting abstruse theoretical investigations. Moreover, one motivation in returning to Germany in 1958 for a decade (1958–1968) was his desire to establish a political science institute in Munich that might have influence in bringing democracy on the American model to a country and continent with little inclination toward, and even less experience with, free government. He believed that "the spirit of American democracy would be a good thing to have in Germany."[14]

It has to be stressed that, while Voegelin expressed grave misgivings about exporting wholesale to unprepared third-world peoples Western constitutions and the trappings of modern democracy, there was no ambiguity about his conviction that Anglo-American representative democracy was the most eligible mode of government available in the modern world, if only the requisite infrastructure somehow could be developed. To be sure there were and remain difficult, perhaps unsurmountable problems to be faced if anything approximating a satisfactory modern "democracy," one assuring liberty under rule of law, is to be attained and preserved. Anglo-American historical development

11. Trans. in *CW* 1, *On the Form of the American Mind.*
12. Voegelin, *AR,* 58–59.
13. Cf. Eric Voegelin, *Anamnesis: Zur Theorie der Geschichte und Politik* (Munich: Piper Verlag, 1966), 350–54.
14. Voegelin, *AR,* 91.

obviously cannot be replicated. And it must be acknowledged that the task verges on difficulty to the point of impossibility in the Middle East where the experiment now is being conducted as the core of American foreign and security policy.[15]

If despite his own misgivings about the likelihood of success Voegelin paradoxically nevertheless vigorously sought to help foster democracy through teaching and writing in Germany during his years at the University of Munich—beginning with the stern strictures laid down in his inaugural lecture—it can only be primarily because no other feasible options were available. From the time of the Allied armies' occupation at the end of the war onward, democracy was ongoing in name and fact in West Germany, and the point was to make it sound if at all possible and not suffer a repeat of the Weimar Republic debacle. Hence, there is a tone of urgency apparent in some of Voegelin's writings at the time on the subject. Moreover, the polity or mixed regime that Aristotle favors in the *Politics* (1295a25–1296b13) as the best practicable constitution readily harmonizes as middle-class government with "democracy" in the modern sense—whatever the distinctions rightly drawn between the ancient Hellenic polis and the modern nation state, ancient and modern republicanism. With allowances for the differences, it is arguably the favored pattern of true or free government from antiquity onward, i.e., one devoted to justice *(salus populi)*, resting on consent of the people and settled rule of law as principles articulated over the centuries by Polybius, Thomas Aquinas, Sir John Fortescue in the name of the English constitution (citing Thomas), and in Charles I's *Answer to the XIX Propositions of Parliament* in 1642.[16] Hence, with appropriate adjustments to time and tradition, representative democracy is a general form of government not unique to any specific culture but capable of great adaptations.

---

15. Cf. Eric Voegelin, "Liberalism and Its History [1960]," trans. Mary and Keith Algozin, *Review of Politics* 36 (1964): 504–20; repr. in *CW* 11:83–99. On the uniqueness of America, see Jack P. Greene, *The Intellectual Construction of America: Exceptionalism and Identity from 1492 to 1800* (Chapel Hill: University of North Carolina Press, 1993). Consult the first four chapters herein for related analysis.

16. See the discussion in Ellis Sandoz, ed., *The Roots of Liberty: Magna Carta, Ancient Constitution, and the Anglo-American Tradition of Rule of Law* (Columbia: University of Missouri Press, 1993), 1–20 and the literature cited therein.

Voegelin's educational effort was launched especially against political indifferentism, the old detached thinking patterns and reluctance to question governmental authority and commands that had grown from a variety of sources in German society. He identified four "anti-" complexes militating against order: "the anti-philosophical, the anti-church, the anti-Christian, and the anti-world complexes." Included notably among these complexes are two factors that deserve particular notice: first, the German Reformation's pietist tradition that lays it down that "power is evil," teaching submission to established authority and political abstinence; and, second, the narcissistic Humboldtian educational reforms that shaped the universities and, in the name of cultural formation *(Bildung)*, effectively ruined the spiritual community by severing it from both the life of faith, in the name of immanent reason, and from the citizen's political duty, in the name of devotion to science. By the time the war was over, these apolitical features of the prevailing climate of opinion in Germany—and they are to be seen elsewhere as well—had been enormously exacerbated by the systematic destruction of the upper strata of society, especially its intellectual leadership, by Hitler and his National Socialists. These factors made possible such grotesque specimens of humanity as the concentration camp commandant who loyally fulfills his murderous duties during the day—because to do otherwise would be unthinkable—and then, since he is an educated man, goes home and listens in the evening to Mozart. As is evident, such anesthetized indifference tended then—and tends now—to cut the root of civic involvement as dirty business beyond individuals' personal concern and, therewith, helped produce the public inertia in leading sectors of society that opened the way for totalitarian disaster and later compounded its effects down to the present day.[17]

---

17. Cf. "Demokratie im Neuen Europe," *Gesellschaft-Staat-Erziehung* 4 (1959): 293–300, where Abraham Lincoln's famous phrase also is quoted and its source in the prologue to John Wyclif's 1384 translation of the Bible is also quoted: I have been unable to verify its presence in that source, however. Also, "Demokratie und Industriegeselleschaft," in *Die unternehmerische Verantwortung in unserer Gesellschaftsordnung*, vol. 4 of the Walter-Raymond-Stiftung meeting (Cologne and Opladen: Westdeutscher Verlag [1964]), 96–114. These essays in translation and related matter can be found in *CW* 11. See also Eric Voegelin, "The German University and the Order of German Society: A Reconsideration of the Nazi Era," in *CW* 12:1–35.

The absence of a sound civic culture in which the truth of reality is conserved is a manifestation of the spiritual debauchery of the society and of the individual persons who are its members which has accrued over a period of decades, even centuries, and it continuously works personal and social deformation of consciousness and estrangement from reality. But remedies for the diagnosed condition are urgently required. As Voegelin observed in 1966,

> the German estrangement from reality has already shaken the world twice in this century, and it doesn't appear as if the world is inclined to let itself be shaken by Germany for yet a third time. Do we want, therefore, to let things reach the point where German society becomes the matrix of a third catastrophe, which in all probability would be the last? . . .
>
> Since the heart of the evil is a pneumopathological condition of consciousness, the first step to recovery would involve making people aware of the evil and opening the situation up to public discussion.

Making the public aware of the diagnosis was his purpose in speaking out, he stated, and "the individual can do no more." Voegelin concluded the lecture, as we have seen, on an ominous tone by quoting Ezekiel 33:7–9.[18]

By this diagnosis, underlying individual attitudes is the general absence of a civic culture, and underlying the absent or vitiated culture is spiritual destruction and disease whose long-term process of deterioration cannot await the luxury of long-term therapy: Emergency measures are needed, beginning immediately with public debate. The complexity of the situation will be appreciated, but the requisite personal reorientation in existence is an urgent matter to be undertaken at once in response to the *True Word* of order and reality—plainly an echo of the philosophers Socrates-Plato and of the prophets of Israel who speak *sub specie aeternitatis*. Diagnosis, therapy, and scope of rational action by individuals, as just summarized, would seem to be pertinent to our own deliberations.

18. Voegelin, "The German University," 34–35. Also quoted in *Hitler and the Germans, CW* 31:200, where he tells the students to memorize the passage.

As a commonsense matter—and he was much impressed by common sense—Voegelin's actions and words show that he would have embraced Winston Churchill's ironic assessment that democracy is the worst form of government, except for all of its alternatives. Not utopian expectation but a process of elimination open to compromise is the realistic mode of governing action through prudence in the pragmatic realm under present-day conditions of political pluralism. This is an attitude emblemized by the Augustinian insights into the human condition and division of reality into the City of God and the City of the World in antiquity. It is an attitude difficult to grasp, a hard lesson to learn, for all righteous reformers of the world—not excluding such noble personalities as Václav Havel and his Charter 77 and Civic Forum associates since 1989 in what is now the Czech Republic. New eras do not obliterate the warts from life in the world, nor should they be expected to do so. But there is no inconsistency in this view and in noting that Voegelin would have concurred with Aleksandr Solzhenitsyn's September 1990 conclusion apropos Russia's government in some new era that seemed to be dawning: as stated earlier, new eras do not alter the human condition itself. Solzhenitsyn wrote: "if we disregard [the possibility of—?] the complete absence of rule (i.e., anarchy, or the rule of every strong individual over every weak one), and avoid falling once more into the trap of totalitarianism, that twentieth-century invention, then we cannot be said to have much of a choice: the whole flow of modern history will unquestionably predispose us to choose democracy."[19]

Such matters lie near the surface of our considerations, of course. Institutions and processes, as we have suggested, do not run themselves but depend upon individual persons, cohesive communities, and habituation anchored in historical usage and tradition. The destruction of the people at the hands of radical modernity before and, with a vengeance, after totalitarianism under national socialism or Soviet communism will have generated the kinds of spiritual disorientation in Central and Eastern Europe that Voegelin diagnosed in the 1960s. Solzhenitsyn has written in a similar vein with respect to Russia. On one side, there is no time to think and discuss, for action is required

19. Aleksandr Solzhenitsyn, *Rebuilding Russia: Reflections and Tentative Proposals,* trans. Alexis Klimoff (New York: Farrar, Strauss, and Giroux, 1991), 62.

every day in the face of multiple crises. But this is not primary, for "the structure of the state is secondary to the spirit of human relations.... Politics must not swallow up all of a people's spiritual and creative energies. Beyond upholding its *rights,* mankind must defend its soul, freeing it for reflection and feeling.... [T]he destruction of our souls over three-quarters of a century is the most terrifying thing of all."[20]

Voegelin in writing of Germany and Solzhenitsyn in writing of Russia are thinking about the same epoch in the history of mankind that we are considering. By this reading, then, it did not suddenly occur in 1989, but its beginnings extend back as far at least as the defeat of the imperial designs of Hitler in World War Two. What connects the rise of democratic Germany and the rise of fledgling democratic states out of the rubble of the Soviet communist empire is the collapse of ideologically identified power structures whose fall, simultaneously, opens the horizon to the establishment of free government. What also connects these manifest events in the power sphere is the underlying pneumopathologies that both paved the way for triumph of the ideological imperialists initially and were exacerbated by them during years and decades of domination and forced indoctrination to effect the blinding of the soul on a massive scale. Because even as the lie is given to official truth (that, increasingly, nobody believed anyway) through the suffering and enforced vacuity of the people under ideological terror, the wake of the lie's demise is littered with a large residue of hollow men as debris, the mass men of the recent past who remain mass men even at liberty. Such human material intended by the old putative masters of mankind for the building of socialism, thus, confronts the new "democratic" reformers who are themselves in search of a new plan by which to govern and, perchance, a new truth by which to live. Remaking souls and societies is hard work. In short, the underlying pneumopathology substantially persists as the root evil of our time even after the tyrants fade from the scene and the new epoch begins. The problems remain that allowed the worst excesses of the old era with its relentless destruction of souls by a swindler's truth.

But this is not the whole story, obviously. Force feeding sometimes

20. Ibid., 48–49, 50.

results in cure by nausea, as Solzhenitsyn observed, and after decades of the socialist din "no voice is strong enough to summon us in that direction anymore." Perhaps. While it may be true that the long-subjugated peoples of the old Soviet empire remain prisoners of their past, socialism for Russians, he wrote, "is a dead dog, while for many people in the West, it is still a living lion."[21] Side by side with the ravages of physical and spiritual destruction, the suffering humanity of our century was effecting a renaissance of the mind and spirit that put the lie to the ostensible masters of the Brave New World of second realities through the recovery of truth, not least of all recovery of that ancient truth that "Man shall not live by bread alone, but by every word that proceeds out of the mouth of God" (Matt. 4:4). Václav Havel has stressed this point by writing that, "Communism was not defeated by military force, but by life, by the human spirit, by conscience, by the resistance of Being and man to manipulation."[22] A distinguished legal scholar and authority on Russia also wrote:

> The collapse of Communism was primarily a moral and spiritual collapse. Soviet socialism preached altruism, social responsibility, honesty—but it practiced self-seeking, corruption, and deception. A primary reason for that failure, it seems to me, was its doctrine of the fundamental goodness, and consequently the self-sufficiency, of man and its lack of belief in a transcendent order, personal salvation, and an eternal life. If honesty is only a virtue and not a divine commandment, it lacks the necessary element of sanctity, and it will be discarded when it becomes inexpedient.... Russia needs to rebuild its legal system "with God as the backbone."[23]

21. Aleksandr I. Solzhenitsyn, *East and West: The Nobel Lecture on Literature, A World Split Apart, Letter to the Soviet Leaders, and an Interview with Aleksandr Solzhenitsyn by Janis Sapiets* (New York: Harper & Row, 1980), 163, 156.
22. Václav Havel, "The End of the Modern Era," *New York Times,* March 1, 1992, Op-Ed page; excerpted from his Feb. 4, 1992, speech to the World Economic Forum in Davos, Switzerland. See also "The Power of the Powerless" and "Stories and Totalitarianism," in *Open Letters: Selected Writings, 1965–1990,* by Václav Havel, ed. Paul Wilson (New York: Vintage Books, 1992), 125–214, 328–50.
23. Harold J. Berman, "Christianity and Democracy in the Soviet Union," *Emory International Law Review* 6 (Spring 1992): 23–34, at 32–33. Internal quote attributed to the "Minister of Justice of the Russian Republic."

§4.

The vast reconstruction of philosophy Voegelin pursued over a half-century in response to the crisis of modernity was actuated by the conviction that "philosophizing seems to me to be in essence the interpretation of experiences of transcendence."[24] The elevation of *Man* as highest being in positivism, scientism, and several varieties of atheistic humanism including Marxism has been decried as the most disastrous idolatry of the age by Solzhenitsyn and Havel, a view emphatically supported by Voegelin. This was to embrace, in Havel's language, "the proud belief that man, as the pinnacle of everything that exists, was capable of... possessing the one and only truth about the world.... Communism was the perverse extreme of this trend."[25] Havel earlier had written: "We are going through a great departure from God which has no parallel in history.... I feel that this arrogant anthropocentrism of modern man, who is convinced he can know everything and bring everything under his control, is somewhere in the background of the present crisis. It seems to me that if the world is to change for the better it must start with a change in human consciousness."[26] Solzhenitsyn in his 1978 Harvard commencement address spoke to similar effect:

> [T]here is a disaster which is already very much with us. I am referring to the calamity of an autonomous, irreligious humanistic consciousness. It has made man the measure of all things on earth—imperfect man, who is never free of pride, self-interest, envy, vanity, and dozens of other defects. We are now paying for the mistakes which were not properly appraised at the beginning of the journey. On the way from the Renaissance to our days we have enriched our experience, but we have lost the concept of a Supreme Complete Entity which used to restrain our passions and our irresponsibility. We have placed too much hope in politics and social reforms, only to find out that we were being deprived

24. Eric Voegelin to Alfred Schütz, Jan. 1, 1953, in *The Philosophy of Order: Essays on History, Consciousness, and Politics: For Eric Voegelin on His 80th Birthday, January 3, 1981*, ed. Peter J. Opitz and Gregor Sebba (Stuttgart: Klett-Cotta, 1981), 450.

25. Václav Havel, *The Art of the Impossible* (New York: Knopf, 1997), 89.

26. Václav Havel, *Disturbing the Peace: A Conversation with Karel Huizdala*, trans. and intro. Paul Wilson (New York: A. A. Knopf, 1990), 11–12.

of our spiritual life. It is trampled by the party mob in the East, by the commercial one in the West. This is the essence of the crisis: the split in the world is less terrifying than the similarity of the disease afflicting its main sections. . . . Today it would be retrogressive to hold on to the ossified formulas of the Enlightenment. Such social dogmatism leaves us helpless before the trials of our times. . . . We cannot avoid reassessing the fundamental definitions of human life and human society. Is it true that man is above everything? Is there no Superior Spirit above him? Is it right that man's life and society's activities should be ruled by material expansion above all? . . . to the detriment of our integral spiritual life? If the world has not approached its end, it has reached a major watershed in history, equal in importance to the turn from the Middle Ages to the Renaissance. It will demand from us a spiritual blaze; we shall have to rise to a new height of vision, to a new level of life, where our physical nature will not be cursed, as in the Middle Ages, but even more importantly, our spiritual being will not be trampled upon, as in the Modern Era.[27]

Voegelin's critical philosophizing generally accords with the views expressed by Havel and Solzhenitsyn. Contrary to radical modernity's tendencies, it analytically condemns humanistic reductionism in all its forms and meditatively reestablishes the experiential and theoretical cogency of divine presence as ontologically paramount on the basis of a unique noetic inquiry.[28] As for modern Gnosticism and other trendy "isms," Voegelin stated in glossing the meaning of *disorder* in the preface to *Order and History:* "Ideology is existence in rebellion against God and man. It is the violation of the First and Tenth Commandments, if we want to use the language of Israelite order; it is the *nosos,* the disease of the spirit, if we want to use the language of Aeschylus and Plato."[29] The principle of selection of materials and their treatment is suggested

27. Aleksandr Solzhenitsyn, "A World Split Apart," in *Solzhenitsyn at Harvard: The Address, Twelve Early Responses, and Six Later Reflections,* ed. Ronald Berman (Washington, DC: Ethics and Public Policy Center of Georgetown University, 1980), 18–20.

28. Cf. Paul Caringella, "Eric Voegelin: Philosopher of Divine Presence," in *Eric Voegelin's Significance for the Modern Mind,* ed. Ellis Sandoz (Baton Rouge: Louisiana State University Press, 1991), 174–205.

29. Eric Voegelin, *OH* I, *Israel and Revelation,* xiv.

by Voegelin's epigraph for his *magnum opus,* taken from Augustine's *De vera religione:* "In consideratione creaturarum non est vana et peritura curiositas exercenda; sed gradus ad immortalia et semper manentia faciendus (In the study of [the] creature one should not exercise a vain and perishing curiosity, but ascend toward what is immortal and everlasting)." This epigraph was not chosen as a display of religious orthodoxy, although it is not wrong to think of Voegelin's work as extending that of Augustine and Aquinas and Eckhart in essential respects. Rather, it was chosen because it communicates Voegelin's deepest-held conviction that the path of philosophizing lies in an individual man's luminous tension toward transcendent divine Being and that modernity, in its most characteristic features, systematically eclipses God. By so doing, it mutilates man and the participatory reality of which he is uniquely the reflective noetic part. It is the diagnosis of, and therapy for, radical modernity's reductionist mutilations—committed in the name of *Man*—that must govern the love of divine wisdom in all true philosophy.

Because of the facts of human freedom and fallibility, man's existence is concretely subject to deformation through forgetfulness, rebellion, the lust for power—or plain crookedness—by concrete persons and societies. Thus, of Karl Marx's prohibition against asking questions regarding the Ground of being, Voegelin wonders: "War Marx ein intellektueller Schwindler?" And he answers the question with emphasis on the next page: "Ja, Marx *war* ein intellektueller Schwindler."[30] There is an experienced openness of both structural and directional dimensions. As a consequence, there can be no permanently valid *institutional* solutions to the question of the *best* order for human society. Institutions are conditioned by time, place, history, and culture as elements caught in the maelstrom of the turbulent process once known as the flux of becoming emblematic of contingent being. The criterion at all times, however, is that any concrete social order be one fit for human habitation—understanding *human* in the differentiated amplitude ascertained through noetic science as a prudential endeavor.

What abides, then, is man and being. What changes is the social and historical context of human existence, located in the metaxy as a highly pluralistic temporal and spacial field open to the mystery of being

30. Voegelin, *WPG,* 38–39, *SPG,* 21.

and the glimmering of an eschatological fulfillment beyond present structure-process.

§5.

So far from man abandoning God, in Voegelin's theory of history and reality, "eternal being realizes itself in time" and the substance of history is the disclosure of knowledge of the truth of divine Being in the reflective consciousness of poets, prophets, philosophers, and contemplatives of all eras who representatively realize its presence in personal, social, and historical reality. Among other things, this means that the movement from the compact experience of the cosmos in myth to the differentiating experience of transcendence philosophy engenders, at the same time, "a consciousness of epoch in the philosophers" to whom the experience happens. "The men in whom philosophy becomes an event are aware that it constitutes an epoch in history, a mark from which one distinguishes between a before and an after." In this respect, philosophy is a constituent of history.[31] By this differentiation, history becomes intelligible as a field of tensions in being, and philosophy simultaneously arises as an event in history that renders it luminous for its meaning. The tensions of decisive interest are those that run in the soul between time and eternity, and the tension in the soul between the before and the after of the experience of transcendence. Linguistic difficulties impose themselves, thus: "Neither the poles of the tensions in being nor the experiences of the tensions or the states of order in being are things in the external world, but rather they are terms in the noetic exegesis in which the ontic event interprets itself." The site of the experience and luminous understanding symbolized is the psyche, specifically that dimension of it Plato and Aristotle named the *Nous*, which is bodily present in a concretely existing human being in temporal reality at some specifiable place and time—e.g., Socrates in Athens in 399 BC. This being indubitably so, there must be something in man that is *non-temporal* through which he participates in

---

31. Eric Voegelin, "Eternal Being in Time," in *Anamnesis*, trans. and ed. Gerhart Niemeyer (1978; repr., Columbia: University of Missouri Press, 1990), 115–16.

eternal being. This is the psyche or soul, which Voegelin describes as the sensorium of transcendence, with the experiences themselves occurring neither in time nor in eternity but in the In-Between *(metaxy)* of the two, as Plato said. The experiences can be dated from the temporal side as events with worldly dates, as suggested by Socrates in 399 BC. These are events that can only be experienced personally and take on their historical status from such personal occurrences. The process of the experience in the metaxy is symbolized with attention to the facts that,

> in the philosophical experience, neither does eternal being become an object in time nor is temporal being transposed into eternity. We remain in the In-Between, in a temporal flow of experience in which eternity is present. This flow cannot be dissected into past, present, and future in the world's time, for at every point in the flow there is the tension toward the transcending, eternal Being. This characteristic of the presence of eternal Being in temporal flow may be best represented by the term *flowing presence.*[32]

To put a period to this intricate analysis, we can cite Voegelin's own summary of this stage of the inquiry:

> [T]he core of philosophy is the experience of the tension of being, from the ordering truth of which the indices radiate toward the complexes of reality. Whenever the tension of being results in a concern with the autonomous world of things, there also is concern with God, without whom, understood as world-transcending, there would be no world of autonomous things. Whenever God and world are kept apart by the experience of being, in which they meet, there also is concern with man who, in the experience of himself as one who experiences order, enters into the knowing truth of his own order. This complex of problems seems to me to be the historically constituted core of all philosophy.[33]

With these lines before us, our inquiry has proceeded far enough to venture a provisional response to the problems of truth and the experience of epoch in history, matters with which the discussion opened.

---

32. Ibid., 133.
33. Ibid., 136. The completion of this line of analysis is given in Voegelin's late writings, especially in *OH* V, *In Search of Order.*

One of the key participants in the Prague underground philosophical seminars of the mid-1980s (whose code name was *Dostál,* since then a prominent figure in Czech academic and political life), in the depths of the bad old days, raised the fundamental question of the age as follows: "Does the natural meaning of life represent the entire reality of human existence, or does not human life per se point to a meaning which transcends its natural setting?"[34] The question can only be answered in favor of transcendence, if we are to believe Václav Havel, Aleksandr Solzhenitsyn, and Eric Voegelin, whose testimony on the subject is unanimous. Of course, we are reminded daily that it is not the unanimous verdict of a public in America or more especially in Europe.

But the world is more than a seminar on philosophy or a college debating society. It is also the *agon* of existence, a life-and-death struggle in power politics and civilizational survival. This is especially true now that all of us are charged with the magnified burdens of responsible citizenship in the face of the amorphous enemy pursuing our personal and civilizational destruction in the mysterious name of the Islamist god and Jihad. The destruction of souls by radical ideologies and the pervasive deculturation of Western societies are continuing and potent factors disrupting the practice of rational politics under extreme conditions now rendered even more acute by an array of factors. To quote one astute observer of the current scene apropos the "War on Terrorism" as of summer 2005:

> While it must sound like a matter of little consequence, the chief weakness that our enemy has found could be summarized in the words, "political correctness". By creating taboos against even discussing various realities (such as the dangers presented by massive Muslim immigration, or the nature of Islam), we have rendered ourselves essentially defenseless against attack. It is worse than that: for from an Islamist view, educated Western society is not only morally rotten, decadent and spineless, but run through with a huge class of what Lenin called "useful idiots". These are the kind of "liberals" who think prison conditions in Guantanamo are something to obsess about. The Islamists would not be attacking

the West, if they did not believe themselves to have discovered a soft underbelly. Their rhetoric makes this clear: that they believe Western people can be induced to panic easily; that when panic spreads, a society will collapse. They are certainly right on this latter point. Hence the terror weapon, which has, incidentally, been the key to Arab war strategy through fourteen centuries.

If America does retreat, the hellgates are open. . . . I think the Islamist analysis of the present state of our societies and rulers is right on the money; that characters like Bush, Blair, and Howard are exceptions. Leaders like José Luis Rodríguez Zapatero, Gerhard Schroeder, and Paul Martin are the rule.[35]

§6. Conclusion

What then can be said about the emergence of a new epoch in history? There is at least some evidence to support the suspicion that the age of ideology has come to a close to be supplanted by a renewal of traditional religiosity as the groundwork of human politics. Plainly the terms of debate have been altered in the past fifteen years.[36] The fallacies of the old "isms" have been so exposed as to be plainly untenable intellectually. The collapse of the Soviet empire removed the political bastion of discredited Marxism-Leninism at least in Eurasia. The world has largely turned to liberty and democracy as the only acceptable modes of political culture and institutionalization. That the United States is earnestly

35. David Warren in the *Ottawa Citizen,* Aug. 14, 2005. Quoted from the Internet Web site.

36. Arnold J. Toynbee toward the conclusion of his massive *A Study of History,* 12 vols. (Oxford: Oxford University Press, 1934–1961), commented: "Whatever the religious future of a Westernizing World might prove to be, a post-Christian chapter of Western history had already made it clear that, in some form, a banished Religion was going to return in any event; for it had not proved so easy, after all, to give the Hound of Heaven the slip. Rather than relinquish His pursuit of His spiritual prey, He had resumed it in the guise of the hell-hound; and a liberal-minded and rational-minded society which had facilely assumed that it had rid itself of fanaticism for ever by exorcizing it on the ecclesiastical plane had lived to see it break out again with seven-fold virulence on political and economic planes on which the complacent watchman had been off his guard. . . . A twentieth-century Western World might either return to a Christian worship of the God who is Love as well as Power, or it might succumb to a Narcissan worship of Man's own hypnotizing image" (Toynbee, "The Prospects of Western Civilization," ibid., vol. 9 [1954]: 406–640, at 618.

seeking establishment of regimes so based is evident and destined to have far-reaching consequences. How successful as policy this initiative will eventually be and what specific forms it may take over the decades of the present century no one can predict. But there is some logic to it in seizing the moment as part of the process of modernization. And significant political power (driven by generally valid estimates of imperative national interests) is dedicated to the success of what one may call a grand experiment—or high-stakes gamble—that remains non-imperialistic, not apocalyptic, and dedicated to maintaining peace and to preserving national security. Time will tell the outcome of the hope and the policy. The impenetrable iron curtain of the future allows for little more than this. We remember, however, that war is as old as the human race; peace is the new idea. A renewal of religious fervor among multiple communities of conviction, each one nursing its uniqueness and truth (an inevitably pluralist field), is not necessarily an augury that a peaceful world free of violence is just around the corner.

At the educational and theoretical levels, however, we can espouse toleration without abandoning convictions and remain mindful that philosophically the "fact of revelation is its content," as Voegelin wrote fifty-odd years ago. This is to notice the experiential ground for affirming the *reality* of divine Being that revelation and noesis both provide. This can also lead to a readiness to tolerate rival symbolizations and creedal interpretations of ultimate Truth as a bedrock political lesson, one that opens the possibility of compromise instead of fanaticism, the *sine qua non* of politics: "Think ye are men, deem it not impossible for to err: sift unpartialy your own hearts, whether it be force of reason, or vehemency of affection, which hath bred, and still doth feed these opinions in you," the judicious Hooker begged the fanatics of his own age.[37] There also are major implications for the conception of *history* itself. For through the witness of prophets, philosophers, apostles, and meditatives there arises the abiding insight that

> the substance of history consists in the experiences in which man gains the understanding of his humanity and together with it the understanding of its limits. Philosophy and Christianity have

---

37. Richard Hooker, *Of the Laws of Ecclesiastical Polity,* preface 9.1, in Cambridge Texts in the History of Political Thought, ed. Arthur S. McGrade (Cambridge: Cambridge University Press, 1989), 49.

endowed man with the stature that enables him, with historical effectiveness, to play the role of rational contemplator and pragmatic master of a nature which has lost its demonic terrors. With equal historical effectiveness, however, limits were placed on human grandeur; for Christianity has concentrated demonism into the permanent danger of a fall from the spirit—that is man's only by the grace of God—into the autonomy of his own self, from the *amor Dei* to the *amor sui*. The insight that man in his mere humanity, without the *fides caritate formata,* is demonic nothingness has been brought by Christianity to the ultimate border of clarity which by tradition is called revelation.[38]

The recovery in public consciousness of truth about the transcendent divine Ground of being by a substantial number of living men and women through vital experience, after a period of centuries in which one false ground after another has been trumpeted as official coercive truth in a long succession of idolatries, is palpable in our time and empirically ascertained. This may indeed be such a watershed of history (as Solzhenitsyn supposed in 1978) as to be ranked with the shift from the Middle Ages to the Renaissance. To extrapolate criteria beyond mere memberships and affiliations: If the spiritual outburst of the age is widely experienced; if it is such as to differentiate the interpenetration of noetic and pneumatic experiences-symbolisms as reciprocally articulating representative truth of the Truth beyond representation; if it regenerates philosophy by demonstrating its spiritual authority, and regenerates religion by demonstrating its rational coherence, into a new science of consciousness-reality, with its order and disorders; if the spiritual irruption is such as to demand a new historiography to cope with the before-and-after of the events in the spheres of mind and spirit, of history, and of the political power constellations now fragmenting the ideological empires into religious-ethnic national units looking to divine Providence for blessing of their existence—*then* it seems at least possible that the world may, indeed, be embarked upon a significantly new era, and we may be participant in a transition in human affairs to a post-imperial order unencumbered by stop-history systems.

Political existence necessarily demands action, of course. Even an epochal moment is not the *end* of anything, certainly not the end of

38. Voegelin, *NSP,* 78–79.

history, much less an eschatological fulfillment. Indeed, as a recovery of the truth of differentiated reality gradually propagated in a flourishing public consciousness, it must be understood to be the very opposite of both. Exacerbating every consideration and clouding every calculation is the looming intercivilizational strife with radicalized and militant Islam. And just around the corner from that lies the rise of China as a major and potentially expansionist world power. Auguries of a new epoch, to be sure, but of what order and texture one can only surmise.

The narrower question thus remains: What shall we *do* to preserve any gains we may have made and not allow them to slip through our fingers like water? The *mache athanatos* of Plato comes to mind by way of answer.[39] Whether there is or is not a salutary new epoch in historical prospect, this ancient counsel retains its enduring validity in a sphere of action potentially within personal and political reach. It affirms that the philosopher and all other persons of judgment and goodwill are "obliged to recognize the [undying struggle for order and truth] as the movement toward the experienced *eschaton* of immortality and yet not to indulge in the dreamer's fantasy of an eschatological transfiguration to be pleromatically accomplished by his own dreams and actions."[40]

39. Plato *Laws* 906A.
40. Eric Voegelin, "Wisdom and the Magic of the Extreme," 287, quoted from Sandoz, *VR*, 251.

Bibliographical Appendix

COLLECTED WORKS OF ERIC VOEGELIN
(listed by volume number)

1. *On the Form of the American Mind.* Translated from the German by Ruth Hein. Edited with an introduction by Jürgen Gebhardt and Barry Cooper. 1995. 336 pp.
2. *Race and State.* Translated from the German by Ruth Hein. Edited with an introduction by Klaus Vondung. 1997. 256 pp.
3. *History of the Race Idea: From Ray to Carus.* Translated from the German by Ruth Hein. Edited with an introduction by Klaus Vondung. 1998. 216 pp.
4. *The Authoritarian State: An Essay on the Problem of the Austrian State.* Translated from the German by Ruth Hein. Edited with an introduction by Gilbert Weiss. Historical commentary on the period by Erika Weinzierl. 1999. 408 pp.
5. *Modernity without Restraint: The Political Religions; The New Science of Politics; and Science, Politics, and Gnosticism.* Edited with an introduction by Manfred Henningsen. 1999. 352 pp.
6. *Anamnesis: On the Theory of History and Politics.* Edited with an introduction by David Walsh. Translated from the German by M. J. Hanak. Based upon the abbreviated version originally translated by Gerhart Niemeyer. 2002. 448 pp.
7. *Published Essays, 1922–1928.* Translated from the German by M. J. Hanak. Edited with an introduction by Thomas W. Heilke and John von Heyking. 2003. 376 pp.
8. *Published Essays, 1929–1933.* Translated from the German by M. J. Hanak and Jodi Cockerill. Edited with an introduction by Thomas W. Heilke and John von Heyking. 2004. 264 pp.
9. *Published Essays, 1934–1939.* Translated from the German by M. J. Hanak. Edited with an introduction by Thomas W. Heilke. 2000. 184 pp.

10. *Published Essays, 1940–1952.* Edited with an introduction by Ellis Sandoz. 2000. 272 pp.
11. *Published Essays, 1953–1965.* Edited with an introduction by Ellis Sandoz. 2000. 288 pp.
12. *Published Essays, 1966–1985.* Edited with an introduction by Ellis Sandoz. 1990. 440 pp.
13. *Selected Book Reviews.* Edited and translated by Jodi Cockerill and Barry Cooper. Introduction by Barry Cooper. 2002. 232 pp.
14. *Order and History,* Volume I, *Israel and Revelation.* Edited with an introduction by Maurice P. Hogan. 2001. 616 pp.
15. *Order and History,* Volume II, *The World of the Polis.* Edited with an introduction by Athanasios Moulakis. 2000. 488 pp.
16. *Order and History,* Volume III, *Plato and Aristotle.* Edited with an introduction by Dante Germino. 1999. 464 pp.
17. *Order and History,* Volume IV, *The Ecumenic Age.* Edited with an introduction by Michael Franz. 2000. 456 pp.
18. *Order and History,* Volume V, *In Search of Order.* Edited with an introduction by Ellis Sandoz. 2000. 160 pp.
19. *History of Political Ideas,* Volume I, *Hellenism, Rome, and Early Christianity.* Edited with an introduction by Athanasios Moulakis. General introduction by Thomas A. Hollweck and Ellis Sandoz. 1997. 296 pp.
20. *History of Political Ideas,* Volume II, *The Middle Ages to Aquinas.* Edited with an introduction by Peter von Sivers. 1998. 264 pp.
21. *History of Political Ideas,* Volume III, *The Later Middle Ages.* Edited with an introduction by David Walsh. 1998. 296 pp.
22. *History of Political Ideas,* Volume IV, *Renaissance and Reformation.* Edited with an introduction by David L. Morse and William M. Thompson. 1998. 320 pp.
23. *History of Political Ideas,* Volume V, *Religion and the Rise of Modernity.* Edited with an introduction by James L. Wiser. 1998. 280 pp.
24. *History of Political Ideas,* Volume VI, *Revolution and the New Science.* Edited with an introduction by Barry Cooper. 1999. 240 pp.
25. *History of Political Ideas,* Volume VII, *The New Order and Last Orientation.* Edited with an introduction by Jürgen Gebhardt and Thomas A. Hollweck. 1999. 336 pp.
26. *History of Political Ideas,* Volume VIII, *Crisis and the Apocalypse of Man.* Edited with an introduction by David Walsh. 1999. 520 pp.

27. *Nature of the Law and Related Legal Writings.* Edited with an introduction by Robert Anthony Pascal, James Lee Babin, and John William Corrington. 1991. 144 pp.

28. *What Is History? and Other Late Unpublished Writings.* Edited with an introduction by Thomas A. Hollweck and Paul Caringella. 1990. 296 pp.

29. *Selected Correspondence.* (In preparation.)

30. *Selected Correspondence. 1950–1984.* Translated, edited, and with an introduction by Thomas A. Hollweck. 2006.

31. *Hitler and the Germans.* Translated, edited, and with an introduction by Detlev Clemens and Brendan Purcell. 1999. 296 pp.

32. *The Theory of Governance and Other Miscellaneous Papers, 1921–1938.* Translated from the German by Sue Bollans, Jodi Cockerill, M. J. Hanak, Ingrid Heldt, Elisabeth von Lochner, and William Petropulos. Edited with an introduction by William Petropulos and Gilbert Weiss. 2004. 544 pp.

33. *The Drama of Humanity and Other Miscellaneous Papers, 1939–1985.* Edited with an introduction by William Petropulos and Gilbert Weiss. 2004. 496 pp.

34. *Autobiographical Reflections.* Revised edition, with a Voegelin glossary and cumulative index. Edited with introductions by Ellis Sandoz. 2006. 592 pp.

Index

occupation of, 15; on saints, 26. *See also specific epistles*

Payson, Rev. Phillips, 64*n*24

Peirce, Charles Sanders, 36

Peitho, 132

Pellicani, Luciano, 2*n*3

Penn, William, 43*n*95

Periechon, 163

Perry, Ralph Barton, 29

Persecution and the Art of Writing (Strauss), 124*n*4, 139*n*35, 140*nn*39–40

Peter, First Letter of, 13, 18, 108*n*7

Peter, Second Letter of, 14, 31

Petition of Right (1628), 61, 62–63, 69, 75, 111

Petropulos, William, 158*n*4, 173*n*34, 177

Phaedrus, 89

Phenomenology (Hegel), 148

Philia, 27, 132, 160

Philia politike, 133

Philippians, Letter to, 17*n*36, 20*n*43, 21, 23*n*49

Philosophes, 38, 46–47*n*103

Philosophy: Averroës on, 141, 141*n*43; Common Sense philosophy, 27, 90, 90*n*38, 191; consciousness of epoch in philosophers, 201–4; and meditation, 177; Plato on philosopher, 146; Scholastic philosophy, 11, 33, 147; Spinoza on, 139–40; Voegelin on, 135–36, 146–49, 165, 175, 179–80, 202, 205–6; Voegelin-Strauss debate on meaning of, 121–44. *See also specific philosophers*

Philosophy and Law (Strauss), 129, 136

"Philosophy of Existence, The" (Voegelin), 126*n*7

Philosophy of Jesus, The (Jefferson), 81

Phronesis, 132, 161, 176

Physics (Aristotle), 143

Pistis, 129, 131*n*23

Plato: on *Agathon,* 28; Aristotle's critique of Plato's community of women, children, and property, 38, 39; Averroës on, 141; on *epekeina,* 161, 163, 171, 185–86; on *fides,* 169; on God, 163, 165; on *homonoia,* 17*n*36; on human erotic orientation to divine Being, 130; on In-Between *(metaxy),* 202; influence of, on American founders, 95; on

mache athanatos, 207; Madison's education in, 89; on *noesis,* 33; on *nosos,* 199; on *nous/Nous,* 118, 201; on order and reality, 194; on *peitho,* 132; on philosopher, 146, 180; on *polis,* 39; radical empiricism of, 177; on reason, 132–33; Strauss on, 127, 134, 138, 142; Voegelin on, 122, 125–28, 131–33, 135–36, 138, 147, 152, 160, 163; on wise men, 10

—works: *Gorgias,* 125–26, 163; *Laws,* 106, 163, 207*n*39; *Republic,* 17*n*36, 38, 39, 129*n*17, 163; *Statesman,* 17*n*36; *Symposium,* 176*n*41; *Timaeus,* 157*n*3, 163, 164, 169

Plato and Aristotle (Voegelin), 17*n*36, 124*n*5, 160*n*7

Platonism, 28, 34. *See also* Plato

Plotinus, 136, 143, 164, 167

Pneumatic experiences, 28, 28*n*64, 206

Pneumopathology, 151, 177

Polis, 39

Political Religions (Voegelin), 2*n*3, 115, 175, 180*n*49, 187

Politics (Aristotle), 5, 17*n*36, 38*n*84, 47*n*104, 71–72, 90, 91, 192

Polizzotto, Lorenzo, 43*n*95

Polybius, 5, 90, 192

Poor Richard's Almanac (Franklin), 111

Popular sovereignty, 60

Positivism, 30, 51, 148, 149, 160*n*7, 198

Post-modernism, 113

Power: Acton on, 72

Prayer: and Anselm, 166; Franklin on, 111; national days of, 40, 40*n*88, 66, 108, 108–9*n*8. *See also* Religion

Presbyterian Church, 67, 68, 82, 85, 92

Price, Geoffrey L., 152*n*13

Pritchard, James B., 122*n*2

Privacy rights, 71

Private property, and liberty, 64

Prodigal Son parable, 108

Property, 64

Proslogion (Anselm), 166

Protestantism. *See* Religion

Providence of God, 107–8, 111, 206. *See also* God

Psalms, Book of, 18, 19*n*43, 47, 108, 163, 167, 168, 172, 172*n*33, 177*n*42

LaVergne, TN USA
28 September 2009
159190LV00003B/4/A